Firm Footsteps

Firm Footsteps

Seven Timeless Christian Practices
for Journeying Disciples

Joseph T. LaBelle

WIPF & STOCK · Eugene, Oregon

FIRM FOOTSTEPS
Seven Timeless Christian Practices for Journeying Disciples

Copyright © 2025 Joseph T. LaBelle. All rights reserved. Except for brief quotations in critical publications or reviews, no part of this book may be reproduced in any manner without prior written permission from the publisher. Write: Permissions, Wipf and Stock Publishers, 199 W. 8th Ave., Suite 3, Eugene, OR 97401.

Wipf & Stock
An Imprint of Wipf and Stock Publishers
199 W. 8th Ave., Suite 3
Eugene, OR 97401

www.wipfandstock.com

PAPERBACK ISBN: 979-8-3852-2997-0
HARDCOVER ISBN: 979-8-3852-2998-7
EBOOK ISBN: 979-8-3852-2999-4

VERSION NUMBER 01/29/25

Scripture quotations are from New Revised Standard Version Bible, copyright © 1989 National Council of the Churches of Christ in the United States of America. Used by permission. All rights reserved worldwide.

*Therefore we have been buried with him by baptism into death,
so that, just as Christ was raised from the dead by the glory of the Father,
so we too might walk in newness of life.*

—Romans 6:4

Contents

Acknowledgments | ix
List of Abbreviations and Terms | xi
Introduction | xiii

1. Opening Our Lives to God in Prayer | 1
2. Awakening to God's Loving Presence | 28
3. Christian Spiritual Discernment | 53
4. Trusting in God's Abiding Love | 77
5. Asceticism and Christian Discipleship | 100
6. Charity as the Gift of Self for Others | 129
7. The Challenging Practice of Christian Nonviolence | 153

Bibliography | 181
Name Index | 189

Acknowledgments

There are many faculty members, fellow Missionary Oblates, family, and friends with whom I have shared my ideas over the course of writing this book, for which I am grateful. A few in particular, however, deserve special mention.

I thank the members of my volunteer editorial staff for their attentiveness during the writing phase. Raymond Cook, OMI, DMin, was helpful with his suggestions before being named as superior of the Missionary Oblate province of the United States but has continued to offer ongoing encouragement. Thanks also to Linda Gibler, OP, PhD, for her advice and keen eye for content, structure, and grammar support and to Rose Marden, DMin, for her academic and pastorally grounded contributions.

I thank the many Missionary Oblates in communities scattered around the United States with whom I sojourned for different lengths of time, notably the provincial residence in Washington, DC, the Immaculate Heart of Mary community in eastern Massachusetts, and the La Parra community in deep-south Texas. A special word of thanks goes to my Oblate brothers currently living with me at the St. Eugene de Mazenod residence in San Antonio who have listened to my ideas, struggles, and hopes.

Looking beyond the Oblate world, my siblings—Mary, Judith, John, and David—have been sources of inspiration and encouragement as they navigate the joys and stresses of their family lives.

Thanks again to all of you, along with others whom I fail to mention. Writers can sometimes speak of the personal transformative effects of their journey. Space is too short here, so, Lord willing, I look forward to sharing more of this later.

List of Abbreviations and Glossary Terms

ACW	*Ancient Christian Writers.* 76 vols. (1949–). Newman (Westminster, MD) and Paulist (New York and Mahwah, NJ) alternated publishing different volumes. Newman: vols. 1–26, 31–40, 45, 47, 49–50, 61. Paulist: vols. 27–30, 41–44, 46, 48, 50–60, 62–76.
ANF	*Ante-Nicene Fathers: The Writings of the Fathers Down to A.D. 325.* Edited by Alexander Roberts and James Donaldson. 10 vols. Peabody, MA: Hendrickson, 1994.
asceticism	Originally a Greek military term meaning to practice or struggle; Christian ascetics dedicate their lives to following the way of Jesus.
b.	born
Baker	*Baker Encyclopedic Dictionary of the Bible.* Edited by Walter A. Elwell et al. 4 vols. Grand Rapids: Baker, 1997.
ca.	circa, approximately
consecrated life	Organizations of men or women who dedicate their lives to growing in prayer and charity through professing religious vows (celibate chastity, poverty, obedience).
d.	died

DS	*Dictionnaire de Spiritualité: Ascétique et Mystique, Doctrine et Histoire.* Edited by Marcel Viller et al. 17 vols. Paris: G. Beauchesne et ses fils, 1932–95.
FC	*Fathers of the Church.* 147 vols. by various publishers between 1947 and 2013.
laity, lay	Members of some Christian denominations who are not ordained as bishops, priests, or deacons.
LW	*Luther's Works.* Edited by Robert C. Schultz and Helmut T. Lehmann. 55 vols. Philadelphia: Fortress, 1967.
no.	number
NPNF[1]	*The Nicene and Post-Nicene Fathers.* First Series. Edited by Philip Schaff. 14 vols. Peabody, MA: Hendrickson, 1994.
NPNF[2]	*The Nicene and Post-Nicene Fathers.* Second Series. Edited by Philip Schaff and Henry Wace. 14 vols. Grand Rapids: Eerdmans, 1968.
para.	paragraph
RB	*St. Benedict's Rule for Monasteries*
WSA	*The Works of Saint Augustine: A Translation for the 21st Century.* Edited by John E. Rotelle. Translated by Maria Boulding. 45 vols. Hyde Park, NY: New City Press, 1997–.

Introduction

THERE ARE MANY HUMAN activities that are difficult for some people to appreciate; for others, though, the diversions become worthwhile pursuits with benefits and blessings for daily life. Recreational hiking in a rugged forest woodland is one example. An indifferent person may think of wilderness hiking as merely walking for long periods, hardly worth the trouble and mosquitos. But those who enjoy the diversion will be attentive to improving their ability and look for ways to further their enjoyment. They will give attention to detail and how they do things. Without proper footwear, for instance, a hiker invites callouses, painful blisters, or maybe even a sprained ankle. Choosing too soft a walking trail might produce awkward mud-clumped shoes during the rainy spring season, while traversing very rocky terrain may prove too preoccupying to enjoy one's surroundings. Wearing proper clothes will affect one's enjoyment in extremes of wilting summer heat and bitter winter cold. A poorly marked trail at sunset can lead the hiker to become lost and immobilized in rapidly approaching darkness. Experience, a great teacher, gradually provides the wisdom that makes all the difference between enjoyment and frustration, and trail hiking soon becomes like second nature.

Sooner or later, Christians on their individual life-journeys with Jesus search for some meaningful ways to enhance their experience through integrating their spiritual beliefs with the rest of their lives. But who or what can offer them guidance? Many disciples seek to follow their Christian faith while not identifying with any particular worship community, asking themselves, "Why should I commit myself to a local church congregation or parish that doesn't help me to really live my faith each day?" Other followers content themselves with reciting a few prayers or devotions learned from their parents, unaware of the many other expressions of Christian prayer that have nurtured past Christian generations to mature into living examples of Jesus and the gospel message. Still other persons may be drawn to esoteric spiritual practices that can be contrary to basic Christian beliefs and even harmful to themselves. A frequent result is that one's relationship with Christ becomes dry and dormant, and what could be a fuller and truly human existence loses much of its joy and wonder.

The aim of *Firm Footsteps* is to examine and suggest for the reader seven important and time-honored personal Christian practices that can aid disciples in their journey to a deeper and more mature life as followers of Jesus. Christian spirituality concerns itself with opening one's heart to Jesus and the Gospels and allowing that experience to influence his or her daily life. Several time-honored ways of concretely living one's Christian spirituality have emerged in response to real-life challenges throughout Christian history. Over time, innumerable disciples have adopted concrete practices to make visible the love of Jesus through them in their particular moment, whether during Christianity's first centuries as a marginalized and often persecuted religion, facing the many challenges to remain faithful during the social upheavals and corruptions of medieval society, living as faithful disciples during the Enlightenment centuries that began to value mind over creation, or in present-day challenges. Following Jesus's way of praising his heavenly Father through practical observances helps to nurture disciples' lives as living witnesses to his message of love in the world, in response to the Holy Spirit that prompts and nudges the hearts of all believers.

Each of this book's seven chapters first examines how a given practice developed over the centuries beginning from Jesus's time continuing through the centuries of the patristic (AD 30–600), medieval (600–1500), and "modern" (1500–1940) eras, including accounts of notable individuals who have exemplified the practice. The first chapter studies the richness of the *Christian prayer* tradition and its many expressions, certainly a foundational element for any disciple. Then, *becoming aware of God's presence in life* will sharpen our sensitivity to God's continual accompaniment in life each day. *Spiritual discernment* offers ways to appraise whether choices in daily life will lead us closer to God's love or away from it, an especially important and useful practice when having to make significant life decisions. *Deepening one's trust in God's love* helps us to mature in our discipleship by cultivating Jesus's lifelong trust in the mysterious love that he shared with his heavenly Father. A proper and healthy understanding

INTRODUCTION

of *Christian asceticism* is invaluable for developing good habits and attitudes along the Christian way as we journey along the slow and sometimes difficult process of becoming as Christ. *Exercising charity toward others* helps us to grow in sharing with others the love that Jesus has for all of us by finding practical means to do this. Finally, practicing some degree of *Christian nonviolence* extends beyond avoiding physical bloodshed; it is a pervasive interior attitude that, when adopted, proclaims Jesus's teaching to love and respect one another as children of God. Each chapter includes reflection questions and suggested readings for additional study of the topic, along with a copious supply of footnotes pointing to both printed and online sources, making the book ideal for individual reading or as members of Christian faith-enrichment groups.

A word about the author: As a practicing Roman Catholic missionary and priest, I have endeavored to present these activities in a nondenominational voice while remaining grounded in traditional Christian principles and sources. In no way do I mean to deny the importance of the Eucharist, sacraments, or other practices that are among the riches of the Roman Catholic faith tradition. I have tried to anticipate places where reader objections may arise toward one or another practice, offering contextual and explanatory information in a respectful and inclusive way. The many expressions and practices of our shared Christian spiritual tradition form a rather broad arc of ways to live the gospel message; that is part of its wonder, although I realize that a given practice may not resonate with a particular reader's belief or experience.

May the chapters of *Firm Footsteps* provide means to strengthen and support you as Christian disciples on your unique journey, called as you are to enflesh the timeless loving message of Jesus and the gospel in your own time and place.

1

Opening Our Lives to God in Prayer

JUDGING BY THE WEALTH of books written on the subject, Christian prayer may be very popular but perhaps not well understood. Some readers may ask questions like "Just what *is* Christian prayer? What sets Christian prayer apart from other religious forms? How did so many types of prayer come about?" Ever since the time of Jesus, various prayer expressions have emerged as Christian disciples have sought to live their faith while facing the challenges of their time.

There are several good descriptions of what constitutes Christian prayer. The eighth-century bishop John of Damascus (c. 675–749) described it simply as "an ascent of the mind to God, or the asking God for things which are fitting."[1] In the nineteenth century, the French Carmelite nun Thérèse of Lisieux (1873–1897) wrote, "For me, prayer is an aspiration of the heart, it is a simple glance directed to heaven, it is a cry of gratitude and love in the midst of trial as well as joy."[2] Thomas Merton (1915–1968), who spent much of his life as a Trappist monk searching for an integral prayer to relate his inner self with the world around him, noted that "we do not want to be beginners. But let us be convinced of the fact that we will never be anything else but beginners, all our life!"[3] Christian praying

---

1. John of Damascus, *De fide orth.* 3.24.
2. Thérèse of Lisieux, *Story of a Soul* (manuscript C, ch. 11), 242.
3. Merton, *Contemplative Prayer*, 37.

disciples will always encounter new challenges beckoning them to follow and live more fully in the light and love of our Creator.

In this chapter, we examine forms of popular Christian prayer that have emerged from the time of Jesus and the first disciples within two general though interrelated areas: personal prayer in its vocal and meditative forms and the early development of communal practices that, together with individual personal prayer, make up the church at prayer (its "liturgy"). The final section offers a few suggestions that can help to strengthen a contemporary life of prayer.

Part One: Christian Prayer Through the Centuries

Prayer Insights from the Scriptures

Old Testament Roots of Christian Prayer

A look at some of the prayer expressions and attitudes found in the Old Testament provides a foundation for appreciating later Christian prayer developments.

Jewish understandings of prayer in the Hebrew Scriptures coalesce around five primary areas that persist into the New Testament. The closest interpretation of prayer is to intercede for another person.[4] Other senses include asking God for a favor, or God's mercy. These understandings support one basic reason for prayer as a petition to God for some need. One also finds prayers expressing supplication (praying for one's own need), praise and adoration of God and God's greatness, and expressions of thanksgiving to God for something received. There is a fifth type of prayer, lamentation, which we shall consider later. Each of these types of prayer would find future echoes through history into present-day Christian prayer expressions.

Among God's people of the Old Testament, we also find that prayers of the Jewish people contained at least five noteworthy qualities of their relationship with God:

God's might and compassion. God, awesome in majesty and insensible, was also very close to his chosen people. The compassionate God who heard the Hebrews crying out for release from their bondage was also the mighty God who rescued and accompanied them from their slavery in a cloud by

---

4. Helm, "Prayer," 1474.

day and a column of fire by night (Exod 13:21). The Old Testament psalms typically reveal the closeness of the people to God as they would express in prayer their heartfelt needs, frustrations, sufferings, and happiness.

Prayer as both personal and communal. The people prayed to God in both individual and communal settings. Individual and communal prayer complemented each other within the Hebrew understanding of community prayer and worship. One person's prayer and needs were rooted in the prayer and needs of the wider body of believers.

Gratitude toward God. God's people sought divine assistance and blessing as they went about their daily living and struggles as God's beloved while recalling God's steadfast love for them. Even in times of hardship and apparent defeat, they would proclaim and give thanks for God's continual accompaniment. Psalm 41, for example, expresses the plight of an afflicted man but not without recalling God's past goodness: "As for me, I said, 'O Lord, be gracious to me; heal me, for I have sinned against you'"; yet it also calls out, "But you, O Lord, be gracious to me, and raise me up, that I may repay them. . . . You have upheld me because of my integrity, and set me in your presence forever."[5]

Trust in divine faithfulness. People prayed to God humbly yet with great confidence that they were heard, recalling both communally and individually the many times that God had intervened in their past history.

Prayer and body posture. Praying to God with all of one's being included attention to bodily posture in prayer. Listening to God's proclaimed word, for example, merited an attitude of respectful attentiveness. Holding open one's arms while praying was a beseeching gesture or being vulnerable to God. A person's face-down prostration on the ground (sometimes by kneeling) could express humility, sorrow for sin, or the desire to repent, all physical expressions of their inner attitude toward their Creator.[6]

Expressions of Jewish prayer at the time of Jesus form three basic sets. Numerous forms of *berakah* prayer expressed blessing and praise to God (prayers beginning with phrases such as "Blessed are you, Lord God almighty"). Then there were the numerous shorter prayers uttered as part of one's many daily practices such as rising in the morning, before and after meals, and before sleep. Third and especially notable are the collection of psalms, sung or recited either as a praying community or from memory in moments of private prayer. The various Old Testament psalms expressed

---

5. Ps 41:4, 10–12.
6. Hagan, "Prayer in the Old Testament," 13–14.

a wide range of emotions, many intoned to a lyre or harp. These prayer expressions typically invoked God's intervention on behalf of the praying person (often quite expressively) with confidence that God heard them, finally recalling God's salvation and past blessings on the people.

Prayer Insights from the New Testament

Jesus was a young Jewish man and the Gospel examples of him at prayer reveal evidence of his spiritual heritage. The Gospel of Luke is an especially rich source. By his very life, we find in the person of Jesus the greatest example of God participating in the lives of the Chosen People through his ministry of teaching, healing, and deliverance. Jesus customarily attended public prayer at synagogue gatherings (such as at Nazareth in Luke 4:16). He would also pray alone (as in 22:39 at the Mount of Olives), notably when having to make important decisions (before naming the Twelve [6:12]). He gave his disciples a simple form of prayer that invoked supplication and praise of the Father (Luke's version of the "Lord's Prayer" in 11:2–4), underscoring the importance of simplicity, persistence, and confidence in prayer (11:5–13; 12:22–31; 18:1–8). Finally, while not found in Luke's Gospel, both Mark 15:34 and Matt 27:46 reveal Jesus crying out in lamentation from the cross ("My God, my God, why have you forsaken me?" from Ps 22).

Other persons in Luke's Gospel proclaim their praise and trust in God's intervention with his chosen people. Mary, the mother of Jesus, praises God while visiting Elizabeth in a voice that is at once hers and all Israel awaiting the messiah (Luke 1:46–55). Zechariah, the father of John the Baptist, praises God's fidelity to the people upon the restoration of his voice (1:67–79). As in many psalms, praising God in Luke often appears with a remembrance of past blessings and faithfulness.

The New Testament writings of the apostle Paul offer some insight into the different prayer expressions for this great missionary. Paul's letters typically offer an opening note of praise or thanksgiving to God for the faith present in the new communities, such as "Blessed be the God and Father of our Lord Jesus Christ, who has blessed us in Christ with every spiritual blessing in the heavenly places" (Eph 1:3). Paul frequently utters spontaneous prayers on behalf of his audience, such as "May the Lord direct your hearts toward the love of God and the steadfastness of Christ" (2 Thess 3:5). The Pauline writings also make use of what we might term "confessions" that are longer expressions of praise, likely intended to evoke praise of God from his audience (2 Cor 1:3–11). In all, the writings reveal a spiritually vibrant and heartfelt dimension of his prayer.

Scriptures and Prayer: Some Gleanings

Our brief foray into the Old and New Testaments concerning prayer offers many insights into prayer practices during the time of Jesus and the primitive Christian church, echoing their Jewish heritage. Some key central themes that will influence the subsequent Christian prayer tradition include:

God of power and love. Almighty God was also the God who was concerned for God's people and accompanied them through their travails. We find this modeled especially in the life of Jesus who taught his disciples to trust in the Father's love for their daily needs.

Simplicity of prayer. Jesus counseled his disciples that true prayer to God was simply opening of their hearts or expressing their deepest needs to God without an extensive recitation of words, as their heavenly Father already knew what they truly needed. Brevity and sincerity in prayer expressions were important (Luke 11:1–4; Matt 6:5–13).

Different prayer expressions. Prayer in the Scriptures typically expresses at least one of the four basic types of prayer (adoration and praise, petition, intercession, and thanksgiving). The Lord's Prayer embraces each of these qualities, traditionally following the version of Matthew's Gospel (6:9–13) that has endured through two thousand years of the Christian prayer tradition and remains a Christian mainstay.

Prayer to God could be passionate. Scriptural prayer also offers moments of lamentation prayer, crying out to God in times of suffering and confusion. Present-day Christian disciples need not be fearful of expressing such raw human expression. God has heard emotionally charged words of prayer since Old Testament times and is not offended if we pour out our inner emotional maelstrom to the One who created us and loves us in our weakness.[7]

---

7. Leonard, *Why Bother Praying?*, 34–36.

Prayer in the Early Patristic Era

The early Christian churches encountered many challenges that helped shape their developing prayer tradition. Initially regarded as a Jewish sect, the late first century found Christians excluded from Jewish community prayer life. This alienation from their religious identity left Christians vulnerable to calumnies and other acts of persecution from Jewish and pagan adversaries. The increasing percentage of Greek-speaking and other non-Jewish converts challenged their traditional understanding of God and themselves as people of God. Also, the cultural differences of regional Christian populations (Jerusalem, Antioch, Ephesus, Alexandria, and Rome), although generally holding to Christian beliefs, sometimes experienced bitter doctrinal arguments between them.

Early Communal Worship

Available historical evidence reveals that Christian communal prayer practices had begun to form cohesive rituals by the second century. Christian communities would gather discreetly in willing households or perhaps outdoors on "the Lord's Day" (Sunday, the first day of the week), contrary to the Jewish Sabbath observance on the last day. Reading Paul (1 Cor 11:20–23) suggests that the earliest eucharistic observances were simple moments of offering and sharing of bread and wine among families and guests, likely adjoined to a household meal and invoking Jesus's words of the Last Supper. Before long, however, the eucharistic observance began forming into a ritual that centered on Jesus's four actions at the Last Supper: *taking* (into his hands), *giving thanks* to God as source of the gifts, *saying* a few words in the form of a Jewish blessing, and *giving* or sharing with the others present.[8] By the time of the third-century collection of Christian teachings and discipline, the *Apostolic Tradition*, we find these four underlying actions along with some form of established communal dialogue prayer between congregants and their appointed leader-presider (more frequently an appointed bishop-leader).[9] Prayers of blessing and thanksgiving also accompanied the presentation of other gifts offered for the needy such as oil, wine, or cheese.

Ritual practices also developed to admit converts into the Christian community through baptism, those appointed to ministry leadership, and

---

8. Cabié, *The Eucharist*, 9.
9. Hippolytus, *Trad. Ap.* 4.

a more protracted set of observances to reconcile notorious sinners with both God and community.

Personal or Individual Bodily Forms and Prayer

Only a few instructions on early Christian prayer are on record. The most notable private prayer form was the Lord's Prayer that new Christian converts in Syria were instructed to pray three times daily.[10] Other early writers among the fathers of the church taught their local communities about prayer, with some attention to modesty in bodily adornment and posture while praying. For example, the bishop Tertullian of Carthage in North Africa (d. ca. 220) asserted that praying Christians should present themselves simply before God, using only a few words, without concern for the Jewish practices of wearing the customary mantel and ritual hand washing.[11] It was appropriate for one to pray daily at the third, sixth, and ninth hour (midmorning, midday, and midafternoon) and give thanks before and after meals. Reverence for God suggested that standing was an appropriate prayer posture rather than sitting, unless kneeling at special moments.[12]

The *Apostolic Tradition* also reveals a growing structure and a deepening link of prayer with Jesus's passion and death. Third-hour prayer (roughly midmorning) should focus on Jesus's crucifixion, his agony under the dark afternoon skies from the sixth hour (midday), and his death on the cross at the ninth (midafternoon). The document also indicates times of additional prayer at dawn, before retiring, and even in the middle of the night when one could pray amid the stillness and attentiveness of God's resting creation.[13] Fasting could accompany prayer, especially among those in recognized groups of widows and virgins who had dedicated their lives to practicing prayer and virtues.

Prayer Developments in the Later Patristic Era

The legal recognition of Christianity in 313 by Emperor Constantine and his favor extended to Christians brought a great change to their lives.

---

10. *Did.* 8.
11. Tertullian, *Or.* 13–15.
12. Tertullian, *Or.* 16.
13. Hippolytus, *Trad. Ap.* 36.

Public worship could now emerge from the safety of small home gatherings or predawn outdoor services. The decree also helped to foster greater social acceptance of Christians, a growing Christian influence upon the surrounding cultures, and deeper and more ritual expressions of worship and prayer.

Growth of Public Worship Buildings and Ritual

The fourth century witnessed an increased number of formal public worship structures, notably the numerous massive church structures called *basilicas*.[14] With Christianity's increased prominence, emperors built large structures to accommodate the large crowds and to promote Christianity's grandeur and its public prayer life.

The collective public prayer life of the Christian churches fostered an increasing sense of pageantry in their various expressions of prayer and worship. While Sunday participation was not yet a strict obligation, the eucharistic celebration soon grew in its beauty and intricacy of celebration, order, and adornment. Christian liturgy also included more modest services of public and private community prayer at regular times each day. These "hours" (in Latin, *horae*), initially at dawn and sunset, manifested praise of God at regular times each day. The local clergy officially observed these services that also attracted a wide participation of faithful. The basilica formed the prayer center for all the surrounding neighborhoods, whose Christian members were encouraged to participate, especially before dawn of the new workday. Communal prayer participation included recitation of psalms, a scriptural reading with a homily, and prayers of petition.[15]

Prayer in Early Desert Monasticism

The legalization of Christianity in 313 and removal of the specter of sudden persecution proved to be both a blessing and a curse for those desiring to follow God more intently. The social acceptance of Christianity opened the way for a gradual softening of fervor for Christian life and virtue among the faithful. Some disciples, recalling the hardships of the

---

14. *Basilica* originally referred to large government buildings of the Roman Empire. Early Christians adopted the name for the expansive Christian church centers built by the early pro-Christian emperors.

15. Jungmann, *Christian Prayer*, 14–17.

persecution years, yearned to follow a more ascetically demanding Christianity, far away from the threat of spiritual mediocrity. These ardent followers discovered a way to do so by entering a new arena of solitude and physical hardship as solitary monks in the desert wilderness of Egypt, Palestine, and Syria. While not separating themselves entirely from the wider Christian body, monks sought to focus their energy on making their lives a continual praise of God through diligent solitary prayer, detachment from material goods, and social isolation.

Early monastic prayer was rooted in the Scriptures (especially the psalms) and individual prayer experiences, seeking to achieve St. Paul's exhortation to "pray always" (1 Thess 5:17). Daily recitation of memorized psalms and some form of manual labor occupied their days, along with aids to personal prayer such as fasting and rising in the middle of the night for periods of "vigil prayer." Origen of Alexandria (185–254) taught a three-level method of scriptural study through which a disciple would advance from reading the text literally, then gradually applying a text morally (letting the words guide their use of created goods), and finally entering a deeper allegorical or "mystical" meditation on the text. The monastic pursuit of God placed a greater emphasis on individual prayer growth and deeper spiritual experiences than its earlier Jewish heritage and would influence subsequent Christian spirituality.

The desert monastic tradition of Eastern Christianity led to communal or cenobitic forms of monastic life and prayer. These arrived in the West through the contributions of monastic-minded individuals such as John Cassian (360–435) and Benedict of Nursia (d. 547). Cenobitic monasteries continued the communal and individual prayer observances and the ideal of regularly praising God throughout the day through prayer and ascetical practices. Monastic experiences and expressions of prayer would prove to be very influential in the developing traditions within Christian spirituality.

Prayer Developments Through the Medieval Era

Medieval Western Christianity produced a wealth of insight for the tradition of Christian prayer, though not without its challenges. Monasteries were the chief spiritual centers for this development through the twelfth century. The rise in concern for church reform from the thirteenth century resulted in the growing appreciation for deeper prayer among faithful Christians.

Celtic Christian Monasticism and Lorica Prayers[16]

Recent decades have witnessed growing interest in how Christianity has been influenced by early medieval Celtic spirituality from different regions of the British Isles. Although Roman in faith, expressions of Celtic Christian spiritual life and monasticism were quite distant both culturally and geographically from the less-isolated communities of the European mainland. This separation helped Celtic Christian prayer to maintain a good measure of its local Celtic flavor that held a special sensitivity for nature and the peculiar and harsh characteristics of the land. Celtic Christianity was heavily marked by its considerable monastic presence and priestly character. Most monks were priests, and priests had a special responsibility to make prolonged daily prayer through extensive memorizing and recitation of the psalms.

One lasting prayer expression of Celtic Christianity that emerged from this need for heavy memorization was a particular prayer form known as Lorica prayer. Belief in and fear of demons and evil spirits were a part of ancient Celtic spirituality. Professions of faith in the Holy Trinity (Father, Son, and Holy Spirit) and other Christian beliefs reinforced disciples' doctrinal grasp of the faith and continually invoked divine protection from the many spiritual and other dangers of medieval life. Lorica ("breastplate") prayers reflected these traits, as we find among the verses of the lengthy "Breastplate of Saint Patrick":

> I arise today
> Through a mighty strength, the invocation of the Trinity,
> Through belief in the Threeness,
> Through confession of the Oneness
> of the Creator of creation.
> I arise today
> Through the strength of Christ's birth with His baptism,
> Through the strength of His crucifixion with His burial,
> Through the strength of His resurrection with His ascension,
> Through the strength of His descent for the judgment of doom....
> I arise today, through
> The strength of heaven,
> The light of the sun,
> The radiance of the moon,

16. Webb, "What Is Celtic Spirituality?"

> The splendor of fire,
> The speed of lightning,
> The swiftness of wind,
> The depth of the sea,
> The stability of the earth,
> The firmness of rock . . .
> I arise today, through
> God's strength to pilot me,
> God's might to uphold me,
> God's wisdom to guide me,
> God's eye to look before me,
> God's ear to hear me,
> God's word to speak for me,
> God's hand to guard me,
> God's shield to protect me,
> God's host to save me
> From snares of devils,
> From temptation of vices.

Likely written during the eighth century, this stirring prayer expression has been the source of many renditions found among contemporary Christian hymns and prayers.[17]

Eastern Christian Religious Icons and Prayer

Eastern Orthodox Christianity has deeply influenced Western Christian spiritual thought from its beginning. One notable influence was the eighth-century introduction of sacred icons into the West that initially brought a bitter tension between Rome and Constantinople.

While early medieval icons were well known among Eastern Christians, the West was hesitant to accept them. The ninth-century "Iconoclast Controversy" caused a bitter dispute between Christians who condemned icons as idolatrous (the *iconoclasts*) and those who supported their use. The reaction was so painful that two periods of separation (*schisms*) developed between Rome and Constantinople. Both sides finally reached a common positive understanding by the year 843, though with provisions. Icons could be displayed and venerated for teaching and bringing persons

---

17. "St. Patrick's Breastplate," *IrishCentral*, Mar. 9, 2023.

to a deeper love of God and the saints, but not as objects of adoration reserved to God alone.

For contemporary Orthodox Christians, icons of God, Christ, the Trinity, and the saints are more than ordinary paintings. These works of art are regarded as sacred since they hold, within the image, something of its sacred nature from the figure represented. Iconographers create their works according to strict rules concerning, for instance, the materials used and the symbolism found in the icon. In all, there is a deep reverence for their creation, typically produced by Eastern monks.

Devotional Prayer to Mary and Other Saints

Twelfth-century Western Christian prayer shifted its focus from the glorified Christ of the resurrection to a more affective appreciation for the humanity of Jesus and several events of his earthly life, notably his birth and his final suffering.[18] This new energy in devotional prayer also considered the people who shared Jesus's life and ministry, most notably his mother and "the Twelve" or first apostles who continued his mission.

Devotional prayer to Mary, the mother of Jesus, has early roots in Christian piety with a long and complex development beginning in the earliest Christian centuries. Each Gospel identifies her as the mother of Jesus, while Luke and John notably present Mary as a faith-filled daughter of Israel. Mary, through her life of faithful trust in God's steadfast love, personifies Israel's covenant relationship with God. When she accepts her role in salvation history at the annunciation, Luke's Gospel presents Mary as a "highly favored" woman who would give birth to the messiah (1:28). Her visit with cousin Elizabeth further supports the belief that Mary possessed some preexisting condition of holiness granted her in light of her future motherly role in the incarnation.

Events in the fourth and fifth centuries strengthened this popular devotional attitude toward Mary. The church council of Nicea (325) proclaimed the belief that Jesus shared the divine eternal essence of his heavenly Father, while a later council at Ephesus (431) reaffirmed devotion to Mary as "Mother of God" resulting from that belief. Given the universal sense of maternal love between mother and son, Mary became popularly acclaimed as an approachable intercessor to Jesus, to whom Christians could pray with their needs and sorrows of medieval life. However, some eccentric

18. Jungmann, *Christian Prayer*, 63.

expressions of medieval Marian devotion promoted an unbalanced view of her role and portrayed her as possessing almost quasi-divine attributes that do not resonate with contemporary Christian devotion to her.[19]

Besides devotion to Mary, medieval Christian piety also honored the sanctity of many apostles, early martyrs, and other renowned disciples for their spiritual maturity. Christians recognized in the martyrs an all-consuming identification with Jesus to the point of their suffering and death. The martyrs' steadfast dedication led to their veneration by later Christians through praying at martyrdom and tomb sites. The normalization of Christianity in the fourth century brought an end to the early martyrdom period; from then, there developed an understanding of what constituted saintly holiness. Other individuals over the ensuing centuries, without necessarily dying as martyrs, became recognized for their total dedication to growth in holiness by embodying the life qualities of Jesus and his life of loving faith and trust in his heavenly Father.

Medieval Christians believed saints to be special members of the Christian community or what is called the "Mystical Body of Christ" who could also intercede for them before the heavenly throne. Unfortunately, many practicing Christians lacked an adequate understanding of the saints as worthy of veneration and imitation, leading to accusations of superstition and improper adoration belonging to God alone.[20]

Other Devotional Prayer Practices

Other later medieval expressions of devotional prayer focused on the consecrated Eucharist. The new intellectual approach to theology (Scholasticism) helped to feed a growing popular fascination with the eucharistic body and blood of Christ by raising questions such as "When did the transformation from bread and wine into the consecrated elements occur in the Mass?" or "how are these elements changed?" This more analytical approach to

---

19. Contemporary Christian devotion honors and respects Mary both as the mother of the Son of God and as an exemplary Christian disciple. Proper Christian devotion to Mary would never consider her as divine. Mary's deep trust in God's love showed her to be one of God's truly faithful people, worthy of Christian respect and admiration (*veneration*) without offering her adoration that is due to God alone. To love Mary as Jesus's earthly mother is to love whom Jesus loved, another way of expressing love for him.

20. Contemporary veneration of Mary or any other saintly images replicated in icons, statues, or shrines serve to recall the lives of these spiritual heroes, while remembering God as the true source of all blessing and goodness.

Christian worship helped to foster devotional practices focusing on the consecrated body and blood of Christ in the elements. Groups of Christian faithful reportedly hurried from church to church to observe as the priest held up the bread and wine during their consecration, when they believed the moment of change occurred. Another eucharistic devotion, much more reverent, was the prayerful and often festively adorned "Body of Christ" processions through villages or around parish churches while displaying a large consecrated host in a beautifully laden display or *monstrance*, moving people to maintain long prayerful vigils of eucharistic adoration.[21]

Fourteenth-Century Christian Mysticism

The fourteenth century produced a notable interest in the ancient experiences of Christian mysticism. The recorded experiences and insight from primitive and later monasticism provided much of the foundation for an enduring spiritual tradition.

Christian mystical prayer refers to the interior supernatural experiences and effects of God's transforming love within a person, a component of any Christian prayer practice. The numerous spiritual writings of figures such as Catherine of Siena, followed later by Teresa of Avila and John of the Cross, testify to the basic dynamics found in positive effects of the Christian mystical way. Generally, one's growing experience in prayer can facilitate this inner dynamic as prayer moves to a deepening interior attitude of quiet and rest. Over time, a prayerful relationship with God in prayer tends to dispose praying disciples to God's love that, among other things, slowly liberates them from natural human selfishness. The process can slowly transform disciples more and more completely into the unique personal image and likeness of Christ that each Christian possesses.

Lectio Divina *as a Way of Prayer*

This ancient prayer method of meditating on sacred literature began among the early Christian monks as a means of plumbing the deeper riches of the Scriptures in their daily search for God.[22] Besides scriptural

---

21. Roman Catholic tradition has long taught that the consecrated Eucharist holds the sacred essence of the body and blood of Jesus Christ under the appearance of bread and wine, fulfilling his words at the Last Supper: "This is my body . . . this is my blood."

22. The scriptural scholar and ascetic Jerome (342–420) was one notable proponent

reading, *lectio divina* can also draw from other respected spiritual writings of the Christian tradition.

The method contains four stages whose misleading Latin names need explanation. *Lectio* is more than simple reading. Scriptural passages are slowly read and softly vocalized until one word or phrase catches the attention of the one praying and invites them to pause and ponder the textual meaning, initially for only a few moments. Before long, the individual may begin to exercise the second stage, *meditatio*, the intellectual ruminating or "chewing" on the text for deeper insight into it. After some experience, praying disciples may experience the third stage, *oratio*, a spontaneous welling-up of praise and thanksgiving to God from the inner depths of the spiritual heart. After sufficient experience, the one praying may be moved interiorly to periods of quiet resting in the silence of the divine presence. This stage of *contemplatio* includes a tendency to lose self-awareness in a patient and joyful resting before God, with a self-forgetful exchange of love between creature and Creator.[23]

A variation of the four-part *lectio divina* tradition recognizes that a prayerful encounter with God, if authentic, normally affects some form of change or spiritual fruitfulness toward action in a person's life. Such is the meaning of the Latin word *actio*. At this fifth stage, praying persons integrate and bring into concrete effect whatever insight or other spiritual fruitfulness that they have appropriated from prayer. Any Christian prayer, notably deeper prayer, will incite growth or development in some aspect of one's interior spiritual life and discipleship. This is no less true of *lectio divina* and what it can provide in terms of deeper appreciation for the words of Scripture. The responses will vary depending on the individual. Preachers may realize a deeper insight of the scriptural reading that can impact proclaiming or preaching God's word. Another person may be led to greater engagement in Christian outreach for the needy, or a third may be moved to seek a long-overdue reconciliation with someone. An inner prompt leading to some form of *actio* results from our reception of God's word; as God spoke through the prophet, "so shall my word be that goes out from my mouth; it shall not return to me empty" (Isa 55:11).

Contemporary praying disciples who might wish to explore the tradition of *lectio divina* should note that, while the methodical list of stages

---

of such works.

23. More information on *lectio divina* prayer can be found in Studzinski, "Lectio Divina," 201–21.

imply an easy linear progression from lower to higher (following a popular medieval image of a ladder or stairway of prayer), in reality their duration usually varies from person to person. Daily commitment to perhaps a half-hour is essential for advancing in this prayer form. Sharing one's experience with another knowledgeable person or other like-minded members of a prayer group would be of great value to avoid any inner confusion and self-deception that may arise, especially for disciples who are inexperienced or new to Christian meditative prayer.

The later medieval centuries witnessed a growing engagement of ordinary lay Christians with the prayer tradition, no longer the exclusive practice of monastic and other forms of consecrated religious life. The modern era will continue to witness this growth and practice that has led into the present day.

Modern-Era Developments

Christian prayer practices weathered several challenges during the centuries of the modern era. The many expressions of devotional prayer, while beneficial for countless praying individuals, developed for others into eccentric practices that raised criticism of being superstitious or trying to manipulate God's favorable response to petitionary prayer. Imprudent misunderstandings of meditative and mystical prayer practices also fostered episodes of aberrant pseudo-mystical experiences that caused much confusion, divisive theological opinions, and even moral sinfulness.[24]

Despite difficulties and controversies, the sixteenth and seventeenth centuries experienced a third major collection of Western Christian mystical prayer experiences in Spain (notably with John of the Cross [1542–1591] and Teresa of Avila [or Teresa of Jesus, 1515–1582]), France (Magdalen of Saint Joseph, 1578–1637), and several mystics of the Italian peninsula. Their written accounts of prayer experiences and struggles to walk ever more closely with Jesus have enriched the Christian mystical prayer tradition.

Teresa of Avila made significant contributions to the Christian prayer tradition. She entered the Avila Carmelite Convent of the Incarnation around 1535 but shortly thereafter suffered a severe illness and three years'

---

24. Many praying persons misinterpreted their prayer experiences, leading some into misguided spiritual movements such as Quietism and other undesirable consequences of what became known as "passive prayer."

convalescence.[25] Teresa matured in recollection prayer during this time, but, resuming her normal convent life, she returned to a state of spiritual tepidity for some fifteen years until experiencing a renewed zeal and commitment to her Carmelite vocation of prayer and penance in 1555 and her decision to establish several reformed Carmelite convent communities. Besides her *Life*, Teresa wrote her *Way of Perfection* as a guide to prayer and other practices for her reformed community of women, while she recounts her maturing growth in mystical prayer in a later work, *The Interior Castle*. Teresa's influence greatly affected Carmelite orders of both women and men and remains a source of spiritual nourishment for present-day Christians.

A note of caution to contemporary readers of written accounts from medieval and modern-era mystics concerning prayer and reported cases of exceptional physical phenomena: Experiences of genuine Christian mystical prayer should not be confused with sensational images of personal bodily levitation, hearing divine voices, and the like. The long Christian tradition has revealed that such incidental phenomena in prayer can arise when a praying person's inner self is exposed to the overwhelming divine fire of God's searing love, purifying a disciple's imperfect love. Such exterior phenomena should be regarded as merely incidental to a prayer life and one should never seek them merely for the experience. They are certainly not signs of the recipient's degree of holiness nor divine favor. The next chapter of this book has more to say on the dynamics of Christian mystical prayer.

Influences from the Protestant and Anglican Reform Movements

Among many changes to Christian spiritual practices sparked by the Protestant Reformation and subsequent reformers, Martin Luther (1483–1546) was a particular influence. His desire to correct several areas of church abuses, leading to his ninety-five propositions nailed to the door of Wittenberg Cathedral, also moved him to greater sympathy for ordinary praying Christians. His concern for greater popular access to Scriptures resulted in the first Bible printed in a vernacular (German) language. Luther also composed numerous hymns that were inspirational and educational, and his work *A Simple Way to Pray* offered to Luther's good friend several suggestions for enkindling prayer. One considers a

---

25. Teresa recounts in her autobiography (her *Life*) about her early life and Carmelite years of challenge and renewed commitment.

common problem for praying disciples struggling to observe some periods of daily prayer, noting early in the writing:

> It is a good thing to let prayer be the first business of the morning and the last at night. Guard yourself carefully against those false, deluding ideas which tell you, "Wait a little while. I will pray in an hour; first I must attend to this or that." Such thoughts get you away from prayer into other affairs which so hold your attention and involve you that nothing comes of prayer for that day.[26]

Luther also offers meditations focusing on the six petitions of the Lord's Prayer and a simple format of methodical prayer that he applied to meditations on the Ten Commandments.

A significant contribution from the English church reformers was the Anglican *Book of Common Prayer*. Often called simply "the Prayer Book," the work has undergone different renditions since its original publication under the inspiration of Thomas Cranmer (1489–1556) and continues to influence contemporary churches of the Anglican communion.[27] The *Book of Common Prayer* is a compendium of prayers for both private daily practice and congregational services such as Eucharist, marriages, and funerals. Even today, the "Prayer Book" serves to underscore the relationship of individual and communal prayer.[28]

Modern-Era "Spiritual Exercises" and Prayer Methods

Even before the emergence of the Protestant Reformation, many Christian disciples sought means to help them lead prayerful lives in everyday life. Several well-known works of so-called methodical prayer emerged that led praying disciples through guided prayer sessions of vocal and meditative prayer. Perhaps the most popular and enduring writing has been the *Spiritual Exercises* of Ignatius of Loyola (1491–1556), founder of the Society of Jesus (Jesuits). Originally intended as a guide for discerning whether to become a Jesuit missionary, the *Spiritual Exercises* typically led participants through four weeks of daily meditations. The exercise ideally brought them to a moment of spiritual freedom from conflicting interior feelings or "indifference" for embracing either one option or the other in an act of faith

---

26. Luther, *Simple Way to Pray*, 193.
27. Wakefield, "Anglican Spirituality," 259–63.
28. Steele and Davis, "Book of Common Prayer."

and love. Several other guides to methodical prayer emerged during these centuries, usually focusing on daily prayer growth, including works by the French Sulpician Jean-Jacques Olier (1608–1657) and the Italian Redemptorist Alphonsus de Liguori (1696–1787). Alphonsus also wrote many works on the topics of prayer and devotion; his *Great Means of Salvation and of Perfection* and his *Glories of Mary* have inspired countless praying Christian disciples through our recent time.

Our overview of the Christian prayer tradition has uncovered many prayer forms and experiences from a variety of spiritual masters; many are still helpful today. Being aware of one's personal temperament and preferences can aid disciples in achieving a more fruitful and sustaining personal prayer life, as the next section illustrates.

Part Two: Contemporary Insights for Growth in Christian Prayer

Why Pray Today?

Convincing busy young adult Christians to invest the time to form and nourish a discipline of regular daily prayer can be a hard sell. In the past, when life was much more mysterious and narrowly understood, people more easily turned to divine assistance and protection. Even more recently, praying that God would heal a sick family member was frequently all that one could do in an age that hadn't yet discovered antibiotics and understood less of the many wonders of human physiology. Airport chapels were more plentiful (and perhaps more used) during the earlier years of travel, when flying was much more precarious than today. People felt more vulnerable, and societal reverence for God was a widely shared reality.

Contemporary Western consideration of God and the need for prayer is less universal. Greater reliance on scientific knowledge, popular doubts about the existence of a loving divine Being that allows evil to coexist with good, or personal images of God as overly moralizing or judgmental have caused much of society to set aside serious thoughts of God in favor of personal self-reliance. That security has its limitations, of course. The renewal in prayer following the September 11, 2001, attacks in New York illustrated that we can feel more confident and self-sufficient until the outbreak of some threatening catastrophic event, reminding us that life isn't so secure and predictable after all.

To whom do we pray? We pray to God, yes, but God for Christians is one divine Being, a community of three divine Persons held together in their interrelationship. God is Love (1 John 4:8), what Augustine of Hippo described as a loving communion of Lover (Father) and Beloved (Son) in an unreserved exchange between them of self-giving Love (Holy Spirit). Praying to God gradually opens our lives to this wonderful divinity, this mysterious community of love who interacts with us in ways that are at once creative, transformative, and strengthening. The Christian vocation or lifelong journey forever beckons us to be transformed into Christ in his stance of steadfast love toward his heavenly Father and toward other persons, our transformation leading us to become ever more strengthened and animated by the Holy Spirit.

Interior Movements to Christian Prayer

While many persons may turn to prayer only in a time of great need or tragedy that leaves them feeling helpless, more reflective Christians may be moved to prayer when struck by the wonders of creation that the Creator-Father has called good. Perhaps it is when beholding the natural beauty of a sunset, a breathtaking landscape, a bird's colorful plumage, or the awe when observing an animal's grace or strength or speed. At such moments, the beholder may perceive something of the divine order in creation, that each created thing is part of a more profound created reality that calls each of us to live in greater respectful harmony with it. Pier Giorgio Frassati (1901–1925), an avid mountaineer and exemplary Christian who died at the young age of twenty-four, reportedly wrote, "Every day, my love for the mountains grows more and more. If my studies permitted, I'd spend whole days in the mountains contemplating the Creator's greatness in that pure air."[29]

For other disciples, thoughts of the great gift of salvation through the death and resurrection of Jesus Christ can be more than enough reason for turning to God in thankful prayer, grateful that God never ceases to call us back whenever we falter through sin or other distraction. A. C. Dixon (1854–1925), considered the founder of Christian Fundamentalism, was especially moved by the thought of God's apparent soft spot for the weak, helpless, and broken:

---

29. Pier Giorgio Frassati, quoted in Smith, "Quotes from Pier Giorgio Frassati," para. 22.

A dear friend of mine who was quite a lover of the chase [hunting], told me the following story: "Rising early one morning," he said, "I heard the baying of a score of deerhounds in pursuit of their quarry. Looking away to a broad, open field in front of me, I saw a young fawn making its way across, and giving signs, moreover, that its race was well—nigh run. Reaching the rails of the enclosure, it leaped over and crouched within ten feet from where I stood. A moment later two of the hounds came over, when the fawn ran in my direction and pushed its head between my legs. I lifted the little thing to my breast, and, swinging round and round, fought off the dogs. I felt, just then, that all the dogs in the West could not, and should not capture that fawn after its weakness had appealed to my strength." So is it, when human helplessness appeals to Almighty God. Well do I remember when the hounds of sin were after my soul, until, at last, I ran into the arms of Almighty God.[30]

Still other persons, vaguely aware of the divine presence in life, may experience a moment of insight into God's great love when treated graciously by a stranger or receiving forgiveness for some serious misdeed.

Perhaps the majority of Christians learned to pray when they were children or teenagers but left the practice aside as the busyness of life unfolded for them, learning prayer forms that are no longer satisfying. The remainder of this chapter offers suggestions for Christian disciples who find themselves awakening to the divine mystery and presence in their lives. Learning to pray as adults offers new possibilities and challenges.

Some Desirable Personal Attitudes for Prayer

In the wake of our brief survey of traditional Christian prayer, we can note a few especially helpful and timeless personal attitudes for praying disciples to nurture. Some especially helpful ones include personal humility, gratitude to God, and confidence in God's never-ending love for us.

Humility

Humility, as it relates to Christian prayer, is the virtue moving us to recognize that God is our Creator and we are God's created one. We place ourselves in prayer before the vast mystery of divine love, the source of

---

30. A. C. Dixon, quoted in Bounds and Hodge, *Necessity of Prayer*, 9.

all life and all that is, who sees all and who knows all, yet whose love for us desires our human flourishing. Our prayer is most sincere and humble when we can approach God as we are, "warts and all," and let ourselves be interiorly vulnerable before God. God knows us better than we know ourselves. This process requires a lifetime, as our habitual life of prayer slowly uncovers more and more of Christ within us.

Gratitude to God for Past Blessings

Any prayer to God is, at heart, acknowledging the source of every blessing and happiness. Old Testament gratitude in prayer was rooted in the memory of God's continual and abiding presence in the lives of the Hebrew people at moments both of joy and suffering, eliciting thankfulness to God as the source of every blessing. Much of communal Christian prayer includes expressions of thanksgiving. Time spent in reflecting on one's gifts and blessings can sharpen our awareness of reasons for thankfulness to God, even if only for the faith and wisdom that come to us through following the life example of Jesus.[31]

Praying with Confidence That God Hears Us and Desires Our Good

One difficulty for praying persons to accept is that, while we may believe that God hears our prayer, often we do not receive the results for which we pray. Nevertheless, the Christian tradition has long held that God's love for us is *providential*, meaning that each of us is held in divine loving hands through all of life's successes, joys, and sorrows. In these moments, more so in times of disappointment, we may discover more about our innermost values and motivations as our faith grows and broadens as we learn to change our perception of how God can act through our lives. A later chapter of this book examines the importance of trusting the divine love and some ways to nurture it.

Personal Temperament and Prayer

How do you pray? What is your best way to pray?

---

31. LaBelle, *From Strength to Strength*, 135–60.

People are different, each one possessing a particular constellation of personal talents and personality traits that affect personal likes and dislikes when interacting with others and, ultimately, reaching out to God in some prayerful means. It is helpful to consider some aspects of your unique personality and what types of prayer expressions might best suit your individuality. This chapter section explores three ways by which you may describe your inner personality and preferences.[32] Awareness of where we fall in each area can help us identify what approaches or aids to prayer may enhance our overall prayer life.

Introvert and Extrovert Personalities

Our first range of classifying persons is whether they are predominantly introverts or extroverts. For this chapter, we understand introverts as people energized within their inner world rather than by heavy social interaction. Introvert personalities can be happy alone or perhaps with one or two other persons, while extensive social engagement with continual interpersonal exchanges becomes emotionally draining. Introverts are the ones who, on entering a crowded room, might quickly identify the room exit and work their way of socializing through the crowd in that direction, having learned how to disappear from large and noisy gatherings. In their prayer life, introverts normally prefer more quiet prayer settings. She or he can participate well in communal prayer but appreciates having short periods of quiet at appropriate times (after listening to a scriptural reading or a congregation hymn, for instance).

Extroverts are more energized by interpersonal exchanges. They come alive in social situations and are among the last to leave a party. Extroverts will also eventually retreat from periods of heavy social engagement but usually later than an introvert and will likely feel the social excitement lingering afterward. Extroverts are more apt to think and talk aloud about a problem when seeking a solution. They enjoy social prayer settings. Their struggle, however, can be to remain quiet during liturgical pauses or

---

32. This chapter section borrows from the personality types explored in a very useful book by David W. Keirsey and Marilyn Bates, *Please Understand Me: Character and Temperament Types*. Numerous online and published works use their eight-attribute study that draws from the well-known Myers-Briggs Personality Indicator, still used today for exploring the influence of personality preferences in areas such as interpersonal relationships, management, and leadership styles.

repetitive ritual prayer since extroverts are more people of outward action and expression, preferring engagement with their surrounding world.

Intuitive and Sensate Personalities

The second way that we relate to the world around us can be described as either primarily intuitive or sensate persons. Intuitives can imagine possibilities in persons, projects, or in social development. They tend to be people of ideas, perhaps spending lots of time conceptualizing plans and considering options. Intuitives can occupy themselves with puzzling through a problem to solve and are more comfortable using their inner intuition for making a choice. They are often drawn to interior meditation prayer or deeper contemplation in prayer. Intuitive persons tend to be adept at interiorly engaging symbols or actions in public worship that can open them to a deeper mystical reality.

Individuals who lean toward the sensate descriptor rely more on the human senses and concrete observations in decision-making. They are usually practical-minded, not comfortable with seemingly nebulous intuitive solutions without having supportive sensate and objective facts. They are also more likely to prefer routine to frequent change or innovation. In prayer, sensate persons are drawn to the visual and the tangible; seasonal signs and colors are important to them, as are descriptive words in prayer or sermons and homilies.

The Thinking and Feeling Personalities

Thinking persons prefer to relate to their world more from the perspective of logic. They tend to guard their emotions and are not immediately comfortable with displays of affection. Thinkers tend to compartmentalize their feelings from their decision-making, sometimes earning for themselves an unjust reputation of being somewhat heartless and unfeeling.

Feeling personalities are much more at home by relating to the world through their emotions. They are also sensitive to the feelings of others. However, their ability to make decisions can be clouded and thrown into disarray by their own strongly felt emotions and when they consider the feelings of others whom their decisions may impact.

The three spectra of personal temperaments listed above (introvert-extrovert, intuitive-sensate, thinking-feeling) suggest elements of preference for a disciple's particular prayer style and possible aids to enhance one's prayer life. Of course, each person is a remarkable complexity whom God alone can fathom. In something as personal as prayer, one should pray as one can rather than trying to force-fit a view of how one ought to pray.

The Six Types and Communal Prayer

An individual's awareness of personal preferences can influence both individual and communal prayer growth. Noted spirituality authors Chester Michael and Marie Norrisey note that different temperaments best interact in liturgical services when their dominant functions are engaged, represented by four descriptive words: *Community, Word, Cross,* and *Table*.[33] *Community* suggests just that—fellowship, communion, relationship, concepts that will especially touch feeling personalities. Thinkers may be especially keen on how the *Word* is proclaimed, especially in the content and structure of a sermon or homily. The presence and promotion of sensate objects such as the *Cross* tend to engage the visual ability of sensate-dominant persons. For intuitive persons, finally, *Table* represents the use of symbols that can lead congregants into a deeper perception of divine Mystery unfolding in a communal encounter. The breaking and sharing of bread and wine at the eucharistic table of the Lord, the visible book containing the day's scriptural readings, liturgical symbols accompanying seasons such as Advent and Lent—these and other symbolic items can be particularly fruitful to the symbol-sensitive nature of intuitives. Would that each personality could be well engaged and well fed through public celebrations that are consciously attentive to the wide range of unique individuals attending regular religious services; often enough, though, this is a vain wish. Wise service planners and presiding ministers will be attentive to how they might better engage and spiritually nourish their congregation of various personalities who present themselves for a limited time each week.

A final note: While each personality has a preferred or dominant level of acting within these three ranges of interactions with their outside world, they should not be considered static and everlasting pigeonholes for classifying a person.[34] Each of us has personality traits of introversion

---

33. Michael and Norrisey, *Prayer and Temperament*, 103–20.

34. A more extensive treatment of personality and temperament would include a fourth variable measuring the degree of preferred order or structure in life (relying on a Judging-based personality [J] versus a less structured Perceptive one [P]), also

and extroversion, sensate *and* intuitive, thinking *and* feeling, with one pole from each pair tending to dominate. However, the recessive qualities can be stretched and developed to some degree.

Conclusion

The Christian prayer tradition offers a wide assortment of prayer experiences and expressions, each rooted in a particular historical time but still valuable for contemporary Christians seeking to enhance their prayer life. Familiarity with these forms and an awareness of individual personality preferences can lead disciples to a more sincere, more profound, more transforming prayer relationship with God.

---

considered in Keirsey and Bates, *Please Understand Me*. Michael and Norrisey, *Prayer and Temperament*, explores all of these attributes as they affect prayer styles.

Questions for Reflection

1. What is your understanding of prayer? How does it compare with the attitudes toward prayer found in the Old and New Testaments?
2. What is your attitude toward the many forms of Christian devotional prayer? Are you drawn to any of these? Do you see any value in this class of prayer even if you are not personally drawn to it?
3. How would you describe your personality in terms of predominantly introvert/extrovert, sensate/intuitive, thinking/feeling? There are numerous online Myers-Briggs-based tests that can be helpful for you to identify these.

Suggested Further Reading

Jungmann, Joseph A. *Christian Prayer through the Centuries*. Edited by Christopher Irvine. Translated by John Coyne. New York: Paulist, 2007.

Michael, Chester P. and Marie C. Norrisey. *Prayer and Temperament: Different Prayer Forms for Different Personality Types*. Charlottesville, VA: Open Door, 1991.

Raab, Christopher and Harry Hagan, eds. *The Tradition of Catholic Prayer: The Monks of Saint Meinrad*. Collegeville, MN: Liturgical, 2007.

2

Awakening to God's Loving Presence

MOST, IF NOT ALL, Christians at least try to pray with some regularity. Other disciples, though, after experiencing some special moments of divine nearness, find themselves drawn to giving extra effort to dwell in the sunshine of God's abiding presence that embraces all of creation.

The divine overflowing love is at the heart of God's presence. The human capacity to love, challenged throughout life to deepen and mature, finds itself at any one moment somewhere on a continuum between the extremes of total selfishness and near-complete utter self-giving. In contrast, divine unselfish Love simply *is*. We are always held in God's presence by the unfathomable depth of the divine Love for us; as a result, God is always attentive to us. This exquisite and complete divine Love expresses the love of the three Trinitarian persons for each other in one divine Being: the Father's complete love for the Son, the Son's complete love for the Father, and the Holy Spirit that coexists as the result of this absolute love between Father and Son. The three divine Persons are totally given to each other in perfect loving interrelationship, totally attentive or "present" to one another, three divine Persons comprising the one God. All creation exists due to this outflowing of creative divine Love that overflows into our material and spiritual world; thus, God, who is attentive Love of the three divine Persons, is also attentive to the fruit of this loving intercommunion. God is continually present to us as participants in the created order.

For our part, we human beings are subject to the sensate attractions, distractions, and temptations of the world around us, causing us much difficulty in maintaining a lasting focused awareness of God's presence in our lives. Christian spiritual life practices, such as regular time for personal prayer and quietly resting in the all-surrounding, divine loving gaze, can strengthen our ability to sustain times of awareness, in part through ordering our natural, though sometimes misplaced, human attractions to our world. The beauty of creation can assist us in growing closer to the Creator; often, however, our distorted admiration and desires for the created world reveal a more selfish form of love that pales in comparison with the divine loving presence surrounding us.

The Christian spiritual tradition offers a wealth of testimony from writers and saintly persons who show us that, while we may not directly perceive God's presence using our human senses, we can develop a greater sensitivity to the divine loving presence through developing our inner awareness and sensitivity to it. Classical philosophers of antiquity and some early Christian spiritual masters sought this through maturing in moral virtues and their rational abilities to approach God through the intellect. A more effective path, though, is the way of approaching the divine by cultivating and expanding our interior capacity to love that can reach beyond our intellect. The Christian tradition has long recognized that the refinement of our love for God offers the better hope of finding greater intimacy with God, with the possibility to soar beyond the limitations of our rational ability.

This chapter explores insights from some of the many Christian spiritual masters who have sought a deeper relationship with God. These experiences offer possible means for contemporary disciples to become more attentive to the life-giving and transforming realities of God's loving presence.

Part One: Seeking God's Presence Throughout Christian Spiritual History

In Scripture

The Old Testament

The Hebrew experiences of God provided much of the foundation for early Christian ideas concerning the divine presence among them. God had chosen the people of the covenant as God's special people and remained with them always, leading them from Egyptian slavery through their desert wandering, always raising leaders and prophets who would recall them to their divine covenant from the time of Abraham.

The various strands of Old Testament literature indicate that the Hebrew people of faith perceived a loving God who was their redeemer, even during times of their suffering and rejection of him. God was hidden from them but whose care for them was made known by sending various beneficent angelic messengers to the people (Exod 14:19; 23:20; 33:2).[1] Different traditional accounts in Genesis illustrate the divine preference for those who "walked with God" through salvation accounts, such as enabling Noah and his family to survive the great flood (Gen 6–9). The book of Exodus accounts recall God summoning Moses to lead his people from Egypt to freedom by parting the Red Sea and destroying Pharaoh's charioteers by restoring the waters (Exod 3–14). God interacted with the people through the divine Spirit who provided strength and guidance, the medium through which God bestowed gifts and blessings (2 Chr 15:1; 20:14; 24:20; Zech 4:6; 6:1–8).[2] God even bestowed the divine glory among the people as expressions of the divine indwelling with them in the form of fire: the mighty consuming blaze on Mount Sinai (Exod 29:43) eventually returned to occupy the tabernacle (Exod 40:34–38). Through such iconic images, God's people carried the memory of the divine presence that accompanied them throughout their history.

The New Testament

The incarnation of the Son of God makes visible and tangible the glory and love of God that was manifested in the Old Testament saga. Matthew's Gospel (1:22–25) identifies Jesus as *Emmanuel*, "God with us," who embodies the divine love, inviting all people to fuller existence by following Jesus's example of living in the reign of God.

Jesus's many miracles attest to the presence of this reign. For example, he announces after casting out the evil spirit from an afflicted man, "If it is by the finger of God that I cast out the demons, then the Kingdom of God has come to you" (Luke 11:20). Through many parables, Jesus reveals that God's love is offered to all: love that is transformative (as in Zaccheus's moment of conversion, Luke 19:1–10), restorative (healing socially isolated

---

1. Thomson, "Presence of God," 1751.
2. Thomson, "Presence of God," 1751.

lepers who subsequently could return to community life, Luke 17:11–19), merciful (with the adulterous woman, John 8:3–11), and superabundant (the father's copious love toward his prodigal son, Luke 15:11–31).

Jesus reveals to the Jews that his ministry to others expresses the love of the One who sent him, for "the Father and I are one" (John 10:30) and "the Father is in me and I in the Father" (John 10:38), revealed most exquisitely in his suffering and death. Jesus embodies the fullest possible human manifestation of God who is Love (1 John 4:8), making this love visible through his many acts of healing and restoration that are at once both physical and spiritual. These moments of renewed life offer the hope for a more durable harmony between people and, by extension, with the rest of creation.

First-Century Christians and "Knowledge" of God

For the earliest Christians, "knowledge" of God came through a personal spiritual experience of the divine love. Paul addressed his Ephesian community, saying, "I pray that the God of our Lord Jesus Christ, the Father of glory, may give you a spirit of wisdom and revelation as you come to know him" (Eph 1:17). He also prayed that "you may have the power to comprehend, with all the saints, what is the breadth and length and height and depth, and to know the love of Christ that surpasses knowledge, so that you may be filled with all the fullness of God" (Eph 3:18–19). Simon Peter in John's Gospel spoke for his co-disciples, saying to Jesus shortly before his death that they would not leave him because "we have come to believe and know that you are the Holy One of God" (John 6:69). "Knowledge" in these instances signals a deeper and more committed faith in Jesus as Son of God and who personifies life in the reign of God.

The early church had to learn that Christ, risen and ascended to the Father, remained with them as they gathered in his name, though he would be present in new ways. Through baptism, Christians have died and risen with Christ into their new life with God, helping to form Christ's new body on earth. Jesus would be present in the center of this new community as they gathered together believing in him when reading Scriptures, in breaking of the bread (Luke 24:13–33), or when gathered together to hear testimonies of Jesus's new life in the upper room (Luke 24:34–53).

First-Century Christians and Seeking the reign of God

"Repent, for the reign of God is at hand!" was Jesus's underlying message to his disciples as he called them to live more fully by divine love. Life in the reign of God invited disciples to pursue lives in harmony with the divine love for each person, love free of self-interest, envy, desire for revenge, and overflowing with mercy toward others. In short, one's human love could gradually mature into an ever-clearer representation of divine love. During the first few centuries, Christians pursued this new life by practicing the religious and moral teaching of the twelve apostles (the "apostolic teaching") while confronting the morally corrupting influence of surrounding pagan practices, the scourge of Jewish anti-Christian antagonism, and periodic Roman persecution.

Jesus taught that the possibility of living in the reign of God was available to all; for those who truly desired to live in this reign with hearts unimpeded, he modeled the practices of material detachment (voluntary poverty) and celibate chastity. By about the year AD 50, Paul was supporting the practice of some unmarried or widowed Corinthian Christians who followed lives of committed virginity in preparation for the anticipated return of Christ and a fuller share of life in God's Reign (1 Cor 7). Early Christian ascetics committed themselves to live ever more fully in the reign of God with unfettered hearts, becoming the forerunners of Christian desert monastics and future expressions of consecrated religious life.[3]

Seeking God's Presence in the Patristic Era

For early Christian writers, cultivating an awareness of God through knowledge of God came through prayerful reflection in light of their basic faith, Scripture, and apostolic teaching, which fed their inner experience and conviction of the divine nearness. Some disciples nurtured their reflections and perception of God's presence that drew from their observation of divine attributes perceptible in creation, gaining insight from reading Greek and Roman classical works. Eventually, earnest followers of Jesus also learned the importance of developing and purifying their relationship of loving attentiveness to God.

---

3. The word *asceticism* borrows from a Greek wrestling term meaning to practice or to struggle, as described in chapter 5. Christian ascetics took the call from Jesus seriously to pursue wholehearted life in the reign of God.

A few early patristic Christian writers cited observations of nature as evidence of the divine activity in creation. Bishop Clement of Rome, in his second-century letter to the fractured Christian community at Corinth, called their attention to the divinely instilled qualities of order found in nature:

> The heavens revolve by His arrangement and are subject to Him in peace. Day and night complete the revolution ordained by Him, and neither interferes in the least with the other. Sun and moon and the starry choirs, obedient to His arrangement, roll on in harmony, without any deviation, through their appointed orbits.[4]

Hoping to heal the division among the Corinthian Christians, Clement also asserted in the letter that reestablishing social order and respect for divinely inspired Christian authority would restore the community to the divinely inspired order for all creation and society, a sign of the divine presence in a unified community. This restoration was possible through following the way of Christ's life and love. The Corinthian agitators could find it by embracing Christ's example of humility in seeking forgiveness and restoration of the divinely ordered shepherds; the leaders, likewise, were exhorted to express Christian love by their humble forgiveness.

Bishop Athanasius of Alexandria (c. 293–373), in his classic work *On the Incarnation of the Word*, provides a reasoned and traditional explanation for why Jesus, the Word of God, came into the material world: to restore humanity's intimacy with God that had been ruptured with the fall of Adam and Eve. Men and women were originally created as embodied spirits who would share eternal life, harmony, and incorruptibility with God as his special creation; alas, humanity inherited the sin of Adam and Eve that set them on the road to further sinfulness, incurring corruption and eternal loss.[5] It was unthinkable that such a good and gracious God, who had imbued humanity with the imprint of God's divine image, should scrap his creation and abandon human beings, the pinnacle of creation.[6] While the image of God remains in each person to this day, our likeness to God that is evident through a virtuous life guided by divine love and grace has been lost and needs restoration somehow. God's immense love became known in the person of Jesus, God's spoken Word to humanity, who entered creation and restored humanity's divine likeness and eternal life with

---

4. Clement of Rome, 1 Clem 20.
5. Athanasius, *Inc.* 4.
6. Athanasius, *Inc.* 6.

God. Jesus Christ assumed human nature to overcome the finality of death through his eventual death as a human being who was perfectly faithful to his Father. Animated by his deepest fatherlike love for all humanity, Jesus restored humanity's intended relationship with God into eternity.[7]

Archbishop John Chrysostom of Constantinople (347–407) expressed the orthodox Christian view that creation was essentially good, issuing from a good God and expressing the divine goodness:

> For [creation] is not wicked, but is both beautiful and a token of the wisdom and power and lovingkindness of God.... Hear, too, Paul saying, "For the invisible things of Him, since the creation of the world, are clearly seen, being perceived through the things that are made" [Rom 1:20]. For each of these by which he spoke declared that the creation leads us to the knowledge of God, because it causes us to know the Master fully.[8]

Bishop Augustine of Hippo in the fourth century also recognized the inherent goodness of creation that only could have been brought into being by a superior, good, and eternal Creator:

> Heaven and earth plainly exist, and by the very fact that they undergo change and variation, they cry out that they were made. If anything was not made, yet exists, there is no element in it that was not present earlier; for change and variation imply that something is made that was not previously there.... And their visible existence is the voice with which they say this. It was you who made them, Lord: you are beautiful, so it must have been you, because they are beautiful; you who are good must have made them, because they are good; you who are, because they are.[9]

The beauty found in creation could only have come from a beautiful and good Creator.

Early Christian Monasticism and Searching for God Through Purity of Heart

Ironically, the legalization of Christianity in the early fourth century brought a spiritual tepidity to Christian religious practice and fervor. Many Christian disciples intent on living more fully in the reign of God considered

---

7. Athanasius, *Inc.* 9–10.
8. John Chrysostom, "Homily 2," section 3.
9. Augustine, *Conf.* 11.6.

this relaxed state as an obstacle for those who truly wished to pursue it.[10] A number of Christians had already begun to flee into desert areas during the late-third-century persecutions; once the religion became socially respectable and commonplace, a few of those desiring a more rigorous and undistracted Christian spiritual program began to move out into deserted regions found in parts of Syria, Palestine, and Egypt. Their purpose became to seek "purity of heart" as envisioned by the Christian ascetic Evagrius of Pontus (346–399), who promoted a rigorous program of self-denial for monks to vanquish what he saw as eight principal temptations that could lead to sin.[11] Gradually becoming free from the pull of passions through sometimes excessive practices of assiduous prayer, humility, and bodily deprivations, monks sought to dispose themselves more fully to God's presence through cultivating an unfettered and continual focus on the divine, following St. Paul's ideal to "pray without ceasing" (1 Thess 5:17). In pursuing this goal, monks such as John Cassian experienced a gradual reorientation of their prayer that led away from self-preoccupation to greater concern for the needs of others and, ultimately, could bring the monk to a loving gaze focused on God alone. This highly refined experience of prayer sometimes resulted in short-lived moments of what Cassian called a "prayer of fire" that captivated monks in moments of interior ecstasy, beholding the divine with attitudes of refined, selfless love.[12]

Cassian also promoted the monastic practice of constantly repeating a short prayerful praise. His preferred verse was the opening of the fiftieth psalm, "O God, come to my assistance / O Lord, make haste to help me," that offered a way for monks to deepen their openness to the divine presence in daily life.

In closing, we note that early Christian experiences of opening to the divine presence gradually developed as Christianity built upon its earliest traditional understandings of God, while sometimes learning from insights gained by observing the created world. Desert monastic experiences of prayer offered the additional insight that the divine presence was also a

---

10. Also addressed in chapter 1.

11. Evagrius identified these as greed, lust, avarice, anger, melancholy, vanity, pride, and *accidie* (the temptation to abandon one's regular spiritual program, leading to sloth). See Evagrius, *Talking Back*.

12. Cassian, *Conf.* 9.25.1. Cassian's meaning of ecstacy was that monks would lose their self-awareness (literally, to be "outside themselves") in periods of deepest loving prayer.

loving presence of God, for those who had spiritual ears to listen. The following centuries will build on some of these earlier experiences.

Seeking God's Presence in the Medieval Era

The monastic pursuit of the reign of God was arguably the most visible vehicle and spiritual influence for those seeking a more focused presence to God in the early medieval period. Several medieval spiritual developments moved Christian spirituality out of the monastic confines toward ways of opening oneself to the divine presence in more ordinary circumstances, which we examine next.

Influences of Celtic Christian Spirituality

The Irish Celtic mingling with Christianity of the region has left some special qualities that help to illustrate the Celtic regard for the divine in the joys and struggles of daily life.

The strong presence of monastic communities greatly influenced the development of early Christianity throughout the region. The monastic ideal of continual prayer also influenced the surrounding Christian communities, encouraging a more continual consciousness of God's presence in life. Recognizing that God oversaw and accompanied them at all times produced many blessing prayers, petitions, and greetings intertwined with everyday and seasonal life. Celtic people were very much people of the land, close to its dangers and uncertainties, at mercy to the elements of weather that varied with changing seasons. The people appreciated that life was especially precarious for them, and imploring divine assistance and protection was a normal attitude. God was not to blame for their lot; the people had a strong awareness of divine love for them that rang out in prayers recalling the Trinity and a pervasive sense of gratitude for God's protective goodness. The Celtic people considered themselves a journeying people with a wandering nature. Perhaps this is what gave early Irish monasticism its missionary quality from the time of the first monks who wandered about forming other Christian settlements, lending to the popular sense of being pilgrims in this life toward their heavenly homeland in the reign of God.

Early Celtic Christian spirituality did not suffer from our contemporary tendency to separate the created world into spiritual/physical/

intellectual divisions. Divinity permeated all of life and time. People integrated routine daily chores and other activities with prayers, whether on awaking, while working the fields, feeding the livestock, or at home cooking or weaving. Village church or monastic bells rang regularly each day, calling its hearers to stop, pray, and recall the divine Being that always accompanied them. Essentially, elements of Celtic Christian life periodically reminded them to "pray always" and helped to maintain awareness of God's spiritual closeness. In short, God seemed closer to the people because the people habitually recalled God's presence among them, the source of all their blessings.

Franciscan Spirituality: Traces of God in One Another and in Creation

The thirteenth century witnessed a growing number of persons who sought to find God while trusting deeply in God's great providential love for them. Francis of Assisi was certainly one excellent example. Francis followed the way of Jesus through putting into practice Jesus's way of total trust in the love of his heavenly Father in a spirit of radical gospel poverty (detachment from material goods), humility, and gratitude for the divine goodness and blessings to him. Through his experiences of trusting in the unseen Trinity, Francis paradoxically came to a deeper awareness of God, as he wrote, "You are security . . . You are the protector, you are our guardian and defender, You are strength; You are refreshment."[13]

Francis sought with all his being to walk in the way of the earthly Jesus who trusted in the Father's love for him. His experiences led him to find Jesus in the people he encountered, especially among the poor and most isolated from society. Francis discovered Jesus by following in the Savior's footprints and adhering to his teaching in the gospel.[14] He grew in his appreciation for the sacrament of the Eucharist, in which Christ repeatedly arrives anew among the people of God.[15] His growing intimacy with the unseen Creator also led Francis to recognize that creation expresses praise to God precisely through its existence and its divinely inspired way of

---

13. Francis of Assisi, *The Praises of God* 4.5, quoted in Cotter, "Franciscan Spirituality," 161.

14. Cotter, "Franciscan Spirituality," 164.

15. For more information on the Eucharist as the body of Christ, see chapter 1, footnote 21.

providing for the needs of its different creatures. We find in his "Canticle of the Sun" (otherwise known as his "Canticle of Creation"):

> Praised be You, my Lord, with all your creatures,
> especially Sir Brother Sun,
> Who is the day and through whom You give us light.
> And he is beautiful and radiant with great splendor;
> and bears a likeness of You, Most High One.
> Praise be You, my Lord, through Sister Moon and the Stars,
> in heaven You formed them clear and precious and beautiful.
> Praised be You, my Lord, through Brother Wind, and through the air, cloudy and serene, and every kind of weather
> through which You give sustenance to Your Creatures.[16]

Franciscan spirituality has enormously influenced Christian awareness of how creation can reveal the divine loving activity and has enjoyed growing popularity and awareness into the twenty-first century.

Dominic of Guzman (1170–1221) founded another consecrated religious order, the Order of Preachers (*Dominicans*), laboring to defend and teach the truths of the Christian faith. The divine light of Christian revelation is the source of Truth itself, offering to all humanity the way to live as God's privileged creation. The Dominicans (both men and women) continue this mission, as before, by placing great emphasis on academic study along with three other pillars undergirding their spiritual life: community life, deep prayer, and sharing the spiritual fruits of their labors through service as educators, preachers, and workers for justice rooted in the reign of God.

The fourteenth century nurtured a further interest in interior prayer and the desire to focus on the simplicity of God's love. At least three principal collections of mystical development occurred within Germany (Meister Eckhart), England (with *The Cloud of Unknowing*), Italy (Catherine of Siena), and in the so-called Modern Devotion movement of present-day Netherlands, Belgium, and Luxembourg (*Imitation of Christ*).

The German Dominican theologian and mystic Meister Eckhart (c. 1230–c. 1328) pursued a path of mystical insight through using his intellectual ability. Eckhart and his followers sought to find union with God interiorly by sharpening awareness of their shared foundational "essence" with God. All creation shares to some degree in this divine essence

---

16. Francis of Assisi, "Canticle of the Sun," in *Francis and Claire*, 38–39.

since creation comes forth through Christ, the Word, from the divine creative activity. Like several other Christian mystics who struggled to describe their spiritual experiences, Eckhart's teaching suffered some misunderstandings. For example, some of his preaching implied that praying mystics could become lost or absorbed into the divine presence and lose their individual created personhood in the eternal sea of the divine. Another concern was Eckhart's assertion that all creation shared something of the divine essence; this could be misinterpreted as a form of pantheism that equated God with created matter. Historians and theologians have restored Eckhart's reputation only during the twentieth century. His thought has subsequently influenced the Christian regard for the sacredness of creation, explored later in this chapter.

The English author of *The Cloud of Unknowing* is anonymous, but many historians believe it was Walter Hilton (1340–1396), an English priest and solitary. Advanced prayer, for the author of *The Cloud*, is ultimately in the "realm of the unknowing," a way of meditation without using images but to be pierced through focusing one's prayer on the love of God by way of prayerful utterances of love for God. The author asserts that images of God or sentiments toward the divine, however holy and good they may be, only obstruct this highest approach to love. To that end, praying disciples should imagine themselves situated between two veiled regions: a lower "cloud of forgetting" under which they should consign any such images or words, and, above them, another "cloud of unknowing" beyond which is the unknowable God. Those seeking to follow the way of unknowing should hold themselves as though sitting before a curtain, aware that someone is on the other side but having no perceptible sense of the Other. He instructs praying persons to release mental "acts of love" (blind stirrings or impulses of love) towards God, taking the form of short, repeated words such as "God" and "love."

For the author of *The Cloud*, interior prayer can lead disciples to discover experiences of deepest joy (moments of loving union with God in love at the core of one's being) and deepest sorrow (when confronting the abyss between the disciple and the One the disciple ultimately loves). To the degree that people love something, they tend to give themselves to its pursuit, such as to money, success, family, or comfort. So it is for praying disciples: their maturing love for God will gradually lead them to give themselves over to God and leave behind all other lesser loves. This inner transformation of disciples will lead to their new life in the resurrected Jesus, an ever-greater share of life within the all-consuming love and guidance of the Trinity.

In Italy, Catherine of Siena (1347–1380) was a lay member of the Dominican order who did not live within the confines and rules of a consecrated religious community. Her biography is difficult to know with certainty as it, like that of Francis of Assisi, was subject to exaggeration by her first biographer and some of her disciples.[17] Her story, though, offers an example of someone who sought closeness to God through practices of interior prayer, personal sacrifice, and charity to others.

Catherine's story relates how she lived to seek God alone. She reportedly had an inner mystical experience at seven years of age that, according to her biographer Raymond of Capua, convinced her to henceforth live in perpetual virginity. At fifteen, over the strong objections of her parents, she renewed her desire not to marry by cutting off her hair in defiance to their wishes. Once her parents consented, Catherine joined a local women's association, the *mantellate*, presumably an order of widows and unmarried women who lived at home but supported and encouraged one another in lives of prayer and charitable service. At eighteen, she took the religious habit of a lay "third-order" Dominican, lived as a praying solitary in her bedroom except for attending daily Mass, and followed a penitential life of prayer and fasting. At twenty-one, Catherine returned to live in her family home, where she pursued a life of solitary contemplative prayer and a more active life of service to the poor and sick. People began to regard her as a mature spiritual figure and sought her for her spiritual wisdom. Leading civic figures of Siena also appealed for her intervention in some political disputes but, in some cases, took advantage of her spiritual reputation and political innocence while pursuing political and economic goals. Catherine subsequently moved to Rome with some of her female followers, subsisting mostly on alms. She met her end in early 1380 when she could no longer swallow food or water, though she would still drag herself to the nearby St. Peter's Basilica for daily Mass and prayer. Through these months, Catherine offered her sufferings and prayers for the church's needs, dying on April 29 at thirty-three. Her body now rests in Rome at the Church of the Minerva

---

17. The Dominican Raymond of Capua (c. 1303–1399), Catherine's disciple and confessor, wrote her earliest biography. Catherine's experiences would later influence the reform of the Dominican order, thanks largely to Raymond's influential writing. The introduction by Suzanne Noffke in *Catherine of Siena: The Dialogue* contains a good summary of her life and teaching.

(a Dominican church and convent) near the Pantheon, while her head is preserved at her childhood home in Siena.

Finally, the close of the fourteenth century produced a very influential writing of what is called the Modern Devotion movement: *The Imitation of Christ*, most likely written by Thomas à Kempis sometime after 1400. The work has proved immensely popular among Roman Catholics and many other Christians through the twentieth century and beyond. The title is misleading as the overall focus is much more on the development of one's interior life, while the final part of the work concerns devotion to the Eucharist. *The Imitation of Christ* encourages an affective devotion and contemplation of Christ's humanity as a means to seek union with God. The work does not seek to bring the reader into the higher levels of mystical prayer but rather the more modest levels of developing habits of asceticism, humility, affective prayer, and liberation of the soul from what impedes its growth.

The book offers a very simple and clear expression of practical charity as the way to holiness. On the negative side, the text also contains a measure of the "contempt for the world" attitude that characterized much writing from the later Modern Devotion period. While the book emphasizes the necessity of self-denial and a call to turn away from worldly distractions, it espouses perennial spiritual qualities of interior renunciation, humility, and patience that remain worthwhile Christian practices.

The high- and later-medieval contributions to Christians seeking a closer life with divine Love would continue to bear fruit into the twentieth century and beyond.

Cultivating Awareness of God During the Modern Era

The first half of the modern era witnessed a great flourishing of interest in practicing deeper interior or contemplative prayer, chiefly in the regions of Spain, Italy, and France. Several spiritual writers also arose during the latter years of this period who encouraged opening to God's presence in more down-to-earth ways. The modern era produced many spiritual guides and writers whose influence is still felt in the Western Christian spirituality tradition.

No longer limited to the confines of monastic or mendicant religious orders, fifteenth-century interior mystical prayer became increasingly popular among lay Spanish Christians. The resulting mystical flourishing in Spain brought a bevy of personal prayer experiences in which people claimed to have entered the realm of spiritual union with God. Many have influenced the Christian mystical tradition in the writings of spiritual masters like Teresa of Avila and John of the Cross. Other mystical experiences of the period, however, spawned much controversy and confusion.[18] The growing popularity of recollection prayer (quiet meditative prayer while learning to quiet interior distractions from senses and the intellect) offered a secure means to train a praying person's attention to the divine loving presence.

Teresa of Avila has become perhaps the best-known follower of recollection prayer, offering a personal road map of her growth in recollection and deeper prayer toward giving her fullest attention to God in love. Teresa greatly desired to learn more about growing in her love for Jesus through her deepening prayer and spiritual friendship with him. Her mysterious experiences of deeper prayer were difficult to explain to others and caused her considerable anxiety. Very few people could offer her advice, but fortunately, she was able to contact and interview spiritually proficient individuals visiting her town. Teresa's autobiography (her *Life*) reveals that her development was not easy. Her prayer experiences convinced her that she was called to reform her Carmelite community, encountering resistance from both consecrated religious and sometimes civic leaders beyond her cloister walls.

In his popular work *An Introduction to the Devout Life*, the saintly Bishop Francis de Sales (1567–1622) gave four possible means for praying disciples to open themselves to God's presence: first, they could recall that the divine presence is everywhere; second, they should remember that while we are always in God's presence, God is also present to us in the center of our inner lives and spiritual hearts, offering strength and courage; third, they should realize that God gazes upon us through the eyes of Jesus, who constantly watches over us; fourth, they can always use their imaginations, looking to Jesus as they would a dear friend who is always ready to listen.[19] The *Introduction to the Devout Life* has remained a welcome aid for Christians who are new to the spiritual life and desire to deepen their relationship in prayer with God.

---

18. One controversial figure of this latter group was the Spanish spiritual director and confessor Miguel de Molinos (1628–1696); his prayer method known as Quietism caused considerable mystical mayhem in Spain and other parts of Europe.

19. de Sales, *Introduction* 2.2.

Brother Lawrence of the Resurrection (c. 1614–1691) is especially remembered for the intimacy he expressed to others concerning his relationship with God.[20] A memorable spiritual experience in his late teens and a few years in the French army strengthened his desire to seek God by entering the French Carmelite order, where he was assigned to the monastery kitchen and repairing sandals. Lawrence developed his rule of spirituality and work amid the tedious chores of cooking, cobbling sandals, and cleaning while at the constant bidding of his superiors.

Lawrence's warm and loving character attracted many to him despite his lowly position in life and his menial work. The wisdom he passed on to them in conversations and letters would later become the basis for the book titled *The Practice of the Presence of God*, compiled and published after his death. It became popular among Catholics, Evangelicals, and Protestants alike. A repetitive theme for Brother Lawrence concerned the loving presence of God at every moment in individual lives, continually inviting them to self-abandonment or surrendering the self in trust to this love. Any daily chore or moment of personal sacrifice could serve as a channel of God's love, no matter how mundane or routine; only the motivation mattered. Brother Lawrence died in relative obscurity in 1691 but his teachings have found a following even among present-day praying Christians.

Attention to Christian mystical life in France and elsewhere in Europe suffered a decline in the eighteenth and nineteenth centuries. Eventually, though, the Christian mystical inclination resurfaced among some individuals; among the best known is the Carmelite sister Thérèse of Lisieux (1873–1897).

Thérèse, the youngest of nine children, was born with delicate health. Perhaps because she was the youngest child, the four-year-old Thérèse was deeply affected by her mother's death. The next eight years or so were sad ones for her, including struggles with scrupulosity. At age ten, she suffered from what was likely a neurological illness (comas, convulsions) for a few months before being cured, which she attributed to Mary, known in a popular Marian devotion as Our Lady of Victories. Thérèse would point to 1886 as a special year of her spiritual awakening at thirteen years of age; shortly afterward, she desired to give her life to God, perhaps even to lose it by serving in the foreign missions. After repeatedly pleading with her father (who withheld permission due to her age) and receiving encouragement in an audience with Pope Leo XIII, Thérèse entered the

---

20. Fanning, *Mystics of the Christian Tradition*, 168–69.

Carmel of Lisieux in 1888 at fifteen, remaining there a scant ten years until her death from tuberculosis.

Thérèse's life became more widely known following her death through her informal autobiography, *The Story of a Soul*, originally intended only for local Carmelite sisters. In the work, Thérèse articulated her spiritual path to God as her "little way" of spiritual childhood, in which she fostered two inner qualities of a young child's love toward a parent. One was to develop a child's naturally unqualified love in response to God's love for her, leading her to deeply trust in God's loving care for her. The second childlike quality is that of a child's weakness due to their dependent and vulnerable state in the world, through which God's power may be manifest.[21] Thérèse practiced trusting in God's mysterious plan for her that she embraced through her various trials of life, giving her full attention to completing whatever daily and most ordinary demand was required from her as a "duty of the present moment." Thérèse's life and opportunities to foster her special closeness to God were ordinary, but she was attentive to her call to grow in faith and love in their midst.

The English laywoman Evelyn Underhill (1875–1941) is an attractive model for Christians who seek to open their hearts to God's presence in the way of everyday mysticism. Her early life was ordinary, but Evelyn accomplished much in the world of her day. The only child of agnostic parents, she attended King's College and embarked on a scholar's career. Evelyn was attracted to Roman Catholicism and the Catholic mystical tradition beginning in 1907 but feared that early twentieth-century Catholic wariness toward science, psychology, and other disciplines might damage her academic reputation. She resigned herself mostly to following her personal mystical insight and experiences, eventually publishing some thirty-nine books and 350 articles on mysticism, during which she wrote her major work, *Mysticism* (1911). Besides her many written compositions, Evelyn became well-recognized through leading retreats and guiding other Christians in interior spiritual growth. She also gave a series of theological presentations at Oxford (1921), and was the first woman Fellow of King's College, Cambridge (1928), as well as the first woman editor of the British journal *Spectator*.

Evelyn Underhill's unique spiritual way and her search for God reveal several characteristics. First, hers was a way of everyday faith, leading to deep encounters with God's love through loving others. Second, she

---

21. Scriptural foundations for this include Prov 9:4; Wis 6:6–9; Isa 40:11; 66:2, 12–13.

did this while also completing the demands of her life as a scholar, researcher, and married woman. Third, her experience of opening to God's love illustrates some of its transformative nature: Evelyn's growing prophetic stance of pacifism in her final years coincided with the outbreak of the Second World War, unpopular at a time of frequent Nazi air force bombing of England.[22]

Opening to the Presence of God in Christian History: Notable Observations

Before leaving the historical part of our inquiry, it would be helpful to summarize some key aspects of how different people have cultivated a sensitivity to God's divine loving presence at different times and moments.

Seeking God has been a timeless practice. Cultivating awareness and remembering the divine presence in life have been important for many practicing Christians. Initially the pursuit of a few through lives of dedicated virginity and monasticism, the Christian thirst for drawing closer to the divine became more widely popular in the medieval period and beyond. The Christian mystical tradition contains the experiences of many well-known spiritual masters and authors, along with accounts of lesser-known disciples, who sought to live more closely in love with the God of the universe.

The need for a degree of interior conditioning. Setting aside the special moments of inbreaking divine love for some individuals, studying the lives of most Christian mystics reveals that they usually incorporated some degree of interior "training" to sharpen their personal sensitivity for perceiving the creative divine love in the surrounding world. This program normally included a degree of personal self-denial using some practices that, to some contemporary readers, might seem too harsh and negative. Their purpose was to foster interior quiet and freedom from daily life's many attractions and distractions. Our fifth chapter considers the element of Christian asceticism as a normal part of Christian discipleship.

Everyday experiences can recall prayerful disciples to the divine nearness. Not restricted to blessed moments of solitary prayer, praying disciples soon came to appreciate that they could direct their love and praise to God while performing mundane daily tasks in an attitude of love for God

---

22. Callahan, *Spiritual Guides for Today*, 25–42.

through attentively and deliberately completing whatever was needed. Attentiveness to the created world around them, also, could offer insight and experiences of the divine goodness.

Part Two: Learning to Notice and Cooperate with God's Loving Presence Today

God as "Totally Elsewhere" Yet "Always with Us"

A recurring paradox for Christians throughout the ages is the tension between two qualities of God that form a spectrum. One extreme view is that God exists as a remote being entirely of the spiritual realm, indifferent to the joys and sorrows of creation, whom we should fear as the one who will render our eternal judgment at the end of time. The other pole is that the relentless divine inclination to foster new life and transformation is indeed mysteriously active in the world through events and persons. This energy is the underlying catalyst for human striving to fuller life, life-giving and truly just social progress, and the natural flourishing of creation, whose creative and sanctifying effects we may perceive through our senses and intellect. Different Christian historical periods have sometimes accentuated one aspect over the other. An exaggerated view of God as "totally elsewhere" can lead to difficulty in accepting that the Son of God was born into the world and could suffer human weakness, pain, and the temptation to sin. Leaning too heavily toward Jesus as "God with us" can risk undermining respect for the divine majesty due to God as the source of all that exists, perhaps rendering a domesticated view of Jesus as merely another special human being.

Jesus's incarnation reveals most visibly how God is wondrously both divinely majestic and active in our world. The divine love is so great that Jesus, the divine Word of Truth, entered into salvation history to redeem and restore humanity's special dignity as created beings. Jesus's earthly life gives the saving and sacred example of how to live in the reign of God that he announced, which is living by divine love that has no limit. His life, passion, and death brought a renewal of the divine destiny for humanity and, through a renewed humanity, the hope for responsible coexistence with all that God has created.

Jesus and the Christian Importance of Human Senses

Jesus, having both fully divine and fully human natures, was born into our world as a human being who communicated with those around him and experienced his heavenly Father's love through his human senses. His voice carried words of salvation; his healing touch conveyed divine love to whomever he healed; he heard the cries of those calling out for mercy and healing. Each year, Jesus would have smelled the aroma of roasted Passover lamb and herbs, reminding him that his was a chosen people meant for holiness; finally, from the cross, he gazed on those who despised him and prayed for their forgiveness. Clearly, Jesus's five senses were fully in play and essential for his redeeming mission as he went about conveying divine love and salvation to the world, always seeking to honor and glorify the Father through them. Jesus was a sensuous human being in the fullest human, rightly ordered, and life-giving manner.

Christian Life as Opening to and Participating in the Divine Creative Mystery

As Christian disciples, our senses are also important in our lives of faith and action. God's revelation to us and our experiences of God's creativity, love, and awesomeness normally come to us through our senses. Even our deeper insights of faith and divine love are greatly influenced by sense impressions gained through reading, the faith testimony of others, the touch of a loved one, the beauty and wonders of nature. Every moment holds an opportunity to awaken to this presence around us.

Our Christian call to participate in the gradual unveiling of the reign of God in the world also challenges us to become sensitive to the divine creative and transforming activity within and around us. This activity issues from the divine loving Mystery at the heart of all creation, indeed the kernel of every human experience we have.[23] As an example, focus your attention on a living tree, a wondrous example of creation and divine creative energy. Consider the divine designer (God) who biologically developed the capillary system for sap and water that provides the means of nurturing every living cell comprising it. Next, behold a small stone and reflect on how it assumed its form and inner composition: the eons of time, immense pressure, and perhaps extreme heat that brought it about,

---

23. Carroll, "Moving Mysticism to the Center," 41–52.

giving testimony to the creative yet patient activity flowing from the divine Mystery that has brought it to your hand at this moment. A third example could be observing a sunset with its many colors, only a few of the many hues of color that arise when receding sunlight strikes the atmosphere, expressing only a tad of the beauty found in the divine Mystery from which creation flows. The created world around us gives witness to God as Love, the source of all life and indeed all that exists.

The divine Mystery at the heart of every human experience, at once creative and transforming all creation, is sometimes difficult to accept. The above experiences offer reflections in more peaceful and pleasant moments; as we all know, not all human experiences are so easy to accept. Personal rejection by another, chronic illness, or the death of someone dear to us are just a few challenging areas. In these moments of desolation, we might ask, "Where is God right now? How could God let this happen?" The divine loving Mystery behind every experience may indeed seem imperceptible or absent altogether, leading many persons into a painful trial of faith. Yet, even at such times, the same active Mystery is at the heart of the experience and beckons our surrender to it, as bitter and repulsive as the experience may be, somehow rendering it into something creative, salvific, and strengthening. Such was Jesus's experience as he underwent his passion and death on the cross, leading incredibly to his new risen and glorified life.

Many, but not all, Christians who become aware of the divine Mystery can find themselves drawn to open their hearts in love to its presence that embraces their lives. All Christians are properly mystics to some degree as Christ continually prompts them to become like him in their lives as they gradually mature from selfishness to self-giving. A large proportion of these we might call "passive mystics" as they go through life unaware of the dynamic. In contrast, those disciples who deliberately seek a deeper relationship with God in love can gradually learn to cooperate ever more fully through their love with the divine Mystery they have discovered. Experiencing deeply an inbreaking of divine love is a "pearl of great price" that gradually leads to disciples giving of themselves in loving acceptance and trust to the divine love at the Mystery's heart. These people come from different walks of life. Many of them rearrange their life priorities and lifestyle to a great extent so that they may more freely cultivate and refine their love for God, similar to what aspiring artists or musicians might do to perfect their craft.

Some Suggestions for Growing in Openness to God's Creative Presence

While each disciple differs in personality and preferences, the following short list offers some ideas for cultivating a deeper awareness of the divine in her or his life. Don't hesitate to try variations of these to suit your particular need and situation.

Find some daily time for personal quiet. Finding quiet moments can be difficult in our busy day and family responsibilities, but finding creative ways to carve out at least some minutes during the day is invaluable for becoming sensitive to the Lord's presence in life.

Designate special privileged spaces for prayer. For many disciples, ritual or habitual actions can assist them in establishing and maintaining regular practices to foster awareness of the divine loving presence.[24] Some people enshrine a Bible or other book of daily scriptural readings on a small yet attractive tabletop in a corner of their bedroom or office where they can visit regularly for some daily reading or reflection. A quiet outdoor park for regular attentive walking or sitting can become a privileged place to be still in the presence of the divine. Sadly, many churches are locked nowadays but some congregations or parishes offer keyed or combination-lock access to a chapel or small prayer space within the building.

Read! Another way to feed the inner spiritual life, reading for spiritual nourishment can comprise a broad range of Christian reading. You might consider some interesting written piece on the Gospels, the experiences and struggles of the early monks, works dealing with the holiness of creation, or more devotional writing that can feed your affective relationship with God. Books abound that explore Christian prayer practices and experiences, classic works in Christian spirituality, insightful reading for Christian meditation or spirituality. The list seems endless!

Other aids that can awaken us to the divine presence. In the past, countless village or neighborhood church bells would ring out at dawn, noontime, or evening, typically following the cadence of the *Angelus* prayer.[25] These spiritual aids offered a reminder for Christians to pause

---

24. Some Christian readers may protest at being called "people of ritual" but I submit that most Christians are so. As an example, simply reflect on Sunday public prayer services that normally contain the same sequence of events from start to finish. Our habitual approaches to prayer and worship allow us to relax and enter into a familiar experience.

25. The *Angelus* developed in the eleventh century; the first lines are "The angel of the Lord declared unto Mary / And she conceived by the Holy Spirit." Ask any Catholic

in their activity and pray for a minute, or at least to listen quietly and recall that the divine accompanies us throughout our day. Today, an attractive cell phone alarm announcing a certain hour could serve that purpose nicely. Another way to recall oneself to God's presence is through attaching something like a small wooden cross to a key chain that, when grasped, can serve as a sudden reminder to pause for a few moments and acknowledge the One who accompanies us always.

Keep a spiritual journal. Spiritual journal-writing is very popular for beginners in the spiritual life or even for more advanced disciples who want to record significant impressions from prayer sessions or other spiritual experiences. Entries can be as short or long as the author wishes. Some people express themselves through poetry that they compose. Don't be afraid to stretch yourself in your journal entries; you may discover within you a latent author or poet!

Finally, *take seriously the potential of transforming divine Love.* Divine Love is powerful. Close approaches to the divine Love slowly tend to move a praying disciple's life toward a greater capacity to love others. This interior transformation of charity may be difficult to accommodate at first, perhaps causing discomfort as the searing and purifying nature of divine Love can raise inner questions about one's life, activity, or earlier presumptions about God. Close encounters with divine Love have set many prophets and religious reformers on their perilous journey (just read the first chapter of Isaiah or Jeremiah, or about Paul's conversion in Acts!). Don't be surprised to find that you may question a previous attitude or course of action (though before making any serious decisions, read the next chapter on spiritual discernment). You may also find a growing need to forgive someone in your life or perhaps ask for their pardon.

Conclusion

At the heart of Christianity is God as divine loving Mystery, whose boundless love is the source and sustainer of all creation. As created human beings, this loving Mystery is actively present through the events of our lives in ways that are at the same time creative, transformative, and strengthening. Noticing the signs and wonders of this active loving presence all around us can draw us ever closer to this same presence that continually moves to transform us into the person of Christ. Our personal

---
of a certain age!

transformation into the likeness of Christ promotes the fuller revelation of the reign of God on earth through our transformed lives, a gradually restored harmony and justice toward other persons, and a more harmonious respect for the rest of creation.

Questions for Reflection

1. Can you describe some moment in your life when you perceived a deep awareness of God's presence?
2. God is both "totally elsewhere" and "always with us." What ramifications has that paradox had in your relationship with God? Do you tend to favor one quality over the other?
3. Can you think of some realistic practices that could help you to develop a greater sensitivity to God's works in your life?

Suggestions for Additional Reading

Callahan, Annice. *Spiritual Guides for Today.* New York: Crossroad, 1992.

Costello, Stephen J., ed. *The Search for Spirituality: Seven Paths within the Catholic Tradition.* Dublin, Ireland: Liffey, 2002.

Fanning, Stephen. *Mystics of the Christian Tradition.* New York and London: Routledge, 2001.

Stendl-Rast, David. *A Listening Heart: The Spirituality of Sacred Sensuousness.* 2nd ed. New York: Crossroad, 1999.

3

Christian Spiritual Discernment

CHRISTIAN DISCIPLES ATTEMPTING TO follow the prompting of divine Love in their lives should ask themselves a question: How can disciples tell whether a remarkable spiritual experience was of special significance in their relationship with God? Perhaps it was a close encounter with the divine loving presence. Or, as Ebenezer Scrooge blamed for his ghostly dreaming, was the experience merely the result of "an undigested bit of beef, a blot of mustard, a crumb of cheese, a fragment of underdone potato"?[1] Learning some principles of spiritual discernment offers traditional means and wisdom to help evaluate the likelihood of whether such experiences or prompting to some action are divinely inspired or arise from other motivations.

Our overarching Christian calling is to live so that we grow ever closer to Christ in love. Our actions and choices, especially life-changing ones, can significantly affect this spiritual quest. Spiritual discernment is appraising a religious experience to assist in judging whether the experience incites a disciple toward or away from a deepening relationship with God. *Discernment of spirits* is a helpful spiritual exercise that offers a traditional means to sift through and evaluate the conflicting interior motivations and feelings that can be in play.

In this chapter, we examine many of the traditional experiences and insights that have shaped the Christian discernment tradition and some ways to implement the practice today.

---

1. Dickens, *A Christmas Carol*, 26.

Part One: Development of Christian Discernment Through History

In Scriptures

The Old Testament

Aside from the occasional practice of drawing lots for seeking to know a divine intention (as in Josh 18:6–10 or 1 Chron 24:5, 31), the Old Testament offers little for the discernment tradition. There were many occasions in which people had to make choices in life in light of the demands of obedience to divine laws. Many navigated this task successfully and chose well, while others did not. These were normally clear choices between some obvious good or evil action, between obedience to divine commands or straying from them due to sin and human weakness.

However, a few fundamental points emerge from the Hebrew covenant relationship with God. One is that, for the just person, God offers divine counsel. The psalmist proclaims the triumph of living justly, beginning with, "Truly God is good to the upright, to those who are pure in heart"; and later, "I am continually with you; you hold my right hand. You guide me with your counsel, and afterward you will receive me with honor" (Ps 73:1, 23–24). A second point is their recognition of evil in the world, leaving men and women susceptible to deception by various impulses that can emerge; the traditional "first sin" account of Adam and Eve (Gen 3) illustrates that persons who seek to follow the divine laws and teaching are capable of being deceived by apparent goodness and personal desires.

Another discernment aid emerged from the Hebrew religious experiences with prophecy and the need to differentiate between true and false prophets. The prophetic tradition was present among the chosen people in Hebrew history from the time of Moses, some thirteen centuries before Christ. The book of Deuteronomy underscores the gravity of the prophetic vocation to speak in God's name:

> I will raise up for them a prophet like you from among their own people; I will put my words in the mouth of the prophet, who shall speak to them everything that I command. Anyone who does not heed the words that the prophet shall speak in my name, I myself will hold accountable. But any prophet who speaks in the name of other gods, or who presumes to speak in my name a word that I have not commanded the prophet to speak—that prophet shall

die. You may say to yourself, "How can we recognize a word that the LORD has not spoken?" If a prophet speaks in the name of the LORD but the thing does not take place or prove true, it is a word that the LORD has not spoken.[2]

How might the community judge the authenticity of prophetic voices? At least five measures arose by which the people could better judge whether a prophet might truly be speaking God's word.[3] First, did the prophet promote orthodox practices or beliefs? Second, as noted in the psalm, did a given prophecy come to pass (though this was not a foolproof criterion, since some predictions could occur at some later time!)? Third, consider the popular acceptance of the prophetic message: Did the prophet refrain from softening or otherwise presenting the divine message into a more palatable one for the audience? A prophet who courageously went against popular opinion and was willing to suffer for it was more likely a true prophet. Fourth, did the prophet's outward moral behavior correspond with the message proclaimed? Finally, consider the listeners' perspective: Was their ultimate appraisal as true or false founded on a living and fruitful faith, indispensable on their part if they were to accept the prophet's message? Each of these aided in judging whether a prophetic message was divinely inspired.

The Intertestamental Qumran Community

Scrolls discovered from the ascetic Jewish community at Qumran reveal evidence of practiced discernment during the historical period between the latest recognized Old Testament writings and the earliest New Testament letters. An important practice for admitting new members, the Qumran *Community Rule* (also known as the *Manual of Discipline*) was likely a rule of life for this Essene community. Note the two types of spirits of truth (light) and evil (darkness):

> [God] created man for dominion over the earth; and he set in him two spirits for him to set his course by them until the set time of his visitation. They are the spirits of truth and of perversity. In a dwelling of light are the generations of truth and from a well of darkness come the generations of perversity. In the hand of the

---

2. Deut 18:18–22.
3. McNamara, "Discernment Criteria in Israel," 10–13.

prince of lights is the dominion of all sons of righteousness: in the ways of light they will walk.[4]

> When a man enters the covenant to act according to all these statutes, to be united with the community of holiness, they shall examine in community his spirit as between a man and his neighbor. . . . There shall be examination of [members'] spirits and their deeds year by year, to raise each according to his intelligence and the perfection of his way and to lower each according to his defection.[5]

The biblical means to authenticate prophets and these excerpts from the Qumran rule indicate that, at the dawn of Christianity, spiritual discernment had its place within the Jewish social and religious scene.

The New Testament

The New Testament writings offer several foundational points that can help Christians to evaluate and appraise their daily activities as they seek to walk in the light of Christ amid challenging cultural and religious influences. The first three Gospels and the Acts of the Apostles do not directly address the issue of spiritual discernment, being more focused on proclaiming the good news of the risen Christ. The letters of Paul and John are more fruitful for providing some foundational guiding principles.

Paul frequently exhorts his Christian communities to live every aspect of their lives as disciples of Christ, seeking to live ever more fully in the light of divine love and grow in their charity for one another. This lofty though attainable goal calls them to consistently appraise the relative value of daily actions and choices as to whether they would strengthen the disciples' loving relationship with God.[6]

For Paul, Christian disciples gradually mature in their faith through following the lived example of Jesus, responding to Paul's exhortation to "put away your former way of life, your old self . . . and to be renewed in the spirit of your minds, and to clothe yourselves with the new self, created according to the likeness of God in true righteousness and holiness" (Eph

---

4. Qumran rule 3.17b–21, in Leaney, *Rule of Qumran*, 144.
5. Qumran rule 5:20–24, in Leaney, *Rule of Qumran*, 175–76.
6. Sources for this summary of Pauline discernment include Guillet, "Discernement spirituelle," 1238–44; also material from a 1999 course publication by Helewa, *Ascesi paolino*.

4:22–25). Paul underscores here his view of the Christian calling, to live fully in conformity to the teaching of Christ, the way of divine love or charity. A challenge for disciples is how to realize and foster in life this growth in charity for integration of interior moral life and exterior behavior. Paul's answer: By cultivating the gift of spiritual discernment that is theirs through their baptism and life in the Spirit.

Paul's Letter to the Romans offers his view of lifelong spiritual discernment in service to growth in charity:

> I appeal to you therefore, brothers and sisters, by the mercies of God, to present your bodies as a living sacrifice, holy and acceptable to God, which is your spiritual worship. Do not be conformed to this world, but be transformed by the renewing of your minds, so that you may discern what is the will of God—what is good and acceptable and perfect.[7]

This passage contains a wealth of Pauline insight. *"Do not be conformed to this world"*: Paul exhorts his readers to resist letting social and cultural values determine their form of Christian life as they can lead to errors such as vanity, inconsistency, and other non-Christlike behavior. *"But be transformed"*: Paul here is no doubt referring to a disciple's transformation into Christ, whose life free of self-preoccupation and self-preservation proclaimed God's glory. This transformation through divine love affects every level of a disciple's being, more profound than a simple outward change in lifestyle. *"By the renewing of your minds"*: Paul intends that Christians rebuild their rational and moral senses, enabling them to turn away from false or half-truths behind the surrounding non-Christian practices and attitudes. *"[To] discern what is the will of God"*: The Christian's practical goal is to live at all times illuminated by the divine Truth and be guided in the direction of continual growth in charity. *"What is good"*: Christians are called to discern what is good when evaluated against the spiritual wisdom and intelligence given them in Jesus Christ (Col 1:9–10). *"Pleasing"*: Maturing disciples grow in their ability to imitate Jesus's entire self-giving life as a sacrificial offering or host pleasing to his Father. *"Perfect"*: "Perfection" for Paul is to arrive at full Christian maturity, finding the fullness of life in the Spirit to which the divine love impels disciples; how "perfect" an action is will become evident in their increasing daily life of charity toward God and others.

---

7. Rom 12:23.

Finally, disciples' successful discernment normally results in some enhanced spiritual fruitfulness through their fuller life in Christ. These blessings facilitate lives more attuned to the Spirit rather than according to the flesh, leading to greater freedom as sons or daughters of God.[8] This new life becomes evident through their maturing qualities including "love, joy, peace, patience, kindness, generosity, faithfulness, gentleness, and self-control" (Gal 5:22–23). Conversely, one finds attitudes and actions attuned to spiritually death-dealing ways of the flesh: "Fornication, impurity, licentiousness, idolatry, sorcery, enmities, strife, jealousy, anger, quarrels, dissensions, factions . . . and things like these" (Gal 5:19–21).

In conclusion, an examination of Paul's guiding principles of discernment encourages disciples to weigh, in daily situations, the values and actions that would best facilitate the continual divine impulse toward growth in charity. Maturing disciples will experience a growing sensitivity toward which choices or actions can lead to a greater increase in love.

Among the Johannine writings, both the Gospel of John and his first letter suggest some points that arose from the struggles of the early Christian church at Ephesus. The author was concerned that his Christian community should guard against absorbing influences from previous followers of John and other Christians who had not persevered in their faith. John presents Christian life for his listeners as a journey of stark choices while following the example of Jesus.[9]

The Gospel of John emphasizes that following Jesus calls for a clear choice for him. John insists on the clarity and urgency of one's following Jesus through the author's contrasting images of light versus darkness and death versus life. Whereas the earlier synoptic gospels gradually reveal Jesus as Son of God, John's writings treat this as an already accepted reality; Jesus is the Messiah (John 1:41), the glorified Son of Man (John 1:51; 3:13–14), and the only Son of God (John 3:16–18).

The Johannine body of writings also reveals a link between disciples' fidelity to Jesus and their living in the Spirit. Walking in the way of Jesus or not is to live "in the Spirit" or not. Following the Last Supper discourse, Jesus announces the coming of the Holy Spirit to those who are faithful to the teachings of the Word made flesh and his kingdom (John 14:12–17).

---

8. "Flesh" is the English scriptural translation of the Greek word *sarx*, the collection of human attributes that plague the human condition due to human weakness and inclination to sin. Paul lists some spiritually perilous ones.

9. Perkins, "John," 945.

The prologue to John's first letter also shows this clear and sharp distinction, stating, "God is light and in him there is no darkness at all" (1 John 1:5–10). In effect, disciples' actions in life should reflect their radical choice to live more fully in the reign of God.[10]

John's first letter indicates a third principle, the presence of different spirits with which disciples must contend:

> Beloved, do not believe every spirit, but test the spirits to see whether they are from God; for many false prophets have gone out into the world. By this you know the Spirit of God: every spirit that confesses that Jesus Christ has come in the flesh is from God, and every spirit that does not confess Jesus is not from God. And this is the spirit of the antichrist, of which you have heard that it is coming; and now it is already in the world. . . . [Those of the antichrist] are from the world; therefore, what they say is from the world. Whoever knows God listens to us. . . . From this we know the spirit of truth and the spirit of error.[11]

Finally, John reveals in his first letter a guiding principle by which disciples may know that they are following the Spirit of God:

> And this is [God's] commandment, that we should believe in the name of his Son Jesus Christ and love one another, just as he has commanded us. All who obey his commandments abide in him, and he abides in them. And by this we know that he abides in us, by the Spirit that he has given us.[12]

Those who believe in Christ follow Christ's teaching that leads to deeper life in the Spirit; for John, this new life includes both the presence of Christ in the disciple and their greater participation in Christ's love.

In conclusion, both Hebrew and Christian testaments offer foundational elements for practicing some degree of spiritual discernment in their relationship with God. The Old Testament writings offer limited but solid counsels to support and sustain people who would walk in the way of truth, blessing, and righteousness. In the New Testament, both Paul and John present, each in his own way, the importance and signs to observe for disciples earnestly seeking to follow the way of Christ. Disciples walking in the way of Jesus are "living in the Spirit," whose validating sign is their deepening charity to others. Christian discernment is a vital practice for

---

10. Moberly, "'Test the Spirits,'" 304–5.
11. 1 John 4:1–3, 5–6.
12. 1 John 3:23–24.

serious disciples to identify choices and actions that can lead them into a closer loving relationship with God.

Influences on Spiritual Discernment in the Patristic Era

Spiritual discernment was an important and necessary topic in writings of Christian antiquity. Several points of insight developed during this time that guided Christian disciples in pursuits such as sifting true from false prophetic or non-Christian teaching, identifying the influences of good and evil motivations (usually called spirits), learning to recognize early signs of temptations to sin, and how to exercise authority more charitably.

The Pastor of Hermas

The Pastor of Hermas is an apocalyptic pastoral writing from the later first to the mid-second century that calls its readers to repentance and strengthen their spiritual life. The work contains a series of spiritual revelations from a shepherd-like visitor to Hermas, a Christian Roman slave who describes them in a series of five visions, twelve mandates (commandments), and ten similitudes (similar to parables). Highly respected among early Christians, notably catechumens for baptism, *The Pastor* addresses ethical development and growth in virtue.

The work also reveals the important place of spiritual discernment for the Christian disciples intent on following the way of righteousness:

> "Hear now," said [the Pastor], "in regard to faith. There are two angels with a man—one of righteousness, and the other of iniquity." And I said to him, "How, sir, am I to know the powers of these, for both angels dwell with me?" "Hear," said he, and "understand them. The angel of righteousness is gentle and modest, meek and peaceful. When, therefore, he ascends into your heart, forthwith he talks to you of righteousness, purity, chastity, contentment, and of every righteous deed and glorious virtue. When all these ascend into your heart, know that the angel of righteousness is with you. These are the deeds of the angel of righteousness. Trust him, then, and his works."[13]

---

13. Commandment 7. Hermas, *Pastor*, 24.

Next, the Pastor informs Hermas how to recognize the way of darkness:

> "Look now at the works of the angel of iniquity. First, he is wrathful, and bitter, and foolish, and his works are evil, and ruin the servants of God. When, then, he ascends into your heart, know him by his works." And I said to him, "How, sir, I shall perceive him, I do not know." "Hear and understand," said he. "When anger comes upon you, or harshness, know that he is in you; and you will know this to be the case also, when you are attacked by a longing after many transactions, and the richest delicacies, and drunken revels, and divers luxuries, and things improper, and by a hankering after women, and by overreaching, and pride, and blustering, and by whatever is like to these. When these ascend into your heart, know that the angel of iniquity is in you. Now that you know his works, depart from him, and in no respect trust him, because his deeds are evil, and unprofitable to the servants of God."[14]

Despite its visionary and mystical trappings, the primary focus of *The Pastor* concerned the moral and spiritual lives of early Christians. Practicing discernment was necessary for them as they were assailed daily by threats to their faith and community cohesion. Disciples could learn to use their inner positive or negative reactions to evaluate what they encountered.

The learned third-century ascetic Origen of Alexandria contributed significantly to the developing discernment tradition by his years of experience as a solitary in the wilderness. Among his assertions was that a person's thoughts could come only from three supernatural sources: either directly from God (exceedingly rare!), a good spirit, or an evil one. Origen concluded that the presence of the good spirit within an individual led to inner tranquility and peace. In contrast, an evil spirit would be recognizable through an anxious or disrupted inner spirit. Disciples suffering from signs of an evil influence could retrace the sequence of their thoughts leading to their current agitation to identify where an evil spirit might have entered the process. Since these spiritual influences came from beyond the normal human realm, Origen maintained that discernment between spiritual influences was a necessary spiritual gift of the Holy Spirit, available to mature Christian disciples.[15]

---

14. Commandment 6.2. Hermas, *Pastor*, 24.

15. Origen, *Princ.* 3.3–4; as explained by Lienhard, "On 'Discernment of Spirits,'" 511–14.

Early Monastic Insight into Discernment

While shaped by the peculiarities and demands of solitary and communal monastic life, early Christian monasticism left an undeniable mark on the developing tradition of Christian discernment. Monastic personification of evil and temptations with demons gradually yielded to recognizing evil effects and influences as arising from unredeemed human weakness and sin.

The Life of Anthony, authored by Bishop Athanasius of Alexandria around 357, greatly influenced the early Christian monastic tradition. The work focuses on the need for monks to develop the ability for spiritual discernment and recognize the presence of evil demons capable of provoking temptations and discord in a monk's daily life.

Athanasius's account relates some significant temptations that the neophyte Anthony endured, his growing ability to recognize their onset, and how he learned to overcome them. A frequent temptation for monks to abandon their pursuit was a common case; Anthony was not exempt from this as he struggled with thoughts of his past life of ease, along with concerns for his only sibling, a sister whom he had entrusted to a community of virgin ascetics. He learned that such thoughts, if entertained, would lead to lessened zeal in his personal discipline of prayer and penitential practices, ultimately producing a greater temptation for him to abandon his solitary pursuit and return to the world he had left behind.

Anthony's method of dealing with these temptations, developed through his personal experience, had three steps. First, he learned to recognize when thoughts first tended to evoke inner agitation that threatened his normal interior peace and prayerfulness. Second, Anthony always kept in mind that the evil demon always operated upon him in very subtle ways, seeking to remain hidden from discovery, so that he was slow to recognize its presence. Finally, Anthony learned that failures did not mean that God had abandoned him; experiences of failure in the spiritual life were ways that could strengthen his faith and inner resolve. His insights concerning interior influences of malicious spiritual motivations would prove beneficial to the developing spiritual discernment tradition.

Discernment and Monastic "Discretion"

Later writings from various monastic centers reveal a growing appreciation for the practice of discernment in the desert regions of Egypt, Syria, and Palestine. *The Life of Anthony* had already portrayed discernment primarily as an instrument for recognizing the presence of evil by noticing the quality of temptations and the thoughts or disharmony they evoked within a monk. These thoughts later became associated with temptations from one of the so-called "capital sins" that the monk must subdue.[16] A collection of short anecdotes of monastic wisdom, *The Sayings of the Desert Fathers*, contains several examples that consider the practice of monastic "discretion" as one of several desirable virtues.[17] Discernment also became associated with a monk's ability to exercise moderation in areas including their ascetic practices and wisdom to interpret elements of their monastic rule when leading or advising other monks.[18]

John Cassian (360–c. 435) also addresses this application of discernment when guiding other monks.[19] He uses the Latin term *discretio*, translated into English as "discernment" but with a particular meaning for monastic discernment. Cassian associates monastic discretion with prudence in the careful and wise interpretation and application of monastic rules. He criticizes the lack of this discretion in several cases of younger monks in their sometimes excessive bodily austerities of fasting and all-night vigils for prayer, which could destroy their perseverance in their vocation. Cassian's writing no longer attributes sinful temptations to demonic influences; he sees, rather, that these inclinations arise from within a monk's spiritual heart due to excessive pride. He exhorts them to grow in humility, which becomes evident through their willingness to share thoughts and struggles with an elder and their docility in accepting an elder's counsel.[20] Cassian's view of discernment as discretion will later influence the famous monastic rule of Benedict of Nursia and the need for discretion in monks appointed to leadership as abbots.[21]

Although not formally considered a monk, Augustine of Hippo lived a monastic-like existence for most of his Christian life and ministry. Augustine's literature offers no method or program for spiritual discernment but

16. Lienhard, "On 'Discernment of Spirits,'" 519–20.

17. Such as John the Dwarf, anecdote 34. Ward, *Sayings of the Desert Fathers*, 79.

18. Some have afflicted their bodies by asceticism, but they lack discernment, and so they are far from God. Anthony the Great, anecdote 8. Ward, *Sayings of the Desert Fathers*, 2.

19. Cassian, *Conf.* 2.

20. Cassian, *Conf.* 2.

21. Benedict, *RB* 64, notes that discretion is a most desirable quality for abbot-superiors, along with charity and zeal.

does reveal some experiences from his wholehearted quest to follow Christ. One is the importance he places on recognizing himself as sinful and prone to sin. Gradual knowledge of oneself cultivates personal humility as the self realizes its weaknesses and tendency to stray from following Christ. Humility, in turn, brings oneself closer to Christ and a deeper sensitivity to knowing the ways of Christ and discerning his footsteps to follow. In this way, Christian disciples are better equipped to choose between one of two realms or (for Augustine) cities: the City of God and the City of Man. The difference lies in who is glorified, either God or the disciple:

> Accordingly, two cities have been formed by two loves: the earthly by the love of self, even to the contempt of God; the heavenly by the love of God, even to the contempt of self. The former, in a word, glories in itself, the latter in the Lord. For the one seeks glory from men; but the greatest glory of the other is God, the witness of conscience. The one lifts up its head in its own glory; the other says to its God, "You are my glory, and the lifter up of mine head." In the one, the princes and the nations it subdues are ruled by the love of ruling; in the other, the princes and the subjects serve one another in love, the latter obeying, while the former take thought for all. The one delights in its own strength, represented in the persons of its rulers; the other says to its God, "I will love Thee, O Lord, my strength."[22]

The Christian's task is learning how to live in the City of God throughout life, always guided by loving charity and bolstered with humility and prayer.

Spiritual Discernment and Discretion in the Later Medieval Period

The collection of experiences from the patristic centuries formed the foundation for spiritual discernment during the medieval and modern eras. While not many, the medieval centuries have left their own influences on the tradition.

Echoing some of the evangelist Paul's thoughts concerning the human struggle between following the law of the spirit or that of the flesh (Rom 7:14–25), the third part of Thomas à Kempis's fourteenth-century work *The Imitation of Christ* describes the importance of carefully observing in ourselves the diverse movements of human nature and divine

---

22. Augustine, *Civ.* 14.28.

grace.[23] As individuals become more adept at prayer, grow in self-knowledge of their weaknesses, and endeavor to remain completely resigned to God, they experience the tension between these two spiritual energies. A few guiding comparisons between their opposing effects offer a handful of their respective signature signs:

- Nature tends to be crafty and deceitful, while grace walks with simplicity, turns away from all appearance of evil, is not deceitful, and does all things purely for God.
- Nature labors for self-interest, while grace does not consider what may be advantageous or profitable to herself; rather, she considers what may be profitable to many.
- Nature willingly receives honor and respect, but grace faithfully attributes all honor and glory to God.
- Nature is afraid of being put to shame and despised, but grace willingly suffers reproach for the name of Jesus.
- Nature seeks to have things that are fancy and fetching, while grace is pleased with that which is plain and humble.
- Nature places higher value on temporal things, rejoices at earthly gain, is troubled at losses and is provoked at every injurious word, but grace attends to things eternal and does not cling to temporal items, nor is she disturbed at the loss of things or exasperated by harsh words.[24]

Notice that, for Thomas, interior movements of grace should promote in the disciple a greater desire for personal humility, detachment from worldly goods or honors, and overall concern for the things of God rather than those of personal vanities.

Developments from the Modern Era

As noted in the chapter on prayer, *The Spiritual Exercises* of Ignatius Loyola was his great gift to the Christian spiritual tradition. The original intent of *The Spiritual Exercises* was to assist prospective disciples of Ignatius in discerning whether to commit their lives to God as a foreign missionary.

---

23. à Kempis, *Imitation of Christ*, 3.54.
24. à Kempis, *Imitation of Christ*, 3.54–55.

The program can also effectively renew and strengthen a follower's interior spiritual life and Christian commitment.

The final sections of *The Spiritual Exercises* contain two collections of rules that focus on discernment. One set concerns itself with perceiving the movements that good and evil spirits (motivations) can cause in the soul, explaining differences between what Ignatius labeled interior consolations (signs of a good spirit resulting in positive or affirmative feelings including interior peace, calm, and/or perception of inner harmony with the divine spirit) and interior desolations (from an evil spirit causing lack of peace, anxiety, and inciting a disciple not to seek deeper life and harmony with God).[25] The second set comprises Ignatius's rules for discerning between the spirits, normally with the aid of someone adept at leading the *Spiritual Exercises*.[26] The discernment program offers some structured contemporary guidelines, examined toward the end of this chapter.

Protestant Reformation Influences and the Emergence of Communal Discernment

Protestant Christianity has influenced the understanding of spiritual discernment in practical and pastoral ways. The earliest Reformers, with their wariness toward Christian mysticism, set the practice of spiritual discernment on three foundation stones: divine grace available to all, the presence of faith, and Scripture as the unerring word of God. Scripture offered the lens through which Christians could uncover God's will for disciples. A practical result was the application of spiritual discernment as a communal exercise, useful in appraising congregational leadership and seeking responses to local pastoral concerns.

The Religious Society of Friends, also known as Quakers, offers a striking history of a church body seeking a unified community response to surrounding social needs through a form of practicing community-wide spiritual discernment. The Quaker movement's roots reach back to the seventeenth-century English Christian religious dissenters, including their founder, George Fox (1624–1691). Its members sought to live a community life of holy obedience and guided by the Holy Spirit, the principal agent

---

25. Ignatius, *Spiritual Exercises*, 313–27.
26. Ignatius, *Spiritual Exercises*, 328–36.

of discernment.[27] The Quaker tradition continues into the contemporary period, as we shall examine later in this chapter.

A Few Observations Concerning the Historical Practice of Spiritual Discernment

We have uncovered several key traditional insights for practicing spiritual discernment, such as:

Discernment is both a gift of the Holy Spirit and a virtue. Christian tradition has long appreciated that spiritual discernment is a gift (or *charism*) of the Holy Spirit, a quality to cultivate and put into practice. To flourish, however, Christian tradition has long counseled that disciples seeking to practice spiritual discernment do so with attitudes of humility, regular prayer, a fundamental desire to cooperate with how God may be moving them in life, and inner detachment from superfluous material goods. In short, effectively practicing spiritual discernment calls for spiritual maturity.

A disciple's love for God and effective discernment practice are interactive and nourish each other. Practicing discernment for seeking a greater love for God fosters the disciple's growth in love; growing in love likewise sharpens the disciple's proficiency in discernment, raising the likelihood of sharpening the disciple's proficiency in future discernment, leading to deeper love, further discernment, and so on in a continual progression.

The need for sensitivity to signs of divine or evil motivations. In considering the significance of a spiritual movement or a possible course of action that the movement may inspire in a Christian, discerning disciples need some ability to identify supportive or negating interior signs. Divine or enlivening motivations tend to produce "fruits of the Spirit" including a humble awareness of the self as imperfect and needful of God's grace, as well as inner joy, peace, docility to the gospel, and truthfulness. The so-called "evil spirit" is whatever tends to produce at least one of the opposite effects including interior pride, an attitude of self-sufficiency, inner agitation, lack of peace, and dishonesty with oneself or others when assessing one's spiritual relationship with God.

Communal spiritual discernment. Present and effective in community members, the Holy Spirit can and does move Christian communities to show Christ's love to others beyond its limited confines. The practice of communal

---

27. Farrow, "Discernment in the Quaker Tradition," 51–62.

spiritual discernment, found among the first Christians of Acts and later in many Christian church communities following the Protestant Reformation, remains applicable today. Of course, promoting growth in charity and a closer following of Jesus's example should be its principal focus.

Part Two: Practicing Spiritual Discernment Today

The word "discernment" in ordinary conversation frequently refers to making an acceptable decision; it can also refer to seeing a hidden quality of some object or even distinguishing the superiority of one object from others (such as when evaluating a diamond). Christian spiritual discernment is more precise, however, referring to the Holy Spirit's gift of appraisal for Christian living and evaluating whether a spiritual motivation can lead a disciple toward or away from God's love. Some disciples will use the term of general "spiritual discernment" when they mean a more specific "discernment of spirits" and vice-versa. Discernment of spirits, properly speaking, refers to a process of distinguishing and appraising among a variety of conflicting emotions when seeking to choose a particular action or outcome.

Some Key Foundation Stones for Practicing Spiritual Discernment

Christian discernment presumes that disciples earnestly desire to draw closer to the Lord of love through developing a deeper sensitivity to the prompting of the Holy Spirit in their lives. It also presumes a mature degree of faith and ability to trust that God's love for them always desires their greatest good, which is to live ever more fully in harmony with this love.

Some earlier spiritual authors underscored the serious need for learning and complying with the will of God as almost a matter of spiritual life and death. A better reason for cultivating this spiritual sensitivity is that maturing disciples seek to grow in their sensitivity to follow along in what might be described as a lifelong "dance" with God, who leads throughout life. If we must speak of *God's will*, it is the endless divine prompting in the lives of God's daughters and sons that they become most fully alive through cooperating with the movement of divine love offered to each of us. We are free to reject it, and often we do because of willfulness, fear, or simply our insensitivity to the very subtle intuitive loving dance moves with our Beloved. We may fail, perhaps often, to move harmoniously with God's lead. Don't worry if you step on the divine toes now and then and ask for forgiveness; the lead Dancer is very forgiving and will never leave you on the ballroom floor!

Discernment is also challenging because making a choice requires leaving other options behind, an inescapable consequence that is difficult for many people to accept. Remember that discerning persons seek to act in some way that is either "good" or "better" for their lived response to grow in love with God.

The Need for Christian Discernment in Today's World

Spiritual Discernment in a World of Competing Messages

There are at least three reasons why spiritual discernment is especially valuable for Christian disciples today. One is the widespread influence of religious opinions that pretend to be Christian in various religious publications and other self-dubbed "prophetic" media and literature. Perusing the religious and philosophical sections of a local or online bookstore quickly reveals an enormous collection of Christian, pseudo-Christian, non-Christian religious, philosophical, and even semi-politically inspired works. Some of these authors begin with a predetermined agenda, proclaiming their message under a thinly veiled mantel of prophecy that contains only a kernel or two of what we might recognize as authentically Christian. Ironically, earnest disciples today face many of the same challenges as the earliest Christian communities who sought to be faithful to the message of Jesus along their path that included considerable social indifference, derision, and rejection, with many followers incurring persecution and even death for their deep faith.

A second compelling reason for practicing Christian discernment is the heavy contemporary emphasis often placed on individual opinion, especially when reasoned discourse becomes shouted down by someone's final appeal to personal feeling. Wide-scale avoidance or inability to apply reason in conversation, not to mention common sense, has brought a maelstrom of disputed issues in religious, ethical, and political spheres, particularly in issues concerning medical ethics, human sexuality, care for the defenseless, and environmental stewardship. Christians struggling to navigate the rocky shoals of today's Western society while guided by Christian beliefs and centuries-held teaching can greatly benefit from having some facility with the practice of spiritual discernment, so to separate the wheat from weeds and distinguish true gold from deceptive "fool's gold."

A third area concerns Christian faith communities. These are not exempt from having to practice some degree of discernment, since church bodies are comprised of individual Christians who are inescapably affected by their local culture. Cultural pluralism and its frequently uncritical outlook and expressions, if not seriously appraised, can do immense harm to Christian churches wrestling between competing moral views grounded in Christian apostolic teaching and other ideas that rest on shifting sands of trendiness. Left unchecked and un-critiqued, these competing forces can bring mayhem and division into communities, threatening to compromise a communal witness to the saving and healing love of Christ and presence of the Holy Spirit. Christian denominations seeking the immense good of restoring unity within the wider body of Christ can also find themselves challenged to appraise their differing Christian beliefs as they seek to uncover their shared foundation stones.[28]

Both individual and communal Christian discernment surely have an important place as disciples regularly confront our many contemporary challenges and currents.

Principal Avenues of Christian Discernment

Christians have traditionally come to identify three possible applications of spiritual discernment.

Day-to-Day Individual Discernment of Spiritual Movements

This process examines and seeks to appraise whether a given interior experience and possible response to it will lead one closer in love to God and greater life of charity to others. The apostle Paul elaborated on this, as we discovered in the scriptural section, writing that discernment as appraisal was a charism or gift of the Holy Spirit; also, exercising this gift helps to strengthen it.

In addition to Paul's example for individual discernment, examining the lives of notable persons in Christian spirituality suggests that many of

---

28. Ukpong, "Pluralism and the Problem," 421–24.

them were extraordinarily gifted to practice discernment through the gift of God's loving grace, their well-developed inner sensitivity, experience, and usually with guidance from others. Perhaps we could name this first way of discernment the *mystical route* that was especially evident in the lives of medieval disciples like Catherine of Siena, Mechtilde of Magdeburg, or recent ones including Dorothy Day. Their paths seemed to follow the one proposed by the apostle Paul: the fruit of a well-developed interior life, a trusting relationship with God, and past experiences. A disciple's integration of these influences can lead to a unique path of daily discernment that is most authentic and harmonizing. The difficulty with trying to follow their example of discernment is that their subjective and deeply interior experiences offer little helpful structure to follow their unique ways beyond noting their particular use of symbols or naming their operative virtues. Spiritual backgrounds and experiences are unique to each person; only rare individuals, such as Ignatius of Loyola, have provided any systematic process of their discernment method.

Communal Discernment

As we have seen, communal discernment may be practiced by a community of believers who seek a corporate response to some pastoral or other need. Communal discernment would consider the particular community and Christian denomination, size of the discerning group, and other issues. Much has been written on this in recent decades.[29]

Quakerism, mentioned earlier in this chapter, is a communal yet interior-based spirituality that draws from the "one heart and one soul" ideal valued by the earliest Christian community of Jerusalem. True Christian life in the Spirit should incite in disciples a growing sensitivity to social needs and a Christian responsibility to alleviate them. Rather than focusing upon or examining religious experience itself, or upon its supernatural dimension, meetings at the communal level seek unity among its followers through achieving an acceptable unity of mind and heart. Quaker communities rely heavily on humility and especially patience as they discern a unified vision and response to how they should address needs in the wider society. Quakers are popularly known for their history of social activism, being instrumental in the campaign against the transatlantic slave trade before the twentieth century, and their more

---

29. See, for example, Hall and Tonna, *God's Plans for Us*, and Orsy, *Discernment*.

recent campaigns for the rights of minorities, such as women, prisoners, and LGBTQ+ concerns. Quaker communal discernment and participation have also helped to form several leading contemporary charities, including Oxfam and Amnesty International.

Discerning Complex Personal Choices: The "Discernment of Spirits"

Spiritual discernment is an important practice for intentional living as Jesus's disciples and growing in spiritual maturity. Christian disciples seek to follow the prompting of the Holy Spirit that incites them to ever-greater love. They often must contend with the pressures of various inner motivations, desires, and conflicts that can align with or deviate from the foundational divine inspiration to grow in charity.

Most Christians will someday confront a significant and life-changing choice. A very common one would be deciding whether marriage is indeed the best path for a disciple's journey with Christ and, if so, eventually discerning whether to marry a particular person. Other weighty decisions include life options such as uprooting a family and relocating to a faraway career promotion or new employment. Hopefully, Christians would consider the question, "Which option is more in line with how God is leading me (along with my family) to grow in love through my particular life circumstances?" For such occasions, the traditional practice known as *discernment of spirits* can be an invaluable and enlightening exercise.

A wealth of printed and online material focuses on the discernment of spirits that draws from the sixteenth-century experiences of Ignatius of Loyola in his *Spiritual Exercises*. The work offers a systematic way to rationally appraise the many conflicting impressions that can besiege and sometimes paralyze one's decision-making process.[30] Discernment of spirits is certainly not a cold rational activity that ignores one's emotions. Still, variations of Ignatius's program offer ways to address conflicting motivations

---

30. Ignatius's *Spiritual Exercises*, second week, numbers 179–183. A second series of propositions (184–188) engage the discerner's imaginative faculty. It is written with the sixteenth-century understanding of God, the gravity of following God's will, and the weighty discernment of whether or not to embrace a lifelong and far-flung missionary vocation. A contemporary approach is found in Liebert, *Way of Discernment*, offering a wholistic approach for the discerning person that considers other signals arising from a disciple's body, senses, internal physiology, intellect, and emotions that can influence and inform a discernment.

and help defuse some of the emotional energy while identifying inner motivations that can tug and tear at one's heart.

Below is a practical interpretation of the traditional steps for the discernment of spirits involving a substantial choice in life.[31] These nine steps normally would occur over many days or several weeks, depending on the individual. Having someone with whom to share your impressions and struggles along the way, especially one experienced in this discernment process, would be a great blessing.

Place yourself in God's presence. Place yourself quietly before God in an attitude of quiet prayer, letting yourself calmly begin the process. Recall what you are about to do while remembering your underlying desire to walk more closely in God's love through your ultimate discernment.

Collect available information. By now you've probably begun searching for informative data concerning aspects of your discernment issue. If not, you should be looking for anything that would offer additional insight about your question. Some people find themselves endlessly looking for more information. Give reasonable energy to this search but try not to become paralyzed in an endless search for more!

Put your question into a simple form. The process is more manageable if you reduce the question to simple "yes" or "no" queries. Your original issue for discernment may have more than one question to address. For example, the question of "Should I move from Portland to Peoria?" might better be broken into two questions to discern: "Should I move from Portland?" and "Should I move to Peoria?" Only if you discern a strong enough "yes" for the first would you have reason to determine the second. Remember, break the discernment problem into smaller, manageable segments.

Take a sheet of paper and form two columns labeled "Consolations" and "Desolations." Suppose you are moved to reply "yes" to your discernment question. List what reasons affect you positively as "consolations," such as giving you feelings of inner peacefulness, calm, and the sense of your choice being in harmony with the Divine Spirit within you. Then, consider any "desolations"—reasons that leave you feeling anxious, fearful, perhaps not being one with yourself as you seek to follow the Spirit's prompting. You can carry this exercise during the next week or so, jotting down reasons on the appropriate list.

---

31. This process is a modified version of the one found in Liebert, *Way of Discernment*, 19–21.

Evaluate your entries. When you feel you have listed all significant reasons for consolation or desolation, take these to prayer for a few days and reflect on their gravity for your life. You may find that some of them are truly significant and bring strong feelings; others can seem trivial after a while, or you may recognize them as simple personal preferences. Eventually, you will find yourself crossing out some of your less-significant entries.

Evaluate your final lists. Examine your list of remaining entries. Which ones are truly significant for you? Which ones are of lesser importance? Review this list periodically for several days and bring it to prayer, asking the Holy Spirit to enlighten your mind toward arriving at a final discernment.

Make a tentative decision and notice its effect on you. Take your decision to prayer for a few days and jot down your experiences or impressions. Offer this tentative decision to God and see how it sits with you. Over time, do you find that you experience inner peace and "ownership" of your decision? Does it seem to harmonize with the divine energy within you?

Conversely, does your tentative decision make you feel unsettled, anxious, and uncertain? A weighty decision can be frightening and unsettling but, if what you propose harmonizes with the "divine dance," these feelings should give way to a greater conviction that your discernment is true. If not, return to your initial lists and review them, or identify and list other possible hidden reasons. Otherwise, continue to the next step.

Make a firmer decision and notice its effects. Begin to take some early steps toward enacting your previous discernment, such as talking about your approaching decision with someone you trust who would be affected by your discernment. Once again, hold this in prayer for a few days to see what feelings or energies surface within you. This period allows your discernment, if agreeable, to mature into a firmer intention.

You may have made your earlier tentative decision prematurely, hoping to find relief from your constant focus on the question. Once again, if you find yourself with bothersome feelings leading you to question your earlier discernment, return to your comparison sheet for further reflection in prayer and listening and reconsider your tentative decision.

Finally, decide! Your earlier steps of seeking a tentative and firmer discernment should allow you to step forward in faith with an enlightened sense of your topic and a reasonable degree of confidence that your discernment would lead you into a more loving relationship with God and others. The passage of time should gradually affirm this for you.

Conclusion

God, the divine loving Mystery, continually draws Christian disciples into an ever-closer relationship through their growing capacity to love as Jesus. Those disciples eager to draw closer will find some degree of practicing spiritual discernment, or at least being familiar with it, a great help. Small or great, our daily choices will affect, to some degree, our loving relationship with God and others.

Exercises and Questions for Reflection

1. Name a few contemporary persons or social movements that others in society might claim to be "prophetic." As a Christian disciple, examine them in light of the prophetic discernment criteria mentioned earlier. Can you name any authenticating qualities that might indicate them to be "true" or "false" prophets?

2. Try your hand at individual spiritual discernment for some imaginary case such as "Should I accept a new job in another city?" or "Should I give more time to serving others in some way?" Remember to break the question into manageable "yes" or "no" answers. What competing motivations arise for you while conducting this discernment?

3. For group or class settings: Just as an experiment, imagine a group project that your Christian community might consider to undertake (working at a soup kitchen or thrift shop, spending time with inner-city youth, or another one). After time for prayer, discuss among yourselves the following: What were some of your positive and affirming impressions of the proposal? Do your "community members" suggest what may seem to be immovable blocks to adopting the project? What would be some of your reservations toward doing this as an interdependent community of disciples? Remember that community discernment of serious questions might take several prayer meeting sessions before arriving at an agreeable conclusion.

Suggested Further Reading

Barry, William. *Paying Attention to God: Discernment in Prayer.* Notre Dame, IN: Ave Maria, 1990.

Liebert, Elizabeth. *The Way of Discernment: Spiritual Practices for Decision Making.* Louisville, KY: Westminster John Knox, 2008.

4

Trusting in God's Abiding Love

TRUST OR HAVING CONFIDENCE in God's love for us (God's *providential* love) refers to how well we can trust in God's pervading goodness and abiding love for us and all of creation as we navigate the different challenges of life. Early Christians understood that trust in God should normally arise from faith. The Reformation concept of *assurance* expresses this idea, a "confident and enduring faith in God, trust in the promises of God, and the state of security that results from unreserved commitment to God's will."[1] The long Roman Catholic tradition holds that our ability to trust in God's love forms a concrete expression of the supernatural virtue of hope.

This chapter first considers the importance of Christians' trust in God that is present throughout Scripture.

Part One: Trusting God Through the Centuries

In Scripture

The Old Testament

Examining some Jewish attitudes of life and prayer reveals that the Old Testament people closely associate their Jewish faith with trusting in God and God's desire for their wellbeing.[2] God's faithfulness to the Hebrew

1. Perdue, "Assurance," 71.
2. Mercer, "Faith," 289.

nation is a core theme of the Hebrew Scriptures, found in the accounts and trials of Abram/Abraham, Moses leading the exodus from Egypt, the many prophets whom God calls to rekindle the people's covenant relationship, and through the feats of Esther and Judith, who save the Hebrew people from adversaries. All of these events serve to keep alive the memory that God has never abandoned them in the past and merits their trust. God's covenant with them ratifies that the people would be God's special and blessed people whom God will never abandon; the people, in turn, are to honor the covenant through their faithful and trusting obedience to God and the terms of the Jewish law.

The psalms frequently project the people's sense of trust in God, recalling God's past greatness and who would surely do so again. For example,

> I love you, O Lord, my strength.
>
> The Lord is my rock, my fortress, and my deliverer; God, my rock in whom I take refuge, my shield, and the horn of my salvation, my stronghold.
>
> I call upon the Lord, who is worthy to be praised, so I shall be saved from my enemies.[3]

The prophetic literature is less abundant with its appeals to trusting in God, but they are still present. Jeremiah, for one, proclaims that trust in the divine ways is a bulwark in times of hardship:

> Blessed are those who trust in the Lord, whose trust is the Lord. They shall be like a tree planted by water, sending out its roots by the stream. It shall not fear when heat comes, and its leaves shall stay green; in the year of drought it is not anxious, and it does not cease to bear fruit.[4]

The prophet Isaiah announces, "Those of steadfast mind you keep in peace—in peace because they trust in you. Trust in the Lord forever, for in the Lord God you have an everlasting rock."[5]

Among the wisdom literature writings, the author of Proverbs exhorts his listener always to remember that trust in God is more dependable than in one's limited wisdom:

---

3. Ps 18:1–3; see also Ps 22 and 24.
4. Jer 17:7–8.
5. Isa 26:3–4.

> Trust in the LORD with all your heart, and do not rely on your own insight. In all your ways acknowledge him, and he will make straight your paths. Do not be wise in your own eyes; fear the LORD, and turn away from evil. It will be a healing for your flesh and a refreshment for your body.[6]

The book of Job offers another story of trusting in God but with deeper insight into the reality that the divine provident love is mysterious. Trust in God's ways does not guarantee that God will act in expected ways. The joys and sorrows of life do not always indicate God's favor toward individuals for their otherwise righteous lives, a vexing irony in the wisdom literature tradition.

Trust in God among the Old Testament people of faith finds its strength in God's past saving interventions. Trusting in the mysterious divine wisdom is more dependable than human wisdom, abilities, and resources.

The New Testament

The New Testament understanding of trust in God has its roots in the traditional Hebrew beliefs in God's providential love and the importance of confidence in one's prayer. From its beginning, the Christian tradition has believed that this providential love finds its greatest human expression in the saving life and death of Jesus Christ.

The Gospel of Luke reflects throughout that confidence in God is tied to one's fullness of life in God's Spirit. Mary's trusting "yes" in reply to the angel announcing her blessed role (Luke 1:26–38) enables Jesus's conception and earthly mission. Mary's hymn of praise also reflects her trust in God's abiding presence and love in her as a member of the Jewish nation (1:46–55). Later, Jesus's confidence in his Father's love for him strengthens him to face the perils of his ministry of proclaiming the good news and the hardships of his ultimate rejection, suffering, and death. Jesus, "filled with the power of the Spirit" (4:14), begins his ministry as one with the freedom of a son of God, able to trust in his Father's providential love throughout. He teaches his disciples that their lives are to reflect this, warning them that "foxes have holes, and birds of the air have nests; but the Son of Man has nowhere to lay his head" (9:58). Jesus eventually commissions them to go from town to town preaching the good news while relying on this love, begging for food and shelter, and invoking God's

---

6. Prov 3:5–8.

protection from assailants and other hardships along the way (10:1–11). Using the simple prayer form that Jesus taught them, the disciples asked that God "give [them] each day [their] daily bread" (11:3), everything necessary for their life and mission. As did their Jewish ancestors, the disciples rooted their lives in dependence on God's love, discerning the presence of the Holy Spirit as they preached boldly and confidently amid growing hostility. By so living, the disciples provided a visible and striking testimony to their trust in God's love for them that was possible through their rich life in the Spirit, available to those who commit themselves to living fully in the reign of God that they proclaim.

Jesus's challenge to trust in God's love for the first disciples was a reality from their first glimmer of a divine summons that led them away from the familiar toward something new, promising, and liberating. Ultimately, the challenge also led them to the darkened skies of Calvary that came upon most of them as they hid in fear. Later, the wind and flames of Pentecost gave them great courage to go out and proclaim the good news, trusting in the Spirit of the risen Christ in the face of disappointment, dungeon, and death. Trust in divine providence has been an element of Christian discipleship from its very beginning.

Several New Testament writers addressed the growing delay of Jesus's promised return in the early decades of the struggling churches. As an example, Jesus in Mark 1:14–15 proclaims that "the time is fulfilled, and the Kingdom of God has come near"; the author of Luke seems to exchange this sense of impending fulfillment into an expectation stretching indefinitely into the future, "until the times of the gentiles are fulfilled" (Luke 21:24), signaled by certain events that must first happen.[7] The Acts of the Apostles promotes the interim time of waiting as a time for the "witness of the church" initially to the Jews but ultimately extended to the gentiles.[8]

The pastoral letters of the later first century reflect some concerns raised by the delayed second coming of Jesus (the *parousia*) and the solidifying of the communities' early beliefs and norms.[9] James, for instance, calls his readers to trust God's ways in times of difficulty, whose surpassing wisdom will ultimately emerge:

> My brothers and sisters, whenever you face trials of any kind, consider it nothing but joy, because you know that the testing of your

---

7. Perrin and Duling, *New Testament*, 298.
8. Perrin and Duling, *New Testament*, 299–300.
9. Perrin and Duling, *New Testament*, 371–72.

> faith produces endurance. . . . If any of you is lacking in wisdom, ask God, who gives to all generously and ungrudgingly, and it will be given you. But ask in faith, never doubting, for the one who doubts is like a wave of the sea, driven and tossed by the wind; for the doubter, being double-minded and unstable in every way, must not expect to receive anything from the Lord.[10]

In addition, James calls his listeners to strengthen their hearts, for the coming of the Lord is near (5:8).

The second letter of Peter, bolstering Christian faith and their moral life, reminded the early Christians of the divine promise they had received:

> His divine power has given us everything needed for life and godliness, through the knowledge of him who called us by his own glory and goodness. Thus he has given us, through these things, his precious and very great promises, so that through them you may escape from the corruption that is in the world because of lust, and may become participants of the divine nature.[11]

To summarize this section, both the Hebrew and Christian Testaments revealed the importance of trusting in God, such as having faith in God's invitation to new life, a confident trust in God's providential love, and obedience to the Jewish law. New Testament faith absorbed these principles while focusing primarily on Jesus as the long-awaited Messiah and the fulfillment of the Jewish Scripture, who gave us a lived example of trust in the goodness of his heavenly Father.

Trust in God in the Patristic Era

Among the Fathers of the Church

Early Christians found themselves challenged to trust in God's love for them in at least two notable areas: in asserting their nascent Christian beliefs as superior to Jewish and pagan thought, and in the need to rely on divine providence to sustain them as they encountered waves of persecution and martyrdom.

By the first century, Christianity had already begun to develop beyond its initial identity as a Jewish sect toward a new self-understanding. Christian apologists such as Justin Martyr (ca. 105–ca. 165) defended

---

10. Jas 1:2–3, 5–8.
11. 2 Pet 1:3–4.

apparent oddities of Christian belief in correspondence with emperors, philosophers, and outspoken Christian detractors. In a work addressed to the Christian antagonist Trypho, he laid out the link between the Christian faith and its Jewish roots from which the faith in Jesus was a reasonable and logical conclusion. He argued that, like the Jews, the Christians trusted in God's promises behind the law of the covenant; however, while the Jewish law came through the saving heroic figures of Abraham and Moses, Christians believed that the way of Christ Jesus offered the model for fulfilling that first covenant.[12] Even more boldly, Justin wrote that Christian salvation did not come from the bloody ritual act of Jewish circumcision but has been won for them, through their baptism, the "new circumcision" into the life and death of Christ.[13] In another writing, Justin commended all Christians who could accept this, proclaiming, "Blessed are all they that put their trust in Him."[14] Christian trust in God's faithfulness was important to early disciples as they gradually grew beyond their primarily Jewish identity.

The intermittent periods of Christian persecution before the fourth century challenged Christians to hold fast to their faith amid their sufferings. Two figures from Carthage in North Africa were especially influential in buttressing the trust and faith of afflicted Christians. In his work "On Flight from Persecution," Tertullian (ca. 160–ca. 230) addressed the pressing question of whether Christians facing persecution should stay and face their oppressors rather than flee. He concluded that they should trustfully remain and thus glorify God through whatever outcome emerged. Tertullian also believed that periods of persecution offered moments when one's faith and trust in God could shine most gloriously:

> The one great thing in persecution is the promotion of the glory of God, as He tries and casts away, lays on and takes off. But what concerns the glory of God will surely come to pass by His will. And when is trust in God more strong, than when there is a greater fear of Him, and when persecution breaks out? The Church is awestruck. Then is faith both more zealous in preparation, and better disciplined in fasts, and meetings, and prayers, and lowliness, in brotherly-kindness and love, in holiness and temperance.[15]

---

12. Justin, *Dial.* 11.
13. Justin, *Dial.* 24.
14. Justin, *1 Apol.* 40.
15. Tertullian, *Fuga pers.* 1.

Who could say that God, who is aware of all things, did not wish to use suffering for some greater or otherwise mysterious good, perhaps even through delivering the disciples from their plight? In addition, Christians had to accept that perhaps they really were called through the circumstances of their time to give witness to their faith by way of persecution or death. If disciples fled this moment of suffering, would they be better able to withstand a future moment? In such a threatening situation, they should therefore stay and face their oppressors, trusting that God would bring some good from the evil they faced:

> The matter stands thus—we have either both things in our own power, or they wholly lie with God. If it is ours to confess or to deny, why do we not anticipate the nobler thing, that is, that we shall confess? . . . But if the matter is wholly in God's hand, why do we not leave it to His will, recognizing His might and power in that, just as He can bring us back to trial when we flee, so is He able to screen us when we do not flee? . . . Strange conduct, is it not, to honor God in the matter of flight from persecution, because He can bring you back from your flight to stand before the judgment-seat; but in regard of witness-bearing, to do Him high dishonor by despairing of power at His hands to shield you from danger? Why do you not rather on this, the side of constancy and trust in God, say, I do my part; I depart not; God, if He choose, will Himself be my protector?[16]

Tertullian held that Christians should accept the uncertain outcome of their circumstances.

Bishop Cyprian of Carthage (d. 258) also held that a Christian's trust in Christ's ultimate victory over evil came forth more exquisitely in one's willingness to endure suffering:

> And that the proof might not be the less solid and the confession of Christ might not be a matter of pleasure, they are tried by tortures, by crosses, by many kinds of punishments. Pain, which is the witness of truth, is applied, so that Christ, the Son of God, who is believed to have been given to man for life, might be proclaimed not only by the proclamation of the voice but by the testimony of suffering.[17]

---

16. Tertullian, *Fuga pers.* 5.
17. Cyprian, *Idol.* 15.

Not long after Emperor Constantine legalized Christianity, Augustine of Hippo (354–430) reflected on the virtues of faith, hope, and love in his written work for Christian living. His book follows a theme from the earlier persecutions that the divine will or plan is faultless and always will realize some positive effect; whatever happens, be it good or bad, God permits to occur through what is known as the divine *permissive* will (God's passively allowing events to occur, in contrast to actively willing so). The divine plan is unfathomable, and only in God's own time would it become known:

> Then will be seen in the clearest light of wisdom what holy men now hold by faith in anticipation of grasping it by manifest understanding; namely, how certain and immutable and efficacious is the will of God; how many things He can do but does not will to do, though willing nothing which He cannot do.... Nothing, therefore happens unless the Omnipotent wills it to happen: He either permits it to happen, or He brings it about Himself. Nor are we to doubt that God does well when He permits evil. For He does not permit this except for a just reason, and all that is just is indeed good.... For He is called Almighty for no other reason than that He can do whatever He wills and because the effectiveness of His almighty will cannot be thwarted by the will of any creature whatsoever.[18]

Elsewhere, in his "Exposition of Psalm 120," Augustine preached on the importance of disciples' trusting in God to help them navigate through the perils of this earthly life as they spiritually proceeded to ascend Mount Zion toward their final destiny.[19] At least two points are particularly noteworthy. One is that disciples ascending to the Lord cannot do so through only their own means; humility calls them also to seek divine assistance.[20] Also, disciples must constantly remain vigilant for the full return of the Lord at some unknown moment, while allowing the Lord to be their watchman and guardian to strengthen them in faltering moments along the way.[21]

Augustine reminds his readers that the Lord is like a watchman, overseeing them and ready to guide them while passing through daily temptations and dangers, if they would only let him:

---

18. Augustine, *Enchir.* 95–96.
19. Augustine, *Enarrat. Ps.* 120 (Ps 121 in the NRSV).
20. Augustine, *Enarrat. Ps.* 120.5.
21. Augustine, *Enarrat. Ps.* 120.6–8.

> *May the Lord guard your going in, and your coming out henceforth and for ever.* Notice how it says, *Your coming out henceforth and forever,* whereas your *going in* is only for a time. . . . When we are tempted, we go in; when we conquer the temptation, we come out. . . . Thus humility is your guardian in all temptation, for we are climbing up from the valley of weeping, singing our song of ascents; and the Lord is guarding our entrance that we may go into it and be safe. When temptation comes upon us, let us keep our faith whole and strong. Then he will guard our *coming out henceforth and for ever,* for when we have finally come through all temptation there will be no further temptation to daunt us for all eternity, no concupiscence ever again to make its insolent demands. . . . Guard yourselves, but not by any strength of your own, for the Lord is your defense and your guardian, the Lord who neither grows drowsy nor sleeps.[22]

All the events of one's life, whether joyful or in suffering, take place under the divine gaze that sees all and seeks to bring maturity in faith by trusting in God through any situation, even in moments of temptation.

Insights from the Emerging Monastic Tradition

The early monastic tradition instructs in several places how monks should lean on God for strength in their long solitary vocation while wrestling with their inner spiritual and personal struggles. The first biographer of Anthony of Egypt reports one such instance in the young monk's life:

> There then he passed his life, and endured such great wrestlings, "Not against flesh and blood [Ephesians 6:12]," as it is written, but against opposing demons, as we learned from those who visited him. For there they heard tumults, many voices, and, as it were, the clash of arms. At night they saw the mountain become full of wild beasts, and him also fighting as though against visible beings, and praying against them. And those who came to him he encouraged, while kneeling he contended and prayed to the Lord. Surely it was a marvelous thing that a man, alone in such a desert, feared neither the demons who rose up against him, nor the fierceness of the four-footed beasts and creeping things, for all they were so many. But in truth, as it is written, "He trusted in the Lord as Mount Sion ," with a mind unshaken and undisturbed; so that the demons

---

22. Augustine, *Enarra. Ps.* 120.14. Emphasis original.

> rather fled from him, and the wild beasts, as it is written [Job 5:23], "kept peace with him."[23]

Anthony counsels his fellow monks to avoid self-reliance in their struggles rather than God's strength while persevering in their vocation to seek union with God. Shortly before he died, he counseled his brother monks:

> And do you be watchful and destroy not your long discipline, but as though now making a beginning, zealously preserve your determination. For you know the treachery of the demons, how fierce they are, but how little power they have. Wherefore fear them not, but rather ever breathe Christ, and trust Him. Live as though dying daily.... Therefore be the more earnest always to be followers first of God and then of the Saints; that after death they also may receive you as well-known friends into the eternal habitations.[24]

St. Gregory the Great (540–604), a Benedictine monk at heart even while he reigned as pope, recalled the preface of the Benedictine rule to incline the ear of a monk's heart with a receptive, trustful, and obedient attitude toward finding the divine will in life. One of Gregory's anecdotes on the Benedictine founder, Benedict of Nursia (480–547), related that a poor man came to the monastery begging for a little oil. Although Benedict commanded that the oil be given, the cellarer refused because only a tiny bit was available. If the cellarer gave any oil as alms, there would be none for the monastery. Angry at this distrust of God's providence, Benedict knelt down to pray. As he prayed, a bubbling sound came from inside the oil jar. The monks watched in fascination as oil filled the vessel so much that it overflowed, leaked out beneath the lid and finally pushed the cover off, cascading out onto the floor.[25] His message was that God would always bless a disciple's trust in some way.

Whether in pastoral writings or anecdotal stories, patristic-era Christian writers and teachers conveyed the message that trusting in the divine loving strength was an important quality for Christian discipleship.

---

23. Athanasius, *Vit. Ant.* 51.
24. Athanasius, *Vit. Ant.* 91.
25. Gregory, *Dial.* 2.28–29.

Trust in God in the High- and Late-Medieval Periods (1100–1500)

Franciscan Spirituality

Christian spirituality of the twelfth century looked anew to the humanity of Jesus for insight as to how the church compromised by the world should present itself in the world. There developed a special focus on the simple gospel lives of Jesus and the Twelve, forming a particular interest in the disciples' ability to follow Jesus's attitude of trust in the Father's providential love for them. The life of Francis of Assisi offered perhaps the most striking image of this. A particular element of his spirituality was based on the profound and providential love of the Father that Jesus embraced in his daily existence; Francis believed that the same providential love would also provide for a friar's most basic needs. This attitude was part of the beauty of the mendicant spiritual approach among itinerant preachers like Francis's small band. Francis trained his friars to rely on God's goodness by not carrying money on their journeys, trusting that they would find shelter and adequate food along the way. One can imagine that more than one friar went hungry for a night or two, and others had to sleep in the open during a rainstorm; nonetheless, their deep trust in God's caring for them recalled, in a striking way, the same attitude of Jesus and the Twelve in following their uncertain lifestyle.

The fourteenth-century writing *The Imitation of Christ* remains a popular spiritual aid for Christian prayer and day-to-day living. Originally written for either clerics or monks, countless other Christians since then have benefited from reading it. The work instructs readers to avoid excessive trust in human abilities to bring them to happiness, to "put no confidence in the knowledge you have acquired, or in the skill of any human counselor; rely on God's grace—he brings aid to the humble, and only humiliation to the overly self-confident."[26] Whatever be disciples' plans or personal projects, they should pray to God, asking for success.[27] God is the ultimate source of a person's happiness, regardless of whatever the particular situation.[28] Indeed, much of the work's third book encourages readers to find their strength and trust through trusting in God's love for them.

---

26. à Kempis, *Imitation of Christ*, 1.7.1; see also 3.42.
27. à Kempis, *Imitation of Christ*, 3.15.
28. à Kempis, *Imitation of Christ*, 3.16–17; see also 3.50

Trusting God in the Modern Era

Among Early Protestant Writers

Martin Luther (1483–1546) held that placing one's trust in God went hand-in-hand with one's professed faith. Trusting in something other than the Creator was tantamount to idolatry, an offense against the first commandment. Luther considered this in his *Large Catechism*:

> "You are to have no other gods."
> That is, you are to regard me alone as your God. What does this mean, and how is it to be understood? What does "to have a god" mean, or what is God?
> Answer: A "god" is the term for that to which we are to look for all good and in which we are to find refuge in all need. Therefore, to have a god is nothing else than to trust and believe in that one with your whole heart. As I have often said, it is the trust and faith of the heart alone that make both God and an idol. If your faith and trust are right, then your God is the true one. Conversely, where your trust is false and wrong, there you do not have the true God. For these two belong together, faith and God. Anything on which your heart relies and depends, I say, that is really your God.[29]

For Luther, as for Protestantism generally, trust in God should be a natural consequence of faith in God and God's great love for each person, evidenced through Jesus's redeeming death on the cross. Disciples could hope in God's mercy and salvation based on this faith, while the Roman Catholic tradition has held since the thirteenth century that exercising trust in God belongs to a supernatural virtue of hope.

John Wesley (1703–1791) was a well-known Methodist preacher who proclaimed that faith in divine mercy was the essential foundation stone for one's ability to trust in God:

> We cannot serve God unless we believe in him. This is the only true foundation of serving him. Therefore, believing in God, as "reconciling the world to himself through Christ Jesus," the believing in him, as a loving, pardoning God, is the first great branch of his service. . . .[30]

---

29. Luther, *Large Catechism*, in Kolb and Wengert, *Book of Concord*, 386.
30. Wesley, "Sermon 29.4."

> And thus to believe in God implies, to trust in him as our strength, without whom we can do nothing, who every moment endues us with power from on high, without which it is impossible to please him; as our help, our only help in time of trouble, who compasses us about with songs of deliverance; as our shield, our defender, and the lifter up of our head above all our enemies that are round about us.... [This] implies, to trust in God as our happiness; as the center of spirits; the only rest of our souls; the only good who is adequate to all our capacities, and sufficient to satisfy all the desires he hath given us.[31]

Everything we have and need comes from our God, who loves us, sustains us, and alone is worthy of our trust.

Trust in God in the Years of Roman Catholic Counter-Reformation

The sixteenth through twentieth centuries produced an impressive number of spiritual writers from different parts of the Christian spectrum. One common conviction was the need to accept the reality of some unknowable divine plan for each person, the "will of God." These writers insisted that maturing disciples would learn how to accept this enveloping program with a trusting heart, hence the necessity for them to develop the virtues of humility and trustful obedience as sons or daughters of their heavenly Father. The resulting confidence in God's loving concern for them would guide and strengthen disciples through their many trials and difficulties in actively responding to the spiritual and human needs of others.

Ignatius of Loyola was anything but a timid and retiring person. Ignatius was a man of action throughout his life, first as a soldier seeking honor and glory, then diligently following his newfound Christian convictions as a "soldier of Christ." As a Christian disciple, though, Ignatius realized that to work for God's glory involved two entities: the divine will or plan and Ignatius's cooperation to bring it about. He revealed this in a sixteenth-century letter:

> I consider it an error to trust and hope in any means or efforts in themselves alone; nor do I consider it a safe path to trust the whole matter to God our Lord without desiring to help myself by what he has given me; so that it seems to me in our Lord that I ought to

---

31. Wesley, "Sermon 29.4."

make use of both parts, desiring in all things his greater praise and glory, and nothing else.[32]

One could summarize these two elements of Ignatius's thought in his well-known desire to pray as if everything depended on God, but also to act as if it depended on Ignatius.

Teresa of Avila (1515–1582) enjoyed a relationship of deep closeness and awareness of God's love for her that guided her through the many trying periods of her life. Teresa frequently addressed the need to have confidence in God while maturing in prayer and closeness to God, who would not abandon a persevering disciple. She wrote,

> Have great confidence, for it is necessary not to hold back one's desires, but to believe in God that if we try we shall little by little, even though it may not be soon, reach the state the saints did with his help. For if they had never determined to desire and seek this state little by little in practice they would never have mounted so high.[33]

Several trials and roadblocks challenged Teresa to trust in the divine plan as she went about reforming her Carmelite order. She spent several years navigating the lengthy and confusing process of establishing the reformed convent of San José, her first of many religious houses directed to Carmelite reform, living in prayerful trust while observing a respectful attitude of obedience toward her superiors.[34]

Bishop Francis de Sales (1567–1622) reminds his readers that, when considering the importance of trust in God, disciples must also remember the importance of practicing humility in their relationships with God. An attitude of humility can help remind them of being finite human beings who, for all of their anxiety, concern, and perhaps even scheming, in the end must rely on God's provident love that, alone, can bring about their ultimate happiness, even in defeat. God can bring good from any situation, any loss, any disappointment. Humility, meekness, and remaining close to God through prayer are Francis's key ingredients for a healthy relationship in Christ that support one's trust in the divine plan:

---

32. Ignatius in a 1555 letter to Francis Borgia; quoted in Ignatius and Young, *Letters*, 401.
33. Teresa, *Life*, 13.2.
34. Teresa, *Life*, 32–36.

> In all your affairs rely wholly on God's providence through which alone you must look for success. Nevertheless, strive quietly on your part to cooperate with its designs. You may be sure that if you have firm trust in God, the success that comes to you will always be that which is most useful for you whether it appears good or bad in your private judgement. Imitate little children who with one hand hold fast to their father while with the other they gather strawberries or blackberries from the hedges. So too if you gather and handle the goods of this world with one hand, you must always hold fast with the other to your heavenly Father's hand and turn toward him from time to time to see if your actions or occupations are pleasing to him.[35]

Jean-Pierre de Caussade (1675–1751) situates Christian trust in God as a cornerstone of his well-known counsel of "spiritual abandonment to divine love," a challenging though effective means to grow in trust of God. Caussade begins by noting that the divine order wrought by God in the world and for each person is oriented to the salvation of all people. Every moment of life brings with it both divine blessing and challenge: a blessing in that it issues from God, and a challenge in that disciples must surrender themselves to this belief while attending to their joyful or difficult "duties of the present moment." Caussade illustrates this in recalling Mary's submission to bear the Son of God:

> "The power of the most High shall over-shadow thee" [Luke 1:35], said the angel to Mary. This shadow beneath which the power of God conceals itself in order to bring Jesus Christ to souls, is the duty, attraction or cross which each moment brings.[36]

Disciples' obedient acceptance and cooperation with the divine plan expresses their trusting obedience to God's overarching and mysterious guidance.

Restoring popular trust in God's merciful love was one spiritual focus of the Italian founder of the Redemptorists, Alphonsus de Liguori (1696–1787), during the corrosive decades of Jansenist piety that denied belief in God's divine mercy. Alphonsus wrote that God's divine being, total love, could only love and desire a person's happiness; this desire for one's good remained even in moments of sin, or when suffering the consequences of sin. Alphonsus taught that, in the end, disciples would find their true

---

35. de Sales, *Introduction* 3.10.
36. Caussade, *Abandonment to Divine Providence* 1.1.2.

happiness and peace when they learned to follow their present path with attitudes of obedient and faithful trust.[37]

The Carmelite Thérèse of Lisieux (1873–1897), examined earlier, followed her "little way" of spiritual childhood that led her to deepen in her trust of God's love. It involved turning all of one's life, plans, and desires over to God with the intention to realize God's divine plan for her even in times of poor health. She did this with blind and filial confidence in a "spiritual abandonment" of her desires and plans for God's love, trusting that God's absolute love can use any outcome to strengthen one's living in this love.[38]

Some Traditional Insights on Having Trust in God

Examining the practice of Christian trust in God through Christian history reveals several perennial themes that underscore its importance for Christian disciples seeking to follow the way of Jesus.

Early Christian trust in God was rooted in Scriptures and tempered by hardships. The attitude of trusting in God's love and faithfulness predated Christianity, having been an essential part of Jewish prayer and relationship with God. Early Christianity, drawing from its Jewish roots, also saw its importance and natural place in the early centuries of Christian struggles to survive amid antagonistic and even hostile cultures.

Trust in God is a timeless practice through history. Many traditional Christian writers have indicated that the call to grow in trust in God's love was a normal part of maturing Christian discipleship. Whether in the early centuries of Christian persecution and martyrdom, the medieval trust of itinerant religious orders, or in the many spiritual or charitable pursuits following the Reformation, spiritual masters have exhorted disciples to develop their trust in God's divine love for all people, the God who desires their wellbeing and ultimate happiness that comes with spiritual maturity, even in times of hardship and loss.

Some blessing or good can result from trusting God. Such was the thought of so many faith-filled persons and writers throughout Christian history; a healthy and maturing trust in divine providence is able to accept the vicissitudes and failures in life while believing that one's sincere and trustful love for God can produce unseen fruitfulness.

37. Liguori, *Uniformity with God's Will*, 4.2.
38. Jamart, *Complete Spiritual Doctrine*, 296.

Part Two: Cultivating a Contemporary Christian Trust in God

Socially Conditioned Obstacles to Developing Trust

In whom or what do you place your trust? How easily can you trust in anything?

Broken relationships and shattered traditional values have wreaked havoc on countless individuals who have difficulty trusting others. Most of us realize that the ability to trust is an essential ingredient for any deep and satisfying relationship. A 2020 article from *The Atlantic* about social trust claims that the United States is currently in the grip of a "moral convulsion" that began years before but came to a head during the many particular events of that tumultuous year. As a result, the author noted, we are in a perilous moment:

> Social trust is a measure of the moral quality of a society—of whether the people and institutions in it are trustworthy, whether they keep their promises and work for the common good. When people in a church lose faith or trust in God, the Church collapses. When people in a society lose faith or trust in their institutions and in each other, the nation collapses.[39]

Generations following those of the Great Depression and the later "Baby Boomers" after the Second World War have had good reason to question the sturdiness of social structures and the durability of personal relationships. The earlier age of confidence has morphed into what the author called an "age of precarity."[40]

The lack of social trust has accompanied a remarkable disability for people to trust in other persons. A 2019 study indicates that younger generations, in particular, find it more difficult to do so:

> All told, nearly half of young adults (46%) are what the Center's report defines as "low trusters"—people who, compared with other Americans, are more likely to see others as selfish, exploitative and untrustworthy, rather than helpful, fair and trustworthy. Older Americans are less likely to be low trusters. For example, just 19% of adults ages 65 and older fall into this category, according to the survey, which was conducted in late 2018 among 10,618 U.S. adults.[41]

---

39. Brooks, "Moral Convulsion," para. 7.
40. Brooks, "Moral Convulsion," para. 11.
41. Gramlich, "Young Americans," para. 3.

The further personal heartbreaks and difficulties caused by the reality of broken families resulting from divorce, parental abandonment, and parents of several marriages only add to an already sad and injurious situation.

Another significant reason for the inability to trust in God can be a loss of hope among younger generations to realize future happiness and stability. The impact of the earlier COVID-19 world epidemic is still felt in many countries, leaving stubborn economic instability. Regional wars threaten to ignite into wider conflict involving the growing number of nuclear powers. Concerns over the uncertainties of global climate change that is affecting huge numbers of the world's population are on the rise. Add to these the Western cultural shifts associated with postmodernism, sparking domestic political chaos, it is little wonder that many people begin to develop a subtle though crippling dystopian view of a world that will be very different from what it once was. Hope can seem in short supply, and trusting in something beyond one's own abilities can be a challenge.

Christian hope differs from ordinary hope, however. Christian hope means more than simple optimism; rather, Christian hope "takes the long view" that God is always motivating disciples to mature into a deeper and more authentically human existence as envisioned by our Creator, despite and perhaps even using the challenges of periodic temporal catastrophes and challenges.

Some Latter-Day Christian Models for Building Trust in God

Two stories of contemporary-era Christians illustrate well that trusting in God calls for humility, faith, and courage. While not all Christians (thankfully!) need follow these extremely demanding paths of holiness, the examples of these individuals offer inspiration and hope for living with courageous trust in God's providential love.

Gianna Beretta Molla (1922–1962), from Magenta in northern Italy, enjoyed life during her youth that included hiking, skiing, mountaineering, and joyful service to the elderly and needy. Following her years in university, she was a pediatrician who soon married and became the mother of three children. Two miscarriages followed. Shortly after learning that she was once again expecting a child, a painful fibroid tumor in her uterus required her to have surgery. A hysterectomy abortion would have been a swifter solution for removing the tumor. However, Gianna would not sacrifice the life of her unborn child for her personal health and entrusted herself to prayer and divine providence that she and especially the child would survive despite the medical risks. Doctors removed the tumor and the child was born, six months later, with the mother's namesake; Gianna, however, survived only for a week after the birth and died in great pain at the age of thirty-nine.[42] She was canonized as a Roman Catholic saint in 2006, during which Pope John Paul II noted of Gianna:

> Following the example of Christ, who "having loved his own . . . loved them to the end" (John 13:1), this holy mother of a family remained heroically faithful to the commitment she made on the day of her marriage. The extreme sacrifice she sealed with her life testifies that only those who have the courage to give of themselves totally to God and to others are able to fulfil themselves.[43]

Christian de Chergé along with six fellow Trappist monks of the Our Lady of Atlas monastery in Algeria were murdered in 1996 by Islamic terrorists.[44] Recognized all but officially as Christian martyrs in their deaths for their faith, the monks had sought merely to proclaim the gospel through their Christlike presence of loving accompaniment and living among the surrounding non-Christian people. The monastic community had known in advance that their lives were in danger. Nevertheless, they discerned as a community that their divine call was to be faithful monks among the people with whom they had lived as witnesses to God's love and abiding presence, come what may, following the way of Jesus with his people who "loved them until the end" (John 13:1). Theirs was a wider understanding of Christian witness, not fully understood nor supported by some brother Trappists, which required a deep embrace of trust in the divine plan for them and their mission.[45]

Toward Cultivating a Greater Trust in God Today

Christian disciples living in this time are also challenged to live as people of hope, some at considerable cost or even personal risk. Our tradition offers

---

42. Vatican News Service, "Gianna Beretta Molla (1922–1962)."

43. John Paul II, "Canonization of Six New Saints," 7.

44. The seven monks were Dom Christian de Chergé, Brother Luc (born Paul Dochier), Father Christophe (Lebreton), Brother Michel (Fleury), Father Bruno (born Christian Lemarchand), Father Célestin (Ringeard), and Brother Paul (Favre-Miville).

45. Salenson, *Christian de Chergé*, 153–67.

several perspectives on Christian confidence in God; with more contemporary eyes, let us reflect on a few.

Growing in trust takes time. Trust in a person does not normally happen immediately; more often, it takes some time to develop a living and healthy relationship. Our relationship with Christ, while not exactly of the earthly variety, nonetheless requires time and attention through some regular practice of prayer, reflection, and recalling past experiences of God's love for us.

Christian trust in God implicitly recognizes, in faith, the existence of some divine overview of life and creation. A necessary condition for our mature willingness to trust in God's love is our conviction to desire what God desires for humanity, the world, and by extension, for us as part of this world. Such is the process of building up and uncovering the reign of God on earth. As disciples of Jesus, we are his hands and voices, called to become like him in our day. Similarly, we seek to realize God's unfolding reign, little by little, year by year, while perhaps unable to perceive its growth. In our praying the Lord's Prayer we say "thy kingdom come" while also saying immediately after it "thy will be done on earth as it is in heaven." Can we collaborate with the divine plan of which we are a part, helping to uncover God's reign in our world, even if sometimes we cannot fathom how the state of our world or an apparent personal tragedy or failure could possibly fit into this long-term project?

Faithful trust in God's love for us allows disciples to experience the highs and lows of human life that form the path toward human maturity. Some people seem to have their professional lives figured out early in adulthood, while others follow a longer and rockier road as they must first experience a variety of occupations before finding their best fit. The path of dating and other lasting relationships is an almost universal challenge with its times of bliss and joys as well as its share of disappointments and heartache.

Christian trust draws upon a disciple's willingness to cooperate and act amidst the vagaries of the divine mystery for one's life. Trusting in God does not mean that we are to live passively as fatalistic "Christian Stoics" who shrug our shoulders and leave everything to God. The divine interaction in our world is not without its ultimate goal, contrary to the thought of some contemporary observers who believe that life is more like a colliding sequence of purposeless random events. To Christians, earthly existence is not merely a disparate series of haphazard events, like the indeterminate scatter of billiard balls in an opening break. If we believe that God loves us and that God desires, not only for us but for all people, to experience the fullest human joy possible, to live in the deepest harmony with the utter splendor of divine love cascading into our lives, then we can begin to appreciate the mystery of the divine interaction with our world. Everything that occurs in a disciple's life—*everything*—has the potential for helping to uncover the reign of God. Many events can serve to thwart or temporarily deter its growth; such is frequently the cost of imperfect free will and sin. I may even be driven to the brink of despair at the loss of someone dear or in the face of some financial catastrophe or threat to my health. Still, even these experiences can sprout vines and shoots that ultimately help to strengthen my life of faith and fullness of life in Christ and, hopefully, to nurture the faith life of others. God can bring good from every event, even from sinful actions. Perhaps we do not like the results, preferring another outcome. However, if our trust in God is rooted in a belief that God is ultimately working for the good of all, then we can better embrace and cooperate with this continual intervention in our lives and world.

While in a time of prayer, or simply after finding a quiet place for a few moments, recall times in life when you may have asked yourself, "Where is God in this situation? How could God allow this to happen or to threaten me?" More often than not, it is only in retrospect that we can appreciate that God who seemed silent and absent was indeed with us during our most trying times.

Trusting in God exercises our Christian humility and obedience in life. Those of us entrusting ourselves to the divine gaze that lovingly oversees us have need for at least two key Christian virtues. One is humility, in which we admit that God is the source of all our blessings, life, and every breath we take. This can be a particularly difficult lesson to learn for twenty-first-century Westerners of developed nations, more accustomed to placing trust in what *we* accomplish, what *we* have experienced, and the simplistic belief that if you desire it earnestly enough and work hard enough, it will happen. Again, trust in God's overall supervision does not mean that we should throw up our hands and responsibility in the simple belief that God is in the driver's seat. Our maturing Christian trust in God will slowly teach us, however, that every action, every success, every blessing, and every failure for that matter, occurs within the eternal gaze that sees an individual life and that of all the human race as part of the created order, held in existence as part of the overall divine plan rooted in divine love.[46]

The second virtue, Christian obedience, takes its lead from Jesus's attitude of faithful filial obedience, that of a loving son toward his heavenly Father. True Christian obedience goes further than simply obeying the Ten Commandments and fulfilling basic Christian moral laws. Christian obedience stems from our loving relationship with God formed by God's immense love for us and our love for God in return. The filial obedience that Jesus models for us works toward making every instant of our life into an expression of faithful praise to our heavenly Father, resulting in a life that is animated and guided by this loving relationship and thus more capable of trusting in the divine vision for each person.[47]

Conclusion

Whether in the more ordinary footsteps along the "little way" of Thérèse of Lisieux, the mysterious and costly way of the Trappists from Our Lady of the Atlas, or somewhere in between, a disciple's trust in God's love can be a challenging and sometimes frightful practice. Living by this trust, however, puts into practice the gospel words of Jesus that "unless you become like a little child you shall not enter the Kingdom of Heaven" (Matt 18:3)—the trust of a child becoming, paradoxically, a traditional sign of maturing Christian discipleship.

---

46. LaBelle, *From Strength to Strength*, 23–45.
47. LaBelle, *From Strength to Strength*, 46–67.

Questions for Reflection

1. Recall some personal life experience in which you felt abandoned by God, or perhaps God did not seem near. While acknowledging the difficulty or even pain that may have resulted, can you identify any positive elements of your relationship with God that emerged from the experience?
2. Can you identify within you any personal attributes or experiences that might keep you from maturing in your trust of God's love for you?
3. United States currency is imprinted with the phrase "In God We Trust." Is this still a true statement? How so, or how not?

Suggested Further Reading

Manning, Brennan. *Ruthless Trust: The Ragamuffin's Path to God.* San Francisco: HarperOne, 2002.

5

Asceticism and Christian Discipleship

CHRISTIAN DISCIPLESHIP CALLS US to grow daily in our love for God and others, following Jesus as our model. Christian discipleship is, therefore, an ascetical pursuit. Asceticism finds its roots in the ancient Greek word *asketes*, meaning to condition the body for military combat and honing the needed skills such as spear-throwing, archery, swordsmanship, or other physical exercise requiring focus, effort, and interior discipline. The asceticism of Christianity supports a disciple's lifelong pursuit: personal transformation into Christ, leading to fuller life in the reign of God, leading to an ever-expanding love for God and other people, God's daughters and sons like us.

Christian ascetical exercises can assist us to use and enjoy more wisely the blessings of food, drink, sex, sleep, and other normal pursuits of daily living. Unfortunately, popular misunderstandings of Christian asceticism can fixate on past practices associated with various ascetical practices and "mortifications" to curb sinful temptations and unruliness of the flesh: wearing a scratchy goat-hair shirt for days on end to tame the sensation of touch; adopting a bland or very meager diet to overcome preference for fine food; adopting periods of abstinence from food, alcohol, or sex for the sake of deeper prayer; immersing oneself in icy water to express sorrow for one's sins; or maintaining sleepless vigils for days on end in the misunderstood quest for continuous prayer. Disciples from different periods of Christian spirituality have practiced one or another of these forms, influenced to some degree by their underlying philosophical or religious attitudes concerning personhood, social mores concerning marriage and sexuality, and exaggerated valuation of the spiritual realm over material creation and the human body. The good news is that none of the above extraordinary ascetical practices is essential for Christian discipleship. As we shall find, though, a healthy understanding and appreciation for asceticism is a timeless practice to pursue more freely the way of Jesus.

The tradition of Christian asceticism, for all disciples, focuses on enhancing growth in the three general and interactive areas of self-denial, prayer, and greater love for God and others, helping to foster a disciple's ongoing transformation into Christ. Most disciples seem to fit into what we might call "ordinary" Christian asceticism, observing at least the minimal expected practices of discipleship within their particular denomination. Some followers of Jesus, however, responding to a deeper personal religious experience, yearn to follow more closely Jesus's life of spiritual freedom through self-denial beyond ordinary spiritual means. Traditionally called *ascetics*, these Christian individuals typically follow a more rigorous program of daily life that fosters their inner freedom to follow in Jesus's footsteps. Many Christian ascetics find that adopting limitations to normal human goods such as rightful human possessions, relationships, and self-autonomy can bear fruit in deeper love for God and others in prayer and service.

We have already considered prayer and charity in Christian discipleship. This chapter examines the historical roots and dynamics of various ascetical practices of self-denial within the overall asceticism of Christianity and what contemporary disciples might glean from them.

Part One: Christian Asceticism Through History

Asceticism was not unique to early Christianity, of course. People of Roman and Greek antiquity were acquainted with the need for personal restraint of ordinary human pursuits. Practicing asceticism was a voluntary program that entailed at least the temporary or indefinite renunciations of normally permissible pleasures to realize some worthy achievement.[1] Besides self-discipline for athletics, learning moral restraint to curb one's sexual or other appetites was an expected component of classical philosophical formation and education. Christian asceticism initially absorbed certain

---

1. Staatz, "Asceticism," 131.

practices from earlier Hebrew religious experience, gradually forming its own ascetical collage of practices over the ensuing centuries.

Asceticism in Scripture

The Old Testament

"Be holy, as I am holy" (Lev 19:2), God's message to the people through the words of Moses, established the course of life for God's chosen people. By the time of Jesus's birth, the Old Testament people pursued this holiness through listening to God's word in the Jewish writings and observing the covenant laws that regulated every aspect of Jewish life in their desire to embody the divine holiness and justice toward all God's people. Ritual practices, purity laws, dietary rules, regard for one's spouse and offspring, and showing justice to one another—following these consistently and assiduously became the ideal for the Hebrew people.

Ascetical practices intended to overcome human constraints to holiness found no widespread place among the Old Testament people. However, at least some devout Hebrew persons did engage in practices found here and there in the wider written tradition for entering into deeper prayer, ritual purification, or expressing sorrow for past sin. For instance, the book of Judith relates the story of an extraordinary woman who, in her first years of widowhood, began an intensive period of prayerful and humble attentiveness to God through practicing personal isolation, fasting from certain legitimate goods, and wearing sackcloth and ashes (Jdt 8:4–8). Later, the wisdom literature exhorts its readers to overcome personal faults of pride and avarice while always striving to fulfill the commandment to love God with their whole hearts, souls, and strength (Deut 6:5). The prophetic tradition warned the Jewish people against performing merely exterior acts of repentance and prayer to seek divine favor, however, without pursuing an interior conversion of heart.

The New Testament

As noted in earlier chapters, Jesus's proclamation centered on the immanent reign of God, that pearl of great price found through growing in the practice of divine loving charity or *agape*. Life in the reign of God offers the way to live as sons and daughters of God, free to live according to the selfless divine love extended to them.

Embracing the reign of God challenges disciples to identify and, as much as possible, overcome any personal attachments that impede this deeper life. Jesus's life in the Synoptics embodied this interior self-denial that focused on three particular areas of vulnerability to disciples. Jesus was a man of prayer who fully and unselfishly loved both his heavenly Father and others. He also indicates the difficulties for disciples seeking the reign of God while also being concerned for personal wealth, possessions (Luke 18:24), and obligating relationships (Luke 9:59), as well as insisting on one's personal will over responding to the Spirit's movements within them (Luke 2:49). Jesus's life of complete availability to the reign of God included relinquishing love of his very life to the cross, encapsulating the final cost of life in his reign: "If any wish to come after me, let them deny themselves and take up their cross and follow me" (Mark 8:34).

The evangelist Paul strove always to be attentive to the movements of the Spirit of the risen Christ that accompanied him in his missionary ventures and challenges. Paul used athletic images to describe his attentiveness and dedication to finding the freedom to follow the Spirit's prompting. Paul gave himself to winning the runner's prize (1 Cor 9:24–27), having no interest in cursory attitudes of mere "shadowboxing" in his preparation but always keeping his eye on the contest before him. He recalled before his death that his life's race was ending and he had endured its demands (2 Tim 4:7).

Paul's asceticism was his identification with Christ's suffering through shouldering Jesus's single-minded acceptance of personal hardships, dangers, and suffering, trusting in the divine love and relying on God for his needs. This program reinforced in Paul certain qualities such as his choice to remain unmarried (1 Cor 7:8), his pursuit of personal patience, and especially his growth in humility. In all of these, Paul identified with the sufferings and humiliations of Christ, believing that his struggles would bring him to share in Christ's glory (2 Cor 1:3–7). He admitted at times the hardships and self-denial required by his missionary work were more bearable through observing his ascetical lifestyle, enabling him to go about evangelizing and establishing Christian communities.

The Epistle of James reveals some of the day-to-day moral struggles with which late-first-century Christians had to contend. The author exhorts his listeners to grow in a list of virtues for the sake of individuals and the community, such as endurance, humility, wisdom to resist temptation, and patience. James instructs that personal riches are a special peril for people who hoard them to the neglect of justly paying their workers; nowhere, however, does the author condemn riches in themselves or insist that disciples should dissolve themselves of possessions (5:1–6).

Christian Asceticism in the Early Patristic Period

Early Christian asceticism found its practical expression in the disciples' struggles to identify with Christ and follow his example while living in an unsympathetic and often antagonistic society. In the first three centuries, many Christians were also tested in their experiences of physical suffering and martyrdom. Other followers of Christ sought to follow his way more devotedly by adopting his embrace of virginity, detachment from unnecessary possessions, and self-giving in charitable works for others. The experiences of martyrs and dedicated virgins have impacted how subsequent Christianity came to view the deeper meaning and demands of following Jesus.

Persecution and Martyrdom

Christianity in the first centuries encountered many hardships that tested a disciple's desire to follow Jesus. Originally a Jewish religious sect, the Christian estrangement from Jewish public religious life around AD 70 effectively exposed the followers of Christ as a marginalized religion with many beliefs running counter to those of the Roman empire. Jewish accusations of Christianity being a heretical form of Judaism sometimes brought penalties or hardships from local civic leaders. Countless Christian converts became ostracized by their non-Christian families concerned for their own social standing. Other disciples had to change their livelihood if it clashed with Christian beliefs; soldier-converts, for instance, could no longer be involved in military bloodshed and idolatry, nor could any Christians assist in arena events that resulted in the death of criminals or animals. Following the way of Jesus in the first three centuries was frequently a costly pursuit, becoming much more so during the second- and third-century periods of persecution and martyrdom.

The specter of likely suffering for their faith always hovered over the early Christians. Several bishops urged them to be ready for the day when it would arrive and bring a serious test of their faith and witness. The ascetic Tertullian of Carthage wrote a letter to imprisoned disciples awaiting trial and likely execution, urging them to use their time well in toughening themselves for the impending contest:

> You are about to enter a noble contest in which the living God acts the part of superintendent and the Holy Spirit is your trainer, a contest whose crown is eternity, whose prize is angelic nature, citizenship in heaven and glory for ever and ever. And so your Master, Jesus Christ, who has anointed you with the Holy Spirit and has brought you to this training ground, has resolved, before the day of the contest, to take you from a softer way of life to a harsher treatment that your strength may be increased. For athletes, too, are set apart for more rigid training that they may apply themselves to the building up of their physical strength. They are kept from lavish living, from more tempting dishes, from more pleasurable drinks. They are urged on, they are subjected to torturing toils, they are worn out: the more strenuously they have exerted themselves, the greater is their hope of victory. . . . We who are about to win an eternal one recognize in the prison our training ground, that we may be led forth to the actual contest before the seat of the presiding judge well practiced in all hardships, because strength is built up by austerity, but destroyed by softness.[2]

Christians suffering torture and martyrdom provided the greatest moment of testimony to this; the disciple's preparation for this feat, however, displayed another type of witness: the voluntary loving struggle to follow Christ with an unfettered heart.

Roman Empire persecutions were on-again, off-again affairs, sometimes with a generation or more of peace between them, a false peace that naturally enticed many Christians to relax their spiritual discipline. Bishop Cyprian of Carthage (ca. 200-258) recalled the weak spiritual state and discipline of many Christians at the onset of Emperor Decius's persecution:

> Everyone was eager to increase his estate, and forgetful of what the believers in apostolic times either had done before or always should have done, with the insatiable ardor of covetousness they applied themselves to increasing their possessions. Among the priests there was no devout religion; in their ministries no sound faith, in their works no mercy, in their morals no discipline. Among men the beard was defaced; faces were painted among

---

2. Tertullian, *Mart.* 3-5.

women, eyes were falsified after God's hands had completed them, hair was colored in deception. There were crafty frauds to deceive the hearts of the simple, subtle schemes for circumventing the brethren. They joined with infidels in the bond of matrimony; they prostituted the members of Christ to the gentiles. They not only swore rashly, but committed perjury also; they looked down with haughty arrogance upon those placed over them; they maligned one another with an envenomed tongue; they quarreled with one another with stubborn hatred.[3]

Tertullian, Cyprian, and other church elders warned their unsuspecting fellow Christians to prepare for that possible day when they would be taken to jail and put to the test. This lurking menace called for disciples to consider the priority of their faith over any earthly ties of possessions and family relationships.

Earliest Christian Ascetical Virginity

The Christian desire to live a deeper relationship with Jesus by following his ascetical way of virginity and renunciation of possessions has been a core practice for Christian ascetics from the first century.[4] Ascetical virginity did not originate with the Christians but was also a practice among Jews of the Qumran ascetic community and other sects. The Essenes, another Jewish ascetic sect, included members who were both virgins and spouses agreeing to live continently as brother and sister. Countless early Christians adopted varying degrees of sexual continence as ways to identify with Jesus's lifelong virginity.

Practicing virginity was no small matter in either the Roman Empire or in Judaism. Abstaining from marriage conflicted with the Roman societal view favoring marriage as the source of male offspring needed to maintain the security and institutions of society.[5] The Roman Emperor Augustus, for one, imposed a tax on unmarried men in AD 9.[6] The Jews also regarded marriage as chiefly for procreation, in response to the call in Genesis to multiply and populate the land (Gen 9:1). It was a rare individual

---

3. Cyprian, *Laps.* 6.
4. Bouyer et al., *Spirituality of the New Testament*, 303–5.
5. Brown, *Body and Society*, 5–7.
6. The "bachelor tax" imposed on unmarried males. Brown, *Body and Society*, 6.

who married for love, especially among the higher Roman social classes; marriage was a classic means to cement familial and political alliances.

The apostle Paul had counseled celibacy for disciples seriously desiring to pursue prayer and interior conversion in preparation for Jesus's immanent return (1 Cor 7:25–31). Post-Pauline documents reveal that the practice existed: the Acts of the Apostles recalls the four unmarried and prophesying daughters of Phillip the Evangelist (Acts 21:8–9),[7] while James the Just, known as the brother of Jesus, was remembered as an ascetic.[8] These individuals embraced lifelong abstinence from sexual relations as their way of consecrating (meaning "to set aside") their lives to cultivate wholeheartedly their love of God.

Christian communities began to value the witness of lifelong virginity for numerous pastoral reasons. In their dedication, virgins showed more fully the union of Christ and his spouse, the church. Virginity was a radical sign of the Word of God taking root in disciples' lives and moving them to live in the reign of God where no Christian would take another in marriage. Some early bishops recognized that practicing dedicated virginity served as a countersign to the pagan sexual licentiousness of their time, while others wrote that Christians also valued the ascetical demands of following virginity as a privileged spiritual way to live out martyrdom, not in one moment but day after day.

Christian communities soon recognized that dedicated virgins became channels of spiritual fruitfulness, wisdom, and deeper charitable service to the sick and poor. Many people, drawn to the virgins' virtuous living, sought their social companionship. Christian communities eventually considered virgins as a special group; women would wear a distinctive veil as "brides of Christ" while male virgins were called "continent ones" (*continenti*). Virgins initially lived with their natural family who gave them the time, space, and support to follow their acts of prayer, fasting, and charitable work. The recognized title of "virgin" was a loose classification that could include married couples who agreed to live in separate dwellings so to observe lifelong sexual continence. Widows willing to embrace lifelong celibacy could also adopt this life, considered a new beginning for them to dedicate themselves more fully to works of prayer and charity.

---

7. The fourth-century historian Eusebius recalls this in his *Hist. eccl.* 3.31.
8. Eusebius, *Hist. eccl.* 2.23.

Early Christian Ascetical Eccentricities

Early Christian asceticism produced a few popular movements that eventually spawned eccentricities of general orthodox practices. These aberrations resulted largely from the influence of dualist philosophies that divided reality into the material world dominated by evil and the spiritual world belonging to the divine. Dualist proponents held that material desires, along with the pursuit of basic human sexuality and reproduction, must be set aside in order to find salvation. Elements of spiritual-material dualism were present in Encratism (known as "the abstainers"), which taught that personal salvation required extreme ascetical practices to overcome the evils of created matter (including the human body). They exercised prolonged fasts with abstention from meat and wine, renouncing marriage and procreation as earthly practices corrupted by evil.

Eccentric ascetical practices and claims of prophetic utterances defined a second-century movement called Montanism. Its founders, Montanus and two women, Priscilla and Maximilla, claimed that the Holy Spirit led them into ecstatic trances or whirling about while prophesying in strange voices and personalities. Their message announced that the new age guided by the Paraclete had arrived and Christ's return was imminent. While the movement caught the attention of many Christians, it also caused considerable division among Eastern churches. The prophets' overall message and convulsive-like public displays also ran counter to traditional beliefs of prophetic behavior, resulting in church leaders condemning Montanism in the third century.[9]

The Growing Popularity of Ascetical Virginity over Marriage

By the early fourth century, the social popularity of committed virgins presented a challenge to their life of cultivating prayer and virtue. Several church fathers wrote letters and sermons extolling the lives of virgins while offering guiding principles to help sustain their spiritual gifts to the Christian communities. Bishop Ambrose of Milan (340–397), at the urging of his sister Marcellina, compiled and circulated a collection of at least three sermons addressing the topic.[10] Using edifying examples of others living the lifestyle rather than codifying concrete rules, Ambrose apparently

---

9. Eusebius mentions these in his *Hist. eccl.* 4.27 and 5.16.
10. Ambrose, *De virg.*

presented consecrated virginity in such a persuasive light that mothers would hide his circulated writings from their marriage-aged daughters. Another aid was the growing number of supportive virgin communities, although many virgins continued living with their family as before.

In their zealous desire to promote and defend virginity, however, some writings seemed to place marriage on a lower plane. The scriptural interpreter Jerome (347–420) also offered guidelines for a virgin's prayer, dress, social engagements, fasting, and other practices.[11] While respecting marriage as a divine precept, Jerome held that choosing a life of virginity ranked higher than marriage since all people are first born into virginal purity:

> I praise wedlock, I praise marriage, but it is because they give me virgins. I gather the rose from the thorns, the gold from the earth, the pearl from the shell. . . . Wedlock is the more honored, the more what is born of it is loved. Why, mother, do you grudge your daughter her virginity? She has been reared on your milk, she has come from your womb, she has grown up in your bosom. Your watchful affection has kept her a virgin. Are you angry with her because she chooses to be a king's wife and not a soldier's? She has conferred on you a high privilege; you are now the mother-in-law of God. "Concerning virgins," says the apostle [Paul], "I have no commandment of the Lord." Why was this? Because his own virginity was due, not to a command, but to his free choice.[12]

Embracing one's virginal state could lead to the freedom that Adam and Eve enjoyed in paradise before their disobedience and exile:

> Someone may say, "Do you dare detract from wedlock, which is a state blessed by God?" I do not detract from wedlock when I set virginity before it. No one compares a bad thing with a good. Wedded women may congratulate themselves that they come next to virgins. "Be fruitful," God says, "and multiply, and replenish the earth." He who desires to replenish the earth may increase and multiply if he will. But the train to which you belong is not on earth, but in heaven. The command to increase and multiply first finds fulfilment after the expulsion from paradise, after the nakedness and the fig-leaves which speak of sexual passion. . . . In paradise Eve was a virgin, and it was only after [donning] the coats of skins that she began her married life. Now paradise is

---

11. Jerome to Eustochium, "Letter 22" is one document addressing this.
12. Jerome, "Letter 22.20."

your home too. Keep therefore your birthright and say: "Return unto thy rest, O my soul."[13]

The New Ascetical Arena of Desert Monasticism

The legalization of Christianity in 313 led to a relaxed religious fervor. Many Christian ascetics yearned for a more rigorous and demanding religious life and concluded that the desert wilderness was the place where they could escape the seductions of a spiritually lukewarm church and society. The ascetics gradually ventured further and further away from civilization, giving them the freedom and solitude to cultivate lives of virginity, humility, and detachment from possessions.

The earliest monastic desert solitaries had very little information to guide their quest. Athanasius of Alexandria's work, *The Life of Antony*, offered the wisdom of earlier monastic experiences in overcoming various human temptations. The collection was also useful for solitary monks in learning to recognize any indiscreet ascetical zeal that could lead them to destructive practices of excessive fasting, remaining awake for long night prayer vigils, and prolonged exposure to the desert extremes of heat and cold.

Desert monks began recognizing other ascetics who had matured in experience and wisdom, gradually gathering around these wise desert mothers (*ammas*) and fathers (*abbas*) in arrangements of *lauras* or crowns, suggesting the laurel wreaths awarded to athletic victors. This arrangement offered both mutual safety for the monks and a way to help and support each other in their calling.

Communal development for monastic living developed further into that of *cenobitic* monks, residing in enclosed settings of one or more larger structures. Besides celibate chastity and material detachment, cenobite monks also promised obedience to their elder *abba* (father) or *amma* (mother) in seeking openness to receive their spiritual wisdom. The first principal cenobitic rule, that of Pachomius (292–348), was very detailed and rigorously governed the monk's entire day. Subsequent cenobitic rules of Basil of Caesarea in the East and Benedict of Nursia in the West offered more moderated programs concerning daily monastic living and ascetical practices. Benedict's text noted that obedience to the rule slowly led to growth in humility. Observing prompt and wholehearted obedience to the superior was a monk's way of finding and obeying the will of God:

13. Jerome, "Letter 22.19."

> But this very obedience will be acceptable to God and pleasing to men only if what is commanded is done without hesitation, delay, lukewarmness, grumbling, or objection. For the obedience given to Superiors is given to God, since He Himself has said, "He who hears you, hears Me." And the disciples should offer their obedience with a good will, for "God loves a cheerful giver." For if the disciple obeys with an ill will and murmurs, not necessarily with his lips but simply in his heart, then even though he fulfil the command yet his work will not be acceptable to God, who sees that his heart is murmuring. And, far from gaining a reward for such work as this, he will incur the punishment due to murmurers, unless he amend and make satisfaction.[14]

The fourth chapter of Benedict's rule lists a set of seventy-two "good works" to guide monks in everyday life by ways such as chastening the body, having a love for chastity, and avoiding theft or covetousness; in short, by preferring nothing to the love of Christ.

Ascetical Life of Ordinary Lay Christians

Monks were not the only Christians who performed ascetical practices. Writings and sermons of Basil of Caesarea and John Chrysostom to lay Christians indicate that discipleship called them also to order their lives as they sought to grow in their love of God, though to a less demanding degree than monks. Western bishops also exhorted lay Christians to follow some degree of appropriate personal asceticism, especially during the weeks before celebrating Easter and other penitential seasons. Augustine of Hippo preached to his listeners at the opening of Lent:

> Let us fast, humbling our souls as the day draws near on which the Teacher of humility humbled Himself becoming obedient even to death on a cross. Let us imitate His cross, fastening to it our passions subdued by the nails of abstinence. Let us chastise our body, subjecting it to obedience, and, lest we slip into illicit pleasures through our undisciplined flesh, let us in taming it sometimes withdraw licit pleasures. Self-indulgence and drunkenness ought to be shunned on other days; throughout this season, however, even legitimate eating is to be checked. Adultery and fornication

---

14. Benedict, *RB* 5.

must always be abhorred and avoided, but on these days special restraint must be practiced even by married persons.[15]

Augustine understood the Christian life as a call to continuously grow in love for God along the way of Jesus, a disciple's principal model to follow.

Bishop Caesarius of Arles (d. 542) exhorted lay disciples during Lent to perform charitable deeds such as offering alms to the poor, making peace with their enemies, and washing pilgrims' feet. He also called upon them to refrain from marital relations for a few days before receiving Communion and abstain from sex for the Lenten season. They should also rise early to participate in the traditional predawn vigil prayers and make efforts to attend cathedral prayers at midmorning, noon, and midafternoon.[16]

To summarize this section: Christian ascetical practices by the sixth century had their roots in Christianity's earliest years. Living and professing one's beliefs in the face of social and political adversities called for disciples to develop an interior resolve that required their day-by-day attentiveness and exercise. Such resoluteness in Christian life continued past the trying years of martyrdom, leading many serious ascetic disciples to find other ways to harden their resolve to live more fully the gospel message. Their examples served to remind the wider church that their Christian faith was precious, to be cherished above earthly temptations and attractions, however good and rightful they may be.

Early Medieval Developments in Christian Asceticism

A number of Eastern monks developed reputations for performing almost superhuman exaggerations of ascetical practices. These ascetics, nonetheless, could edify and fascinate the wider body of Christians outside the monasteries in the late patristic and early medieval periods. For example, the Syrian monk Simeon Stylites (also named Simeon the Elder, 390–459) and his followers were called stylites, or "pole dwellers," practicing a form of asceticism involving sitting on a pole high above the ground for extended periods. Simeon gradually increased his height above ground until reaching almost sixty feet, where he remained for some thirty-seven years. Confined to a one-square meter base that was surrounded by a protective railing, Simeon's peculiar austerities earned the admiration and sometimes

---

15. Augustine, "Sermon 207.2."
16. One example is in Caesarius of Arles, "Sermon 196."

the conversion of many visitors.[17] Even with the great number of Christian converts attributed to his diligence, Simeon's practice would no doubt be considered extreme by twenty-first-century standards. Another example was John the Faster (or Abstainer), Patriarch of Constantinople from 582–95, whose life story reveals his widely acknowledged reputation of zeal for his ascetical feats and attending to needs of the poor. These feats dwindled as the early Eastern cenobitic rule of Basil helped to temper the exaggerations of monastic ascetical life, while Benedict's program moderated the zeal of Western ascetic monks.

Confession of Sins and Ascetical Acts of Penance

The early medieval period spawned an additional reason for performing ascetical practices besides seeking self-mastery and growth in virtue. First monks, then other Christians began to perform acts of asceticism to express sorrow and beg forgiveness for sins. Earlier Christian reconciliation for serious sins was a lengthy process that could take many years for the penitent to be reunited with the Christian community. The influence of Irish missionary monasticism introduced collections of *penitentials* in the sixth century that listed specific sins along with recommended prayers and practices to perform as atonement. No longer a humiliating and protracted public spectacle as sometimes occurred in earlier centuries, the penitent would meet one-on-one with a priest who served as a channel of God's forgiveness. The priest could also impose penitential tasks commensurate with the offenses forgiven that gave concrete expression of the penitent's sorrow for sins and desire for reconciliation. These penances typically included some combination of prayer, ascetical practices such as additional fasting, and almsgiving to the poor. Monastic ascetical practices also included more physically demanding and punitive actions to express their sorrow for sins committed, including self-immersion in freezing water for a time, sleeping on the ground or other hard surface, observing a designated period of excommunication from the community, prostration on the ground or floor, and repetitive genuflections.

Christians eventually began assuming one or another exercise to express their ongoing remorse for past sins committed personally, beseeching God in atonement for the sins of others, or thanksgiving for some spiritual favor, a broader understanding of penitential practices that

---

17. "Symeon Stylites," in Theodoret, *Monks of Syria*, 160–76.

extended beyond merely fostering one's growth in virtue. Meritorious at heart, this development helped to spawn errant practices such as seeking church indulgences to further mitigate the offenses of sin, notably through monetary or other material donations. Seeking indulgences put into question the traditional belief in God's readiness to forgive sins, a serious concern of the later Protestant Reformation.

Making pilgrimages, already present from the fourth century, became a more commonly accepted ascetical practice during the medieval period. Christians could journey to many shrines, martyr tombs, or other holy places. Early medieval travel carried considerable personal risk, including uncertainties about food and lodging along the way, safety in the threat of assault and robbery, and the ever-present threat of illness. Whether to fulfill a promise to God in exchange for some blessing received or as an extraordinary penitential expression, the dangers and uncertainties of pilgrim travel also brought opportunities to grow in one's faith and trust in God.

Ascetical Practices in the High- and Later-Medieval Periods

Ascetical Devotion to Jesus's Earthly Virtues and Suffering

Renewed interest in Jesus's sacred humanity and special attention to his earthly life in the Gospels fostered more affective spiritual expressions of love and devotion. Jesus was no longer merely a model to imitate; he was one with whom Christians could relate more personally, with loving regard for Jesus as, for instance, the spouse of one's soul or an understanding and ever-faithful friend.

Devotion to Jesus in his sacred humanity incited a desire among many disciples to imitate and identify with him in special moments of his earthly life. Prayerful and affective attentiveness to Jesus's birth, his ministry episodes, and his passion could lead praying disciples to draw closer to Jesus in love by interiorizing his imagined sentiments of joy, anger, love, and suffering. Spiritual masters such as the Franciscan Bonaventure (1221–1274) composed lists of Jesus's earthly virtues to adopt and put into practice, including his humility, poverty, charity, obedience, and patience.

Exercising ways to experience and unite spiritually with Jesus's physical sufferings from his passion also became popular. The temporal events of Jesus's earthly life had passed, but praying disciples could offer their suffering to his redemptive suffering and death that echo through eternity for all humanity. These practices also led disciples to embrace physical suffering as a way to mortify the flesh and overcome sensual or bodily weaknesses, add a note of sincerity to prayer, or as a further way to exercise penance for oneself or others.

The Rise of Christian Church Reform and Penitential Movements

The Christian church of the high-medieval period acquired an unfortunate reputation as having grown too worldly in accumulating wealth and property to the neglect of pastoral needs among the isolated rural Christians, many of whom had fallen into religious ignorance and superstition. The situation fostered a growing desire among many members to restore in both church and ministers the simplicity and virtues of Jesus and the first disciples. Groups of itinerant and poor lay disciples began to move about the countryside and small villages, seeking to foment church conversion and pastoral renewal. The reform movements produced both positive and negative effects. On the one hand, the various mendicant (begging) movements recalled the early Christian observances of voluntary poverty, humility, and itinerancy, helping to produce the Franciscan religious societies of Francis of Assisi and his followers. Dominic de Guzman, founder of the Order of Preachers (Dominicans), was another fierce defender of voluntary poverty in his order of both religious men and women; more so than the Franciscans, though, Dominican followers could be dispensed from their observance of poverty and other ascetical practices, when necessary, to exercise their ministries of preaching and teaching.

The radical emphases on voluntary poverty and humility also appeared in reform movements that more radically condemned Christian church wealth and immorality. Thirteenth-century mendicant groups of lay men and women, such as the *Humiliati*, practiced penitential mortification for individual repentance and atonement, traveling about their regions while calling for the revitalizing of the institutional church and popular piety. However, some of these so-called penitential movements veered into unorthodox beliefs and eccentric ascetical practices due to a lack of suitable theological or pastoral education.[18] Others, though,

---

18. One notable movement, the Waldensians, sought to form an alternative structure to the universal Christian church with its own sacraments and clerical appointments. Albigensians in southern France and Cathars in other parts of Europe represented a dualist movement stressing the corruption of material creation and exercising rigorous

formed by established consecrated life orders of Franciscans, Dominicans, and several other religious orders, sought to offer better guidance and structure by forming associate or "third order" branches (male consecrated religious comprised the first order, with vowed female religious forming the second). Lay Christian men and women drawn to one of these established spiritualities could follow a modified program of the respective order's daily spiritual program and ascetical practices without the solemn vows of a permanent religious commitment.

Besides the traditional observances of voluntary poverty and renunciation, other practices emerged among disciples desiring to identify with the suffering Jesus to express sorrow for sin. Among these pain-inducing exercises were items that could be worn under clothing and undetected by outsiders, such as a hair shirt of goat fur that caused continual discomfort and belts studded with sharp metal points worn around the waist that would scar flesh. Perhaps the most visible and publicly evocative practice was "taking the discipline" or self-flagellation with a multiple-tailed whip. Zeal for reforming the church and especially her clergy reawakened use of the discipline as a visible expression of personal sorrow for sins and recalling onlookers to renew their relationship with God. Flagellation societies began to form, initially respected for their zeal and edifying resolve, but eventually some proclaimed to be holier than the institutional Christian church. Because of this and other evidence of their misguided zeal, Pope Clement VI officially condemned the association of flagellant societies in the fourteenth century, although a few smaller flagellant groups persisted into the nineteenth. Taking the discipline also became an individual ascetical practice among primarily Roman Catholic disciples in many consecrated life communities but gradually disappeared during the twentieth century.

The fourteenth-century Catherine of Siena believed that she could lovingly unite her various physical sufferings to those of Christ for the spiritual good of other souls and the church, something new for the Christian spiritual tradition. Later contemplatives and recluses would follow Catherine's way of prayer and offering her sufferings for others, a practice that would leave its mark on the later spiritual paths of Teresa of Avila, Thérèse of Lisieux, and countless lay Christians living with chronic afflictions.

Encouraging such dramatic and emotional ascetical feats virtually disappears in the late-medieval *Imitation of Christ*. Not altogether,

---

ascetical practices.

though—the author underscores the twofold struggle of Christian spiritual growth as overcoming exterior and interior faults while also putting Jesus's humility and other virtues into practice. Disciples could hope to do so only by adopting Jesus's way of self-denial to the extent that overcame his instinct for self-preservation, which the work presents to readers as the "royal road of the Holy Cross." *The Imitation* gives no specific physical practices but presumes different moments of self-denial in a disciple's life. The author notes, however, that seemingly mundane opportunities also present themselves in the course of a disciple's daily events, offering occasions for self-denial and encouraging death to one's selfishness:

> You see, the cross is at the root of everything; everything is based upon our dying there. There is no other road to life, to true inward peace, but the road of the cross, of dying daily to self. Walk where you will, seek whatever you have a mind to; you will find no higher road above, no safer road below, than the road of the holy cross. You may make all your plans and arrangements in accordance with your own notions and desires; even so, you will always find you have some suffering to bear, whether you like it or not; you will always find the cross. Either you will be conscious of bodily pain, or your soul will be inwardly in distress.... Sometimes God will leave you to yourself, sometimes your neighbor will get on your nerves; what is worse, you will often become burdensome to your own self.... You must put up with it as long as God so wills.[19]

This attitude would significantly influence later Christian life and the pursuit of holiness for disciples following more active lives of ministry and service, venturing beyond the structures and protection of well-regulated monastic and mendicant lives.

Summary

The paths of ascetical practices during the medieval era substantially developed beyond those of earlier monasticism. Adopting Christian virginity and simplicity developed into professing formal vows of voluntary poverty, chastity, and obedience to God through one's superiors. Disciples seeking to identify with Jesus of the Gospels brought a human dimension to Christian spiritual life. Meditating on his earthly experiences and travails brought a heightened awareness and appreciation for God's great love for

---

19. à Kempis, *Imitation of Christ*, 2.12.3–4.

all people but also, as a consequence, an enhanced fear of divine retribution for human sinfulness. Disciples undertook various penitential practices to promote personal growth in prayer and spiritual life and as ways of expressing sorrow to God for both individual and collective social sins. Prayers carrying notes of endured physical suffering could add a special degree of sincerity to one's beseeching God for a host of needs, including the desire for another's good, reparation for past sins, or atonement for social evil.

Notes on Christian Asceticism from the Modern Era

Reactions against Christian Ascetical Life

The fifteenth century witnessed a sharp reaction against ascetical practices of the preceding centuries, mainly on two fronts. One was a libertine attitude antagonistic to Christian morality, fostered by the years of the Renaissance and its inflated praise and confidence in human wisdom and knowledge. An atmosphere of humanism, which looked to the classical periods and wisdom of pagan Rome and Athens, became popular just as the Christian moral influence and authority became challenged and increasingly dismissed as empty and hypocritical, present even in the corruption and intrigues found in the courts of papal Rome.

The other significant anti-ascetical reaction came from the Protestant Reformation. The first Reformers, left skeptical from the perceived follies of mysticism and the sometimes spectacle-like public penitential manifestations, regarded ascetical practices as having limited value in Christian life. Faith and justification resulting from contact with God's word should be the impetus to taking up any ascetical lifestyle as a disciple's response rather than to increase faith. All Christians, married or not, were called to find holiness by engaging with their world and embracing the ascetical challenges of their everyday lives.[20] Reformers also judged consecrated religious life as meaningless, asserting that the members' "gifts" of vowed poverty, chastity, and obedience were requirements for entering the life rather than freely offered.

However, some seventeenth-century figures began reconsidering the impact of dismissing ascetical practices in Reformed Christian life. Christian religious experiences normally move disciples to modify their lifestyle to reflect their new inner reality more truthfully, a dynamic that

20. Wright, *Hidden Lives*, 22–23.

Protestantism had rejected. Writers such as Johann Arndt (1555–1621) in his *True Christianity* and Christian Hoburg (1607–1675) helped to introduce Christian works including *The Imitation of Christ* and *Sayings of the Desert Fathers* to Protestant readers, offering a more foundational ideal of Christian ascetical life and traditional practices predating the medieval church. Milder expressions of earlier ascetical exercises also appeared later in Christian Pietism[21] and Anglican Christian monasticism.

Roman Catholic Counter-Reform and Ascetical Renewal

From the fifteenth century, Roman Catholic piety and practices increasingly focused on the goal of Christian life as nurturing Christ's love and exercising this love toward others in acts of charity. Devotional and ascetical practices could foster this growth, helping to spawn an incredible number of Catholic congregations of vowed religious from the fifteenth to nineteenth centuries who devoted themselves to charitable works. Public displays of ascetical practices found expression in popular public shows of devotion in processions focusing on Jesus, Mary, and other saints. Other personal methods of fasting and ways of mortifying unruly appetites continued, seeking to expand disciples' capacity for showing charitable love to others in ministry and service to the needy. A plethora of modern-era Catholic Christian spiritual writings also emerged, offering spiritual and ascetical guidance. A small and varied list of principal writers and relevant works include Teresa of Avila (*The Way of Perfection*), Alonso Rodriguez (*The Practice of Christian Perfection*), Francis de Sales (*Introduction to the Devout Life*), and Alphonsus de Liguori's numerous works on Christian life and asceticism for lay disciples, vowed religious, and clergy.

Summarizing Observations Concerning the Christian Ascetical Tradition

Asceticism has been a perennial value in Christian life. Earlier Christian asceticism certainly had its extraordinary exaggerations and, for us, unusual exercises in the pursuit of growing in virtue, prayer, and love for God and others. Distortions aside, however, early adherents pursued

---

21. Christian Pietism, arising from seventeenth-century German Lutheranism, was known for its rigorous personal piety and stressing the importance of personal faith over theology and doctrine.

their practices of self-denial in seeking to subdue whatever could impede a deeper Christian life.

Ascetical practices were shaped by their time, culture, and surroundings. Monks and nuns sought a minimum of worldly distraction in enclosed communities; gradually, with the passing of time, other circumstances arose as Christianity increasingly interacted with its surrounding world and social needs. Many individuals chose to do so by embracing some combination of virginity or sexual continence, voluntary poverty, and limited self-will. Christian ascetical practices were not limited to those in structured religious communities; countless disciples have done so within their particular vocations of marriage and family or other forms of dedicated single living. No matter their circumstances, the goal for them has remained the same: to mature in their relationship with God by following the single-minded way of Christ as fully as possible within their particular life direction.

Life can present the grist for ascetical practice. Especially in more recent centuries, Christian disciples have learned that the demands of their life paths, whether in marriage and family life or some other setting, offer countless opportunities to stretch themselves in becoming more mature loving disciples of God and one another. There is little need for individuals to search for exterior penitential practices beyond faithfully responding to the demands of daily discipleship and self-giving for other persons.

Part Two: Asceticism in Contemporary Christian Life

Let us first consider the presence and worth of asceticism in today's world, and then how disciples might interweave some simple practices of Christian asceticism with daily life.

The Many Ascetical Lives and Lifestyles in Today's World

It would be fair to say that twenty-first-century Western society holds an ambiguous regard for the value of asceticism in ordinary daily life. Ours claims to be an age of liberation that has wrestled itself free from a growing list of traditions imposing various restraints in personal and social behavior. Personally defined understandings of human sexuality and its expression, the whirlwind of media advertisements feeding a mentality of consumerism, or the promotion of personal desire and opinion over what was once considered universal common sense, have all contributed to a collective swarm of attractions and distractions in Christian life. Without at least some degree of reasoned filtering, these daily bombardments of images and attitudes can dull a disciple's sensitivity to the deeper meaning and spiritual dimension of Christian human existence.

Looking around us, however, we find that various religious and secular ascetical actions and structures are very present in our world today in service to some objective. Devout followers of different non-Christian religions observe some measure of asceticism in the search for inner enlightenment and enhanced religious experience. Nonreligious retreats and programs foster life-changing habits to heal the psychic rifts and disharmonies in the interrelationship of body-soul-spirit that hobble Western secular society. Athletes striving to excel readily adopt a rigorous daily schedule to ensure a proper amount of sleep, balanced diet, and abstaining from whatever might impede their pursuit. Military structure and service would be impossible without some ingrained ascetical structure and practices, whether in basic training, professional officer training in service academies, or daily lives of routine structure and discipline for readiness to defend the nation. Students pursuing professional education for a career must employ some degree of self-denial and life structure if they hope to succeed. Each of these ascetical endeavors draws respect and admiration from large segments of society.

Christian discipleship, with its unique objective, also has a place among these movements. The asceticism of Christian living can facilitate disciples' growing in love for God that we pursue through cultivating virtuous habits, attention to regular prayer, and sharing more and more freely God's love for all persons. God has created us for a life of shared love with God that will endure beyond earthly life. Following the lived example that Jesus provides offers us the way to achieve this.

Balanced Christian Asceticism for a Fuller Life as God's Sons and Daughters

Christian disciples need a properly integrated understanding of body, mind, spirit, and their relationship to the rest of creation in order to appreciate the place of Christian asceticism. One does not pursue ascetical practices to weaken or punish the human body, created as good, but rather to curb its many tendencies to deter one from realizing a fuller and richer spiritual life. Influential twentieth-century Christian writers such as C. S. Lewis and Pope John Paul II have written about the rightful place of asceticism in a disciple's daily life.[22] Ascetical activity helps to prepare and enlarge one's interior space and longing for God, at once present yet hidden, to instill in disciples a fuller and more human life.

The historical and literary caricatures of Christian ascetical practices leave many people skeptical about their worth. True Christian asceticism has no place for eccentric theatrical or literary castings of self-mutilating figures such as the albino monk Silas in the film *The Da Vinci Code*. Spiritual writer Nicholas Austin has asserted that Christian ascetical practices can fall prey to three notable distortions, leaving them subject to public dismissal and even ridicule: excess (pursuing exaggerated ascetical acts such as fasting for prolonged periods as personal accomplishments, a form of pride), dualism (falling into the subtle trap of seeing the spiritual component of life as good and the corporeal as tainted with evil or worthy of disdain, requiring punishment into submission), and empty religiosity (seeking favor from God or remaining content with performing personal ascetical and religious acts while neglecting charitable needs to the poor and others in our world).[23] Just as did Christian ascetics of old, contemporary disciples should remember that growth in love for God and others is the goal of any Christian practice, including asceticism.

Ordering Our Love for God amid Our Many Other "Loves"

Our Creator has imbued us with a taste for the transcendent and for reaching out in love beyond ourselves. Our yearning for something beyond ourselves can morph into harmful cases of "love seeking fulfillment." Our greatest fulfillment will be in our shared love with God; failure to discover and pursue this tends to leave us trying to satisfy this loving yearning by settling for less satisfying loves.

Our pursuit of this ultimately satisfying love of God for us often suffers from the immediacy of less worthy loves. It is easy to be distracted by other created goods, passions, and delights of sense and creation. As an illustration, imagine stepping outside the home onto a back porch on some starry, moonless night. We extinguish the electric porch light (a created and useful good) in order to peer into the night sky in search of a faint star; after a while, someone suddenly turns the light back on, pulling us away from our intensive gazing and blinding us for a while to any further searching.

22. Fagerberg, "C. S. Lewis on Asceticism."
23. Austin, "Virtue of Asceticism," paras. 7–19.

ASCETICISM AND CHRISTIAN DISCIPLESHIP

Christian tradition has long recognized three general yet classical temptations that can dampen or obscure our innate yearning for our Creator, thanks to the reality of our disordered human affections:

a. One is our desire to possess *things*, good in themselves, whether a sleek and attractive motor vehicle of some type, financial security, a luxurious house, or even smaller "treasures" such as books, clothing, the latest laptop or cell phone. The list is as long as there are created items.

b. Next, we can seek to satisfy this deepest love in our God-given ability to form *relationships with other persons*, whether in casual social groups, a closer community of persons, or exclusively with one complementary other. Here, too, we can unwittingly desire relationships based on our exaggerated wants and expectations. The most worthwhile relationships gradually mature beyond personal desire and selfishness, moving us from "what do I get from this" into the deepest and most satisfying self-giving love to another, a process in this life that approaches but never reaches the total self-giving love of Jesus. Our God, who is Love, is the source of our self-donation to another. Christianity seeks to foster ever-deeper intimacy with God-as-Love by gradually shedding our sometimes thick and scaly outer layers of human selfishness. Most Christian disciples find that this path coincides with committing themselves to the sacrifices of family life or a freely chosen and single-minded pursuit of loving God as part of some committed religious lifestyle. Even these relationships, though they may seem heaven-sent, will continue to suffer at times while individuals grow in self-giving love and their deepest weaknesses and self-serving desires gradually diminish.

c. The third trap is our understanding of *personal freedom and autonomy* and the sometimes unfettered need to assert our will and desires. Like material possession and relationships, self-determination is a God-given right in service to human flourishing; as Christians, we flourish when our choices lead us to become more living expressions of glory to God by following the example and teaching of Jesus. People today can easily misunderstand a life of total autonomy as the freedom to do what they want and believe what they choose to believe as personal truth. True human freedom, in contrast, should lead us to pursue and love God in prayer and in one another as our greatest good.

Whatever our personalized bundle of distractions and impediments, Christian discipleship will sometimes challenge us to identify these and admit their tendency to weigh us down in our pursuit to follow the way of Jesus as we practice personal virtues, prayer, and charity to others. Following this path will present us with different moments, some more difficult than others, challenging us to evaluate and set aside whatever impedes maturity in discipleship. These events provide us the various moments of accepting the cross of Jesus in life, challenges that can bring us to a deeper and fuller existence.

Christian Discipleship and the Inescapable Cross

Christ crucified expressed Jesus's total gift of self for his Father and for others in a love greater than his innate human love for life. Through his experience of the cross, Jesus lived his fullest expression of love, the complete measure of his self-denial in which he abandoned himself to the Father's profound love for him. Throughout his life, Jesus lived totally disposed to replicate and live in harmony with the love of his heavenly Father for him, visible in his detachment from superfluous material concerns, his other-centered life of relating with others, and his total dedication to following the divine prompting. We who seek to follow Jesus's way should expect to encounter moments when we are called to our own self-sacrifice in faithfully responding to God's love in our lives, calling us to deepen in our love of God and others as God loves them. Moments of looking beyond ourselves for another's sake are calls to follow the way of the cross, ironically a symbol of death but leading to a more abundant life.

The German evangelist Dietrich Bonhoeffer (1906–1945), imprisoned and condemned for preaching that National Socialism was contrary to the gospel, wrote that the Christian way for any true disciple must include the type of self-denial that brought Jesus to the cross. We experience something of this cross whenever we deny our earthly desires because we see Christ as our greatest good, the one on whom we have fixed our vision. Our challenges to accept moments of the cross in life circumstances is an inescapable part of the call to follow Christ's example:

> It is laid on every Christian. The first Christ-suffering that everyone has to experience is the call which summons us away from our attachments to this world. It is the death of the old self in the encounter with Jesus Christ. Those who enter into discipleship enter

into Jesus's death. . . . The cross is not the terrible end of a pious, happy life. Instead, it stands at the beginning of community with Jesus Christ. Whenever Christ calls us, his call leads us to death.[24]

Dying to our old self, that self containing our tendencies to possess and control, is our way to enter more deeply into the life of the risen Christ.

Some Suggestions for Incorporating Ascetical Practices in Daily Life

Pausing and reflecting on the drives and passions of our lives while searching for God can help to reveal what may bind us or perhaps impede our growing relationship with Christ. Each person's assortment will be different, of course. Some impediments reveal themselves only later in life, but each of us can eventually identify at least some of them and how they limit our discipleship. They may take time and inner courage to admit; such is the place and benefit of quiet prayer in God's presence, inviting the Holy Spirit's enlightenment to enter within and illuminate them. This acquired "self-knowledge" of personal weaknesses and obstacles, prized by countless Christian ascetics, is a first step to promote growth in humility and maturity in discipleship.

Some other suggested ways to grow in overall Christian maturity could include the following:

Give some structure to your life. Without becoming neurotic in the process, give thought to your routine daily practices that can affect your life of discipleship. What about basic human needs of rest and recreation for healthy, balanced, and productive Christian living? Are there any other activities that, if unhindered, tend to exclude time for prayer or spiritual reading? How much time do you give to electronic pastimes such as television and casual online activity? Many disciples try to observe a weekly "Sabbath break" from any unnecessary online or electronic activity; try it sometime and notice how deeply our electronic "conveniences" have wormed their way into our lives!

Observe periodic fasting and abstaining from food and other goods. Fasting is the quintessential Christian ascetical practice with scriptural roots. Declining a meal or more in a spirit of prayer can intensify praying to God for one's personal needs, for another person, or to express a

---

24. Bonhoeffer, *Discipleship*, 87.

sincere note of sorrow for sin. A fasting variation would be to determine the amount of money saved by not eating and donate it to others in need, a time-honored practice that combines fasting with almsgiving. God readily forgives the penitent; how deeply do I express my gratitude to God for such a great gift and generosity to me?

Periodically abstain from other goods. Related to fasting would be periodic abstinence or limitation of morally permissible goods that, unguarded and taken for granted, can impede a deeper life of discipleship. Alcohol consumption is one obvious example that, left untethered, can be destructive for the life and wellbeing of individuals and families. Christian-ordered sexual intercourse is another area; mutually accepted temporary sexual abstinence can foster a deeper prayer life for both partners and deepen their appreciation and respect for the great sign of self-giving love and commitment they share.

Accept irritations and hardships of everyday life in a spirit of self-denial. Hidden moments of "suffering in silence" when forced to tolerate an annoying person or some mundane irritation can lead disciples to use their small measure of suffering as an exercise to strengthen patience, their charity toward another, and as a way of following Christ's life example of spiritually fruitful self-denial. Willingly sacrificing one's personal time and energy to share important moments in another person's life, whether joyful or sorrowful, is another form of self-denial. Committed life vocations such as marriage, ministry, or consecrated religious life obviously provide plenty of opportunities for self-denial in the spirit of loving others.

The special path of involuntary suffering. Of course, there is voluntary suffering and then there is *real* suffering, unchosen, that countless individuals must bear each day. Such involuntary suffering can be a fruitful channel of prayer and meditation for identifying with Jesus in his example of accepting unjust mental or emotional suffering, bodily suffering, humiliations, bodily exhaustion, or the active process of dying.[25]

These are just a few practices that can add elements of practiced asceticism to your developing Christian life. Time and events will suggest other forms.

---

25. One experience of how personal suffering can deepen one's relationship with God is by Risner, "When Praying Hurts." Many Roman Catholic disciples who bear chronic illnesses, being homebound, or other forms of social isolation follow some form of this discipline as members of what Catholics know as membership in the mystical body of Christ. Comprised of disciples both living and deceased, they share a spirit of worshiping God and offer prayerful support and intercession for the needs of other members.

Conclusion

Christian discipleship calls us to grow in our relationship with God through refining our love for God and one another. Spiritual masters such as Augustine of Hippo have noted that a life of discipleship is not meant to be static, coming to rest at some spiritual plateau of acceptable goodness; it is, rather, a continual journey of growing ever closer to God in shared love, requiring some effort. Traditional Christianity has sought this growth through different means, some questionable, shaped by their time and place. The Christian way is ours as well, carrying with it the same challenge to find anew the life of the risen Christ; such is the reason for seeking the death of our inner selfishness, day after day.

Questions for Reflection

1. What are some of your personal material "treasures" and your attachment to them that you can identify as possible impediments for growing in your discipleship?
2. The practice of virginity and celibacy among Christian ascetics has never been easy and has often attracted criticism and even scorn. What positive reasons can you see that might justify the practice today? What negative reasons come to mind?
3. Can you identify any real-life events or situations in your daily life, great or small, that offer you opportunities to "die to yourself" for the sake of growing in patience, charity to others, etc.?

Suggested Further Reading

Lewis, C. S. *The Screwtape Letters*. New York: Macmillan, 1970.
Merton, Thomas. "Asceticism and Sacrifice." In *No Man Is an Island*. New York: Harcourt Brace Jovanovich, 1978.
Morneau, Robert. "Principles of Asceticism." In *Spiritual Direction: A Path to Spiritual Maturity*. New York: Crossroad, 1998.

6

Charity as the Gift of Self for Others

WHAT'S IN AN ACT of kindness? For Christians, each action that we do for the benefit of another, whether helping to alleviate one's hunger or thirst, spending time with someone who needs encouragement, or doing something more physical like helping another person to move their possessions from one home to another, is a way to show God's love for that person as a brother or sister in Christ who shares with us a basic human dignity.

Christian discipleship calls each of us to grow in our ability to channel this divine love to others. In fact, one's ongoing growth in showing charitable concern to others is a sign of Christian maturity, putting into concrete practice Jesus's commandment to "love one another as I have loved you" (John 15:12). We are not the source of this love and concern that we show to others; our love for others is but a reflection of God's mysterious and gratuitous love for each person. God's unfathomable love for us became most humanly visible in the life, ministry, suffering, and death of Jesus. Completely immersed in his Father's love for him through his faith and obedience, Jesus responded to that love through his loving fidelity to his Father and through showing that love toward everyone he encountered, even asking the Father's forgiveness of those who crucified him. Following this way of sharing God's endless love for each person through our practice of charity is the pathway to living most completely as human beings, as brothers and sisters in the reign of God.

The history of Christianity contains an extensive list of individuals who opened themselves to sharing this divine love toward others through self-giving in some form of charitable service. Some disciples did this in a heroic way that resulted in their deaths; more often, though, they did so in ways that were not dramatic but called them to great self-denial in showing God's love to others. Each response in charity toward another person occurred in its particular historical context, rooted in the Christian community but calling for individual self-giving and even personal "hands-on" engagement to serve those in need.

This chapter considers the scriptural uses of "love" and what they can reveal about God's love for us, some of the concrete ways that Christians have expressed this love of God toward others through the course of Christian history, and some thoughts on cultivating a spirit of practiced charity in the present day.

Part One: Practiced Charity Through Christian History

Divine Love in Scripture

The Old Testament

The Old Testament employs the concept of love in several contexts. References to sexual love are plentiful among God's people, as in the narratives of Adam and Eve, Jacob and Rachel, and the Song of Songs. Other expressions of love for others include the love between friends (such as between David and Jonathan; 1 Sam 18:1 and 2 Sam 1:26), the love of parents for a child (Jacob for Joseph, Gen 37:3), and a slave's loyalty to the master (Naomi's servants, Ruth 15–22).[1]

The deeper sense of abiding love that Jews express in the word *hesed* is of particular interest to us, carrying with it the sense of commitment and deep faithfulness between God and his chosen people. In the religious context, *hesed* is unselfish love, looking toward the good of another rather than oneself, even toward someone unlikable or an adversary. This type of love expresses God's love for the Jewish people, sealed by their embracing the covenant with Moses. God offered this unfailing gift of love and blessings to the people; in return, the people would follow the laws and norms of the covenant. The covenant set down the conditions for how the people were to live in response to God's love for them in both their relationship with God through prayer, public ritual, and their moral life as a community.

---

1. White, "Love," 1357–60.

The New Testament

The Greek word *agape* expresses the reckless and full-hearted nature of the divine love for others, the model and goal for Christian love of one another. "As you love your God, so love your neighbor" captures Jesus's teaching on the implication of this love. Jesus experienced this love to an intensity and degree of commitment that shocked his surrounding Jewish community, calling his disciples to live this same depth of love at all times. To love the Father as deeply as Jesus did, inflamed by this divine love, can overflow in loving other people unreservedly. Such a response does not come naturally to humans, born with a tendency toward selfishness and self-preservation. Indeed, the Christian spiritual journey includes both prayer and the practice of personal detachment from anything that would impede a disciple's fullest living in the inter-dynamic of divine love. Christianity is a lifelong process of personal conversion from the shackles of self-centeredness into an ever-freer sharing of God's love with others.

Whom, precisely, should disciples love? God the Father above all, but Jesus challenges us to love others as the Father loves them, with full-throttled, self-giving love and concern for them without desire of personal gain. Just as the Father's love offers mercy and forgiveness toward others, so disciples should endeavor to do the same. What's more, the love of God that we are to show is love without limit, even to the point of showing that love and loving concern toward our enemies, as illustrated in the parable of the good Samaritan (Luke 10:29–37). In responding to the query "Who is my neighbor?" Jesus reveals that our "neighbor" is simply the closest person to us in need of God's love and compassion, no matter the quality or rank of the relationship.

This compassion of God that Jesus exhibited in the Gospels had a purpose: to offer the way of eternal life to his people, fuller life in the reign of God. He preached and taught first about the need for one's interior *metanoia* or conversion to living by the law of God's love through following his life example. But he also would act at times to relieve other personal afflictions that could impede one's fullness of life. For some people, Jesus sought to restore individuals to fuller community living such as healing from leprosy (Matt 8:1–4), blindness (Matt 9:27–31), or restoring to life the only son of a widowed mother who, without the son, would have become a marginalized and pitied figure in her society (Luke 7:11–15). Through many Gospel accounts, we find Jesus alleviating the suffering of others so to restore their relationship with God and as members of their faith community.

The earliest Christian community described in the Acts of the Apostles illustrated this ideal of self-giving love for others: "Awe came upon everyone, because many wonders and signs were being done by the apostles. All who believed were together and had all things in common; they would sell their possessions and goods and distribute the proceeds to all, as any had need" (Acts 2:43–45). Also, "There was not a needy person among them, for as many as owned lands or houses sold them and brought the proceeds of what was sold. They laid it at the apostles' feet, and it was distributed to each as any had need" (4:34–35). Physical needs in the community were real, especially for people who had lost family or livelihood in choosing to embrace the good news. Comprising both Jews and gentiles who struggled to live the love of Christ despite cultural and historical difficulties, the charity practiced in the Jerusalem Christian community validated the presence of the Holy Spirit who had first inflamed the community on the day of Pentecost. The spirit of the risen Christ emboldened the disciples to proclaim the gospel through not only their verbal proclamation but also the example of their communal and personal lives.

The writings of St. Paul give additional clarity to actively expressing this love. We love others first of all when we obey the commandments toward them. "You shall not commit adultery; you shall not murder; you shall not steal," for "love does no wrong to a neighbor; therefore, love is the fulfilling of the law" (Rom 13:9–11). Lives guided by divine love should elicit responses such as honesty, willingness to support oneself through honest labor (for sharing whatever was earned with the needy among them), kindliness, and a willingness to forgive one another as God in Christ had forgiven them (Eph 4:25–32). Paul also mentions practical expressions of charity, including monetary contributions ("liberality" in 1 Cor 16:2), hospitality (Rom 12:13), mercy (Rom 11:25–32), forsaking vengeance (Rom 12:19), and avoiding quarrels (2 Tim 2:24–25).[2] The apostle would also beg among the other church communities for alms to help support the Jerusalem community (1 Cor 16:1–4). For Paul, Christian love avoids harming others and does not limit itself in its expressions of goodness.[3]

The early Christian practice of tithing, giving ten percent of one's earning for the needs of church communities, had ancient Jewish roots from the time of the patriarch Jacob (Gen 28:22). Initially, Jewish faithful would donate their monetary offering and from the "first fruits" of

2. Pauline authorship of 2 Tim is disputed among scriptural scholars.
3. White, "Love," 1359.

agricultural produce for annual festal celebrations and needs of the poor in their local community. The shift in payment from local synagogues to the central Jerusalem temple administration developed into an annual monetary contribution known as the "temple tax" that was in effect during Jesus's time.[4] Jesus did not condemn the practice; he did, however, instruct his followers that paying the temple tax was not a divine command of the law.[5] The spiritual merit of paying the tax depended on the individual's disposition of heart in reflecting God's love when alleviating the needs of others. Tithing for the sake of the needy and church administration remained a practice among the early Christian church communities.[6]

To summarize this section: Loving concern for others through practicing charity of some type made visible a vibrant element of the Christian message. The divine love was revealed through the life and voluntary death of Jesus. His was the way of self-giving for others that struck at personal selfishness and egotism, the means to salvation for all believers. Jesus called his disciples to follow the same self-giving for the sake of others as he did.

Practiced Christian Charity in the Patristic Era

Literature from the earliest Christian centuries illustrates some of the many struggles for the young church communities, notably in how Christians met the different church needs in times of persecution wrought by the Roman Empire. Disciples busied themselves in practices of material charity such as attending to Christians in prison, visiting the abandoned, practicing prayer, serving in leadership, and contributing from food and monetary resources. Much of this was honed during the frequent episodes of Christian persecution between AD 60 and 313 and helped to seal the pagan respect for Christian disciples as individuals who could and did suffer for others, following the lived example of Jesus whom they proclaimed.

---

4. Vischer, *Tithing*, 2–4.
5. Vischer, *Tithing*, 11.
6. Vischer, *Tithing*, 12.

Visiting the Imprisoned

Prison conditions in the Roman Empire during the first Christian centuries were horrific.[7] The many accounts of imprisoned and martyred Christians in early Christian literature give a common description of prisons as dark, damp, crowded, and malodorous. Little if any outside light or fresh air penetrated their confines; some inmates were chained in the innermost reaches, making their plight even more intolerable. Prisoners typically did not know how long they would be confined; local authorities held countless early Christians for indeterminate periods, hoping to coerce them into recanting their faith or revealing information about other disciples. Those condemned to die could be killed alone in prison or public settings such as arenas or amphitheaters with little warning and at any time by sword, fire, hungry wild beasts, or other terrifying means.

Christian family members and other concerned community members laudably visited those imprisoned for several practical reasons. One was for want of decent food; while prisons would provide some bare sustenance, offering any supplementary nourishment would have been an invaluable service. Many family members or friends who knew the incarcerated chose to abandon them or avoid visits due to the stigma of knowing or being associated with someone imprisoned. Intrepid Christians would take it upon themselves to confront the harshness of prison life while seeking to alleviate the loneliness, physical suffering, and psychological torment that prisoners undoubtedly endured. In all of these, Christians who braved the horrors of prison life and the dangers of visiting the most abandoned took to heart the words of Jesus: "I was in prison and you visited me."[8]

The years of early church persecution provided many calls to exercise the love and compassion of Christ to those in prison. We know less about prison ministry once Christianity was legitimized in the early fourth century. However, concern to alleviate prisoner suffering was on the mind of at least one early sixth-century bishop, Paulus of Jordan, who oversaw the construction of a more humane institution.[9]

---

7. One interesting source for this description is Wansink, *Chained in Christ*, 27–95.

8. Matt 25:36. The longer passage (25:31–46) is the source for the so-called "seven corporal works of mercy" at the heart of practiced Christian charity.

9. Markschies, *Between Two Worlds*, 171.

Early Christian Charity Expressed in Nonviolence

Jesus instructed his disciples to love their enemies and persecutors (Matt 5:44), giving early roots to the Christian tradition of nonviolence in confronting the evils of society. Several early church leaders held to this teaching and encouraged their fellow Christians to do the same. The second-century Christian apologist Justin Martyr wrote of Christianity's call to live by a nonviolent nature even in times of persecution, noting that in so doing, Christians professed their faith through their example:

> And concerning our being patient of injuries, and ready to serve all, and free from anger, this is what He said: "To him that smitith thee on the one cheek, offer also the other; and him that taketh away thy cloak or coat, forbid not. And whosoever shall be angry, is in danger of the fire. And every one that compelleth thee to go with him a mile, follow him two. And let your good works shine before men, that they, seeing them, may glorify your Father which is in heaven." For we ought not to strive; neither has He desired us to be imitators of wicked men, but He has exhorted us to lead all men, by patience and gentleness, from shame and the love of evil. And this indeed is proved in the case of many who once were of your way of thinking, but have changed their violent and tyrannical disposition, being overcome either by the constancy which they have witnessed in their neighbours' lives, or by the extraordinary forbearance they have observed in their fellow-travellers when defrauded, or by the honesty of those with whom they have transacted business.[10]

Other church fathers held a similar view toward nonviolence. Tertullian of Carthage (ca. 160–ca. 225) took a more radical stance in the question of Christians and nonviolence. Tertullian held that Christians should not serve as legal magistrates with authority to impose death sentences, nor should they take up military arms in support of the Roman Empire. Christians should have nothing to do with bloodshed or violent activity.[11] The pacifist attitude found among several of the church fathers aided in providing a gospel-rooted foundation for applying the principle of nonviolence to the Christian ethic in later centuries.[12]

---

10. Justin, *1 Apol.* 16.

11. Tertullian, *Apol.* 36 and 37, as noted in Ryan, "Rejection of Military Service," 14.

12. The medieval "Peace of God" and "Truce of God" movements developed between the tenth and fourteenth centuries, described in the chapter on nonviolence.

Prayer, Fasting, and Almsgiving

Periodic fasting from food was a way to add urgency to a disciple's prayer to God while also offering a means of showing charity. The earliest church document for daily Christian living, the *Didache*, instructed new disciples, "Do not hesitate to give, and do not give in a grumbling mood. You will find out who is the good Rewarder. Do not turn away from the needy; rather, share everything with your brother, and do not say: 'It is private property.'"[13]

Tertullian of Carthage encouraged his flock to contribute as a way to alleviate the various needs in their community, as well as perform a religious act:

> Their gifts are, as it were, piety's deposit fund. For they are not taken thence and spent on feasts, and drinking bouts, and eating houses, but to support and bury poor people, to supply the wants of boys and girls destitute of parents and of old persons now confined to the house, such, too, as have suffered shipwreck; and if there happen to be any in the mines, or banished to the islands, or shut up in the prisons, for nothing but their fidelity to the cause of God's church, they become the nurselings of their confession.[14]

Other church fathers encouraged Christians to share what they had not consumed with those in need, either produce itself or the equivalent monetary cost. Augustine of Hippo, for example, had much to say about the justice of sharing resources with the needy. Like other church fathers, Augustine held that material wealth was a hazard for wealthy Christians on their journey to eternal life. Since all our blessings come from God, anything of the surplus is not necessary for a Christian and should be given to those in need: "The superfluity of the rich is necessary to the poor. If you hold onto superfluous items, then, you are keeping what belongs to someone else."[15] Some of Augustine's thought, however, helped to instill a practical motive for the wealthy to be charitable; in sharing their riches with the poor, who were among God's special people, the grateful poor would direct prayers to God for the patrons' salvation. This thought led to criticism of Christian charitable practices. One reason was that donors sought a reward for their generosity, whereas actual charitable giving should seek none. Another was that the condition of poverty could

---

13. *Did.* 4.7.
14. Tertullian, *Apol.* 39.6.
15. Augustine, *Enarrat. Ps.* 147.12.

become justified as a necessary means for the salvation of the wealthy; with this thinking, there was little incentive for people of means to seek a lasting solution for social poverty. This criticism would surface centuries later among the Protestant Reformers.

The Emergence of Organized Charitable Structures

The legalization of Christianity in 313 inaugurated a new and lasting peace that allowed the spread of Christian influence throughout the Roman Empire. It also witnessed the empire's gradual collapse so that, by the fifth century, growing masses of poor people needed food. While civil government initially had provided a structure for meeting this demand, the final collapse of the empire and the government administration shift from Rome to the Byzantine East contributed to the Christian church becoming the principal purveyor of various forms of charitable services before the mid-ninth century.[16]

As Christianity began to flourish in earnest following the end of persecutions in the early fourth century, so did its charitable energies to address the needs of the poor and sick. The earliest large-scale Christian facilities for offering foodstuffs (grain especially) to those in need were known as *deaconries*, organized by fourth-century Egyptian monasteries.[17] Local-level church deaconries also developed to supplement the feeding of the poor as the churches assumed more of the responsibility that initially had been the concern of the civil government. Outreach to the poor found its way from the east into parts of southern Italy, arriving in Rome only around the year 750 or so.

Beginning in the mid-third century, Eastern Christianity witnessed a flourishing of houses to care for the needs of strangers and the infirm of society. These residences were normally under the tutelage of the local bishop, offering food and lodging to those who were traveling pilgrims or other strangers to the locale. A *xenodochium* (from the Greek root *xeno* referring to a stranger or foreigner) might also offer basic medical care for those travelers in need. Gradually, though, separate facilities were established to

---

16. Dey, "*Diaconiae, Xenodochia, Hospitalia* and Monasteries," 400.

17. The word *deaconry* is from the Latin and Greek word *diaconae/diakonieae*, carrying the notion of charitable service.

care for individuals suffering from chronic or highly contagious diseases, vulnerable elderly women and men, and orphaned children.[18]

Influential lay women and men also initiated and supported the growth in these establishments as expressions of piety through depleting their family fortunes, actions that oftentimes did not sit well with other family members. Helena (246–330), like her son the Emperor Constantine, provided finances for a range of Christian needs that included the construction of several large churches. Later, the patrician Valeria Melania ("Melania the Younger," 383–439) also illustrated the largesse among some of the more affluent and influential through donations for the poor and several works of church art.[19]

Through the number and diversity of such establishments and the faithful witness of individuals, the love of Christ nurtured within local communities produced charitable fruit through ministering to the needy multitudes, offering visible signs of Jesus's self-giving love to their time and place.

Christian Charity Needs and Deeds in the Medieval Centuries

The seventh and eighth centuries witnessed a notable moral corruption in Western Christianity, with diminished church outreach to those in need. The reign of the Emperor Charlemagne (800–819) oversaw a Christian

---

18. Riquet, *Christian Charity in Action*, 62–71.

19. Riquet, *Christian Charity in Action*, 70–71. Melania was the sole descendent of an ancestral family that included influential senators and consuls and found herself heiress to a vast fortune and collection of properties. At the age of fourteen her family arranged her marriage to Valerius Pinianus, a cousin who also controlled vast wealth; thus would the family holdings be fortified, following the social norms of her time. Valeria had deeply desired to follow in the footsteps of her ancestor Antonia Melania who herself had liquidated her wealth and lived as a poor solitary monk near Jerusalem. Alas, Valeria was compelled to marry but made an agreement with her fiancé that they would eventually live as brother and sister after producing two children. As it happened, both children died while very young. Valeria and her husband, having grown fearful of the glitter and enticements of their vast worldly fortunes, chose to honor their initial agreement by liquidating all of their possessions, establishing hospitals, hospices for the dying, orphanages, monasteries, churches, and facilities to feed the poor. They subsequently entered separate monastic communities of women and men to live as poor though happy individuals dedicated to the pursuit of God in lives of prayer and humility.

church renewal throughout his empire that affected monastic life with a reemphasis on their importance as channels of practical charity.

The Charitable Importance of Monastic Communities

Beginning from its roots in the later fourth century, the proliferation of communal monastic communities evolved into an extensive network of organized Christian outreach. The collapse of the Roman Empire and the social mayhem wrought by barbarian tribes, just at the time when Christianity was expanding into the remote areas of Europe, spawned many social needs that complemented the monastic objective of growth in charity among community members. Their practices of hospitality extended to the traveling needs of pilgrims, strangers, and the poor hungry who would gather at the rear door of the monastery kitchen, providing visible witness to the monastic ideals of material detachment, simple lifestyle, and growth in charity to others. Monasteries also became recognized as centers of education and research in the fields of prayer, ritual, and an increase of collective wisdom in agriculture, medicine, theology, and other general sciences. The monastic ideals of prayerful charity among the monks themselves offered a powerful evangelical witness to laymen and women who established villages in the shadows of the monasteries. Together, their charitable love that bore fruit among monks and faithful had a ripple effect beyond the monastery walls into their surrounding local world.

A more pastorally active branch of monastic life attended specifically to the many needs of the poor and travelers. These Western monks helped to staff and administer grain, oil, clothing, etc., reminiscent of the fourth- and fifth-century Eastern monasteries of Saints Pachomius, Basil of Caesarea, and others. This more active degree of monastic engagement with the outer world contrasted with and gradually gave way to the more traditional image of monastic withdrawal and solitude evoked by the writings of John Cassian and Benedict. Why this shift occurred is a question for scholars. Some scholars have suggested that the traditional, strictly enclosed model of Charlemagne's ninth-century church reforms overshadowed the more "worldly" monks. Perhaps the monasteries' growing renown as powerhouses of prayer held greater sway, especially from the increasing influence of monastic patrons and their requests for masses and prayers for their ancestors.[20] Before long, however, other monastic-like communities of "canons regular" arose,

---

20. Dey, "*Diaconiae, Xenodochia, Hospitalia* and Monasteries," 417–22.

such as the Hospitallers of Saint John, with their more flexible lifestyle that could better serve others beyond the cloister walls.

Meeting the Needs of Pilgrims and the Sick

Concern in the twelfth century to reverse another wave of church moral decline once again inspired disciples to the renewed practice of Christian life. This new focus brought with it calls for greater exercise of charity towards others, both in attention to preaching quality and through addressing the social needs of the time.[21] In the high-medieval period, a large need arose from the increasing pilgrimage among Christian lands that brought greater demands for hospitality to travelers and pilgrims.

Increasing travel to the Holy Land by penitential pilgrims and soldiers of the Crusades also brought greater exposure to leprosy, forcing local communities to isolate and stigmatize its victims. The scourge of medieval leprosy and its rendering victims as social outcasts was already well known from scriptural times. Eleventh- and twelfth-century Christian devotion to the sacred humanity of Jesus and the events of his earthly life began to absorb a new depth of compassion for others, eliciting a desire to suffer with Jesus by serving the poor and outcast. The fourth-century Saint Jerome had described Jesus as "leper-like" due to his severe beatings and social abandonment, thus sharing at least figuratively in the ignominy and social stigma of lepers.[22] Serving the needs of lepers became a special way of ministering to the needs of Christ who had shared in their sufferings of rejection and isolation.[23] This attitude led to the establishment of many *leper houses* (or "lazar-houses") that provided hospitality and attention to both physical and spiritual needs, in many ways paralleling monastic life through maintaining chapel facilities, a regulated prayer schedule, and common garb for the residents.

While bishops and many affluent people provided the financial means to establish facilities ministering to the various poor and sick, countless other Christians, such as Elizabeth of Hungary (1207–1231), also responded to their needs through hands-on performances of ordinary and even lowly tasks. Elizabeth's parents arranged her marriage to a nobleman at fourteen, after which she bore three children and lived

21. Vauchez, *Middle Ages*, 98–99.
22. Jerome, commentary on Isaiah 53:4.
23. "Despised Class," para. 3.

happily with her husband until his death six years later. The twenty-year-old widow Elizabeth eventually relocated to a residence apart from her family, who pressured her to remarry. Inspired by the life and spiritual values of Francis of Assisi, she adopted a life of celibacy, prayer, personal poverty, and charity while establishing a hospital, serving the sick, and donating her material riches to alleviate poverty and hunger. Elizabeth became an outstanding example of charity and today is venerated as a patron saint of the Franciscan lay order.[24]

Other Means of Organized Charitable Outreach

The many medieval merchant and artisan guilds for groups such as blacksmiths, cloth-making, and stone masons, provided other effective instruments of Christian charity. In addition to offering political strength in numbers, these groups also provided relief for distressed guild members during times of economic or other difficulties.

A group deserving special mention developed as a class of consecrated religious life: the so-called ransom orders such as the Trinitarians (Order of the Most Holy Trinity and of the Captives, founded in 1198) and the Mercedarians (Order of Our Lady of Mercy, in 1218). Twelfth- and thirteenth-century western Europe was slowly freeing itself from the presence of Muslims, who had amassed across the Mediterranean Sea in the northern African region of present-day Tunisia.[25] The declining Muslim kingdoms resorted to piracy and kidnapping of Christian sojourners in the western Mediterranean, becoming a constant peril for commercial travel and pilgrimages. Ransom order members performed what was needed to rescue unfortunates held captive by raising ransom money or conducting daring rescue missions into Muslim-held areas of Spain, North Africa, or the Near East, willing to risk their freedom and their lives if necessary.

In closing, we can say that attention to the needy had a special place in medieval Christian spirituality. While the period had its share of social and religious failings, Christian attention to others through charitable activity gave a very visible and important witness to the love of God for all people.

---

24. Davis, "The Charitable Revolution," para. 17.
25. In this book, the contemporary word *Muslim* replaces the medieval *Moslem*.

Practiced Charity in the Modern Era

The dawn of the modern era over the Western church brought its share of social and ecclesiastical hardships. The collapse of medieval feudalism had displaced large numbers of farming peasants, many migrating to the emerging large cities and an economy that depended on money rather than land labor. The Hundred Years' War in France, the Spanish aggression toward Jews and Muslims that led to their expulsion from the Iberian Peninsula, the often violent struggle of Italian city-states to maintain their power and independence from each other, and the political ambitions among German princes all tore at the fabric of Western society.

In addition to the civic difficulties, the generally peaceful interdependent medieval relationship between the two social structures of altar and throne also showed signs of wear and decline. Protestant Reformation figures, including Luther and Calvin, criticized and discounted the practice of Christian charity toward the poor as a means of earning divine grace and repentance and called on civic administration to address it.[26] Sadly, this attitude led to a gradual diminishment of the underlying and fundamentally sound Christian motives underlining the exercise of charity as bringing the love of Jesus to the marginalized and unfortunate, the motivation that has proven so fruitful throughout Christian history.

It must be admitted that much of the Western Christian church of this time merited at least some of the Protestant denouncements. The lengthy Roman Catholic Council of Trent between 1545 and 1563 sought, in part, to address these issues. In several sessions that convened during that time, the council documents called for renewed attention to the church's charitable action and outreach, with greater attention to proper stewardship of funds allocated for the purpose.[27] The renewed call to the three traditional pillars of Christian life—prayer, repentance, and a renewed emphasis on visible charitable outreach to the many needs of society—would bear abundant fruit in the ensuing decades and centuries.

---

26. Lindberg, "No Poor Among You," 149–55.

27. Examples include chapter 15 of the 7th session; Council of Trent and Schroeder, *Canons and Decrees*, 61.

Associations to Meet the Needs of Others

The growing popularity of fourteenth-century lay-inspired organizations, known as *confraternities*, offered a spiritually sustaining way for Christians who desired to follow more intently the life example and teaching of Christ. Similar in some ways to the Christian guilds of the twelfth and thirteenth centuries, confraternities proved to be sustaining and invigorating associations for those who wished to concentrate their efforts in one of three basic types: devotional communities (focusing on devotional activities directed to the Eucharist, the Virgin Mary or some particular saint, etc.), penitential confraternities (for those wishing to follow a more rigorous spiritual program along the lines of the established vowed religious life families), and charitable affiliations. This latter group focused primarily on performing some service of charity that included attending to the needs of the sick, the dying, their bereaved families, catechesis or moral formation of adolescents, or almost any other form of human need.[28] The prayer and penitential observances of affiliation confraternities were in service to their main objective of alleviating the needs of others through deepening their relationship to Jesus. The communal support and regulated spiritual life that were so successful among confraternity groups led to the appearance of other organizations called oratories and societies of clerics regular that fostered spiritual renewal among ordained clergy.

This period also spurred an increasing number of more socially active consecrated religious societies. Giving themselves to growing in love of God through prayer and practicing virtues, these religious congregations also sought to love what God loved through alleviating the various social ills of their time. The Society of Jesus ("Jesuits"), founded by Ignatius Loyola in 1534, was a new model of consecrated religious life, less encumbered by earlier monastic models and thus more able to share the love of Christ in the world. Before long, other groups would emerge to address the needs of the materially poor. Among the most impressive were the Daughters of Charity (1633), cofounded by St. Vincent de Paul and St. Louise de Marillac, focusing on the needs of the sick, orphans, socially marginalized, and imprisoned. Many other groups appeared and endeavored to meet the educational and spiritual formation of neglected and wayward youth, such as the Company of St. Ursula (founded by Angela di Merici in 1535). Similar youth-formation communities were founded that included the Piarists

---

28. Duhr, "Confréries," 1472.

for boys (by Joseph Calasanz in 1617) and, later, the Sisters of the Good Shepherd for wayward girls (Marie Ephrasia Pelletier in 1835), as well as the Congregation of St. Francis Xavier (Theodore James Ryken in 1839).

Christian global expansion between the sixteenth and twentieth centuries elicited sacrifice from countless individuals in the area of foreign missions and the establishment of distant Christian church communities. In addition to missionary preachers and instructors, religious leaders addressed the need for service among the traditional channels of Christian charity outreach by establishing hospitals and health centers, schools, orphanages, centers to assist the poor and hungry, leprosy centers, and other areas of special need. Members of vowed religious orders and clergy normally were the backbone of these institutions but could not have been effective without the assistance of many local individuals. Whether in the Americas, throughout the vast continents of Africa and Asia, or on distant Pacific Island territories, Christian preaching of Christ's love for all people became visibly and materially expressed in meeting the vast needs of so many people who were finding new hope in the gospel.

Summary Observations from Christian Tradition and History

Our historical survey suggests at least five general conclusions concerning the place and practice of charity as part of Christian life through the centuries:

Jesus as the model for charitable love. Individuals practicing charitable works drew their energy from the life of Jesus and his ministry to the poor and marginalized. Jesus was their model to whom they drew closer for the sake of others through prayer and some degree of self-denial.

Responding to needs of their day. Christian charitable outreach emerged in response to needs of a particular historical moment. At different times, Christians have visited Roman prisons; met hospitality needs of strangers, the sick, or foreigners; ransomed or rescued hostages to foreign adversaries; and addressed the educational or moral formation of youth. Whatever the need at whatever historical moment, Christian disciples were energized by the love of God in the life of Jesus and arose to serve others in distress.

Christians from all walks of life integrated practicing charity into their lives. Lay people, monks, other consecrated religious, priests, and deacons—the history of Christianity contains accounts of charitable service from each vocation. There is no one rarified class of professional holy

Christians. God's love challenges disciples to grow in becoming ever more like Jesus through adopting his attitude of loving service in her or his particular life circumstances.

Charitable action emerged as a response to the gospel. Charitable activity offers a validating "second voice" to verbal proclamations of divine mercy and love. God's love for all people takes on a deeper hue of authenticity and becomes visible through disciples' showing this divine concern toward others.

Active participation in concrete ways. Financial and material aid are both worthwhile, but investing one's personal time and labor are invaluable. Countless wealthy Christian patrons throughout history have been willing to donate from their wealth and "get their hands dirty" by giving their time and physical service, sometimes in very lowly and humbling tasks.

With these insights, let us consider how Christians today might consider giving of themselves to serve the needs of others in the present day.

Part Two: Practicing Christian Charity in Our Own Day

Various Understandings of "Charity"

Christian disciples have many possible opportunities to donate time, treasure, or talent. The needs presented to us through the media are endless. Numerous charitable organizations seek monetary donations for causes such as for elderly war victims in eastern Europe; another for victims of a destructive storm or earthquake; yet another may address the needs of the homeless and the hungry around the world or in one's hometown. Aside from financial support, some Christians may offer a few hours' time each week to tutor a student who lacks resources to find professional help or perhaps give one evening each week to provide a hand at the local homeless shelter or food pantry. The possible ways to exercise the love of Christ for the sake of some cause are practically limitless.

The contemporary English understanding of charity has become associated primarily with donating material goods—money, food, clothing, etc. For the remainder of this chapter, let us consider this broad group as "charitable donations," and contributing our time or talents will comprise another group of "charitable services." Both are worthwhile and necessary.

Most principal world religious traditions praise individual generosity as a desirable quality that can win divine favor, blessing, and mercy. As noted earlier in this chapter, Judaism placed a very high and traditional value on attending to the needy and strengthening the weak through a whole range of actions intended to mirror the divine *hesed*. One Islamic resource notes, "Islam stresses that giving charity increases our wealth, and makes the mercy of Allah befall on us. . . . And the outcomes of giving are God's blessing, more rewards, and psychological comfort that can be perceived from happiness and joy of giving as well as self-satisfaction."[29] Buddhism teaches that each person is at some time or other a recipient of another's generosity as part of an interconnected web of humanity; the giver's motivation should be as a reciprocal action in gratitude for what the giver has received.[30] Hinduism instructs that charitable giving has a wider social implication in that it involves sharing even basic resources with others and that persons should not consume more than is necessary for their existence.[31] While these summarizing observations are admittedly superficial, we may conclude that charitable outreach has a significant place in a wide range of religious beliefs, with motives ranging from altruism to the benefactor's wellbeing.

In examining Christian charity, we find that the traditional understanding of charity has two parts. The *virtue* of charity is a human quality that we possess as part of our humanity, though in an immature form. Our openness to God's love through prayer and following the life example of Jesus can gradually transform the basic human capacity into an ever clearer reflection of the divine love toward all persons. For this reason, Christian tradition considers Christian charity as a supernatural capacity or virtue (meaning that God's love is its source). The seed of authentic Christian charity is offered to Christians through baptism and cultivated through a disciple's ongoing life of faith, prayer, and imitation of Christ. The *practice* of Christian charity includes the many concrete ways that Christians respond to the lives and needs of others, fulfilling the words of Jesus: "Whatever you do for the least of my brothers (and sisters), you do to me" (Matt 25:40).

Contemporary Examples of Practiced Christian Charity

While there are many inspiring contemporary examples of practiced Christian charity, let us consider two exemplary figures from opposite sides of

---

29. Baqutayan et al., "Psychology of Giving," para. 1.
30. Joseph, "Traditions of Giving in Buddhism," paras. 1 and 13.
31. Sugirtharajah, "Traditions of Giving in Hinduism," paras. 2 and 12.

the globe, moved by the same Holy Spirit in their very different lives and experiences. The first is Mother Teresa of Calcutta (1910–1997); the other is Dorothy Day (1897–1980) of the United States. Each one illustrates certain qualities at the heart of practiced Christian charity.

Born as Agnes Gonxha Bojaxhiu in Macedonia, Mother Teresa first became oriented to a life of active charity through the example of her pious mother. Agnes accepted the prompting to enter consecrated religious life; adopting the name Teresa, she accepted her first assignment as a teacher in India. The masses of starving, sick, and socially marginalized persons around her reawakened Teresa's initial spiritual attraction to serve whom she saw as the poorest of the poor. Teresa founded the Missionary Sisters of Charity in response to their plight, which grew from a handful of women religious to one of world renown, establishing leper houses, hospices, and orphanages within and beyond India. Mother Teresa weathered frequent criticism and derision for aspects of her vocation, such as inadequate medical resources and training for her sisters. She nonetheless cultivated a life of charity with patience and deep trust in divine providence. Mother Teresa received the 1979 Nobel Peace Prize, which recognized her deep concern to meet the needs of the poor and suffering, and following her death, she was proclaimed a Roman Catholic saint in 2016.[32]

What we know of Dorothy Day's life, with its twists and turns, reveals much of how God can work through the complexities of individuals.[33] Day was born to nominally Christian parents in Brooklyn, New York; early in life, her father's occupation led the family to reside for a time in San Francisco and Chicago. While in college, she became sensitive to the plight of workers and the women's suffrage movement, eventually concluding that American society was incapable of alleviating its many social ills. In early adulthood, Day began searching for a meaningful life that could actively foment social change while integrating her newly found Catholic faith. She discovered a way to do this through meeting writer and activist Peter Maurin (1877–1949), a fervent French Catholic and evangelical. Together they began the Catholic Worker Movement to promote similar ideals for social change while also organizing numerous soup kitchens and hostels for the poor and outcast of their streets.

---

32. Ponio, "How Mother Teresa Changed the World," paras. 7–21.

33. Most of this biographical information is found in Day and Berrigan, *The Long Loneliness*.

We also find in Day's Christian journey that she came to value the Christian counsel to nonviolence. Her gospel-inspired stance of pacifism carried her through many years of social struggle in the United States that were not kind to pacifists: protesting for women's suffrage; for peace during the rocky and adversarial years of the Second World War; against the years of military conflict in Vietnam and southeast Asia; and speaking out against the palpable threat of nuclear holocaust. Day's example of making visible Jesus's nonviolent love of all people also played a prominent part in other Christians' nonviolent witness to the gospel, notably that of the Reverend Martin Luther King Jr. (1929–1968).

In the stories of both Mother Teresa and Dorothy Day, we find both parallels and divergences. The two women sought a closer relationship to Jesus through prayer and serving others, cultivating a deep personal-spiritual relationship with him. Both women were also physically engaged in attending to the needs of the poor they encountered in their respective ministries. They had, however, somewhat different attitudes in advocating for wider social structural change that many Christians hold to be an essential quality of Christian charitable engagement with the world. This activity for change is more apparent in Day's life, while with Teresa it was less visible (though present) and a cause for criticism against her. Teresa maintained at different points in her writings that her call to charity was first and foremost to meet the needs of individual sufferers, to show God's love to *this* man or *that* woman when she encountered them, leaving the political complexities and perils of seeking social change to others. The approaches of both Dorothy and Mother Teresa are valid; each woman responded uniquely to the prompting of the Holy Spirit to make the love of Christ present around her. Also at the heart of both individuals was the strong desire to live according to the love of Christ, the essential ingredient for disciples hoping to transform the world. As Thomas Merton noted, "The only influence that can really upset the injustice and iniquity of men is the power that breathes in the Christian tradition, renewing our participation in the Life that is the Light of men."[34]

---

34. Merton and Kidd, *New Seeds of Contemplation*, 144.

Short-Term and More Committed Ways of Christian Service to Others

Present-day Christian disciples seeking ways to offer their time and abilities through volunteering themselves in some degree of charitable service will find a wide range of possibilities, with commitments ranging from a few hours each week through months-long and even lifelong activity. This chapter segment cannot give an exhaustive list of possibilities, of course, but hopefully will be of use to service-minded disciples with different interests and personal gifts.

It certainly would be helpful to take a little time to learn more about yourself and how much time you could reasonably expect to give in some service to others. What can you say about your personality, your interests, and talents? Would you classify yourself as an extrovert who loves social engagement with others, or perhaps more introverted who prefers working alone or with a few others?[35] Do you like working with your hands in repair projects, cooking, or artistic activities? How much time would you be willing to give each week or month? What about available time to give to serving others in light of career and family responsibilities? (Remember that raising a family is in itself a continual call to active charity!) Would you prefer to work among others who share your faith convictions, or would you rather hold your faith quietly to yourself while offering Christ's love among people who may not share your beliefs? Are you more comfortable serving others in individual acts of charity, or do ideas of societal change and improving levels of social justice burn within you? No doubt you will discover the answer to some of these or other questions during your activity with others, so don't concern yourself with answering all of them; they do, however, raise some points that volunteering Christian disciples should consider.

Short-Term and Periodic Involvement

Many, if not most, Christian faith communities have organized volunteer opportunities that take only a few hours each week or month. Depending on the community, areas of need might include visiting the sick and homebound, assisting at church-run food pantries, and donating time at day-care

---

35. The second part of the prayer chapter offers some useful tips for uncovering individual personality traits.

facilities, to name just a few. Depending on the activity, congregations and parishes will typically require some degree of background-checking and ask for personal references. Also, it usually isn't absolutely necessary for volunteers to be congregation or parish members.

Many Christian disciples can find meaning in volunteering for civic-minded projects. Here you'll find various city- or town-level activities that could include working in soup kitchens or even participating in park and waterway cleanup efforts for persons concerned about nature stewardship. There are even local area blood banks for anyone interested in donating blood for others every few months.

Longer-Term Engagements or Commitments

The culmination of some significant project in life, such as graduation from high school or college, may present the opportunity to invest oneself in longer-term charitable service of perhaps several months to a year or more. The reasons will vary among individuals; for Christians, it can offer the chance to integrate the activity with stretching one's discipleship and relationship with Jesus. Groups like the Jesuit Volunteer Corps or the Maryknoll Lay Missioners, to name just two Catholic organizations, typically offer service opportunities in domestic and foreign arenas that call for various personal talents, such as teaching and health care. Depending on the organization, each offers a living stipend, some degree of community living, and requires a commitment of one or two years. One primarily Protestant organization, Navigators World Missions, offers assignments ranging from several weeks to six months in evangelizing roles of teaching and spreading the gospel.

There are also government-sponsored organizations in the United States, such as the Peace Corps and VISTA (Volunteers to Service in America). Their motivation is to project goodwill in international or domestic settings while showing no partiality to any particular religion or religious affiliation.

More information on these and other service opportunities is available via the internet.

Conclusion

The practice of active Christian charity is a healthy and important component in the spiritual life of any Christian disciple. Many individuals stand out in history who offered service that may be considered heroic, even to the extent of losing their lives in showing the love of Christ to others in need. Others, both past and present, have lost their lives as martyrs in bringing Christ and Christ's love to their surroundings, while some may express their charity in extended self-giving for the chronic care of a parent or child. While most Christians are perhaps not called to such heroic levels of self-giving, contributing something of one's time or possessions for the sake of others expresses our desire to love others as Jesus did. Countless Christians do this in their particular locale, day by day or week by week, meeting the needs of others for food, lodging, and maybe simply giving some time to listen to another. Enacting some charitable activity in life engages us with other people, allowing us to incarnate and make visible something of God's love for others through our action, however imperfect and menial that action may be. Our actions of charity to others, no matter how insignificant they may seem, will have an effect in many ways: in our relationships with God, with others around us, and even as ripples of divine love that can positively affect the surrounding created world.

Questions for Reflection

1. The contemporary section of the chapter briefly mentions some perennial needs calling for Christian charity outreach and service. What other ones can you identify? Are there any that might attract you personally to participate in some way?

2. Invitations to practice charity arise daily. How well do you practice more simple expressions of charity in moments calling for patience or courtesy toward others that you meet each day? How about expressions of hospitality toward visitors in your home?

3. Are there any secular or non-Christian organizations that interest you? How would you relate service in them to your life as a Christian disciple, called to follow the life example of Jesus?

Suggested Further Reading

Elizondo, Virgilio P. *Charity*. Maryknoll, NY: Orbis Books, 2008.
Redeemer Presbyterian Church. *Generosity: Responding to God's Radical Grace in Community Study Guide*. Peabody, MA: Hendrickson Publishers, 2016.

7

The Challenging Practice of Christian Nonviolence

CHRISTIAN NONVIOLENCE IS PERHAPS the most controversial of our seven Christian practices. Disciples practice Christian nonviolence when they seek to respond in nonviolent ways to evil or otherwise unjust threats or actions from others, following the examples and words of Jesus. Over the centuries, many Christian disciples and others, for philosophical reasons, have adopted a personal stance of absolute nonviolence to the extent of embracing pacifism, the refusal to take up arms in military service against other institutions or nations.[1] Several present-day religious denominations, such as the Quakers and Seventh-day Adventists, insist on a total commitment to nonviolence, including pacifism, while other Christian affiliations may leave pacifism as a matter of individual conscience.

Jesus of the Gospels offers a fundamental base for nonviolence that guided the earliest Christian followers in their particular historical moment. Some later disciples would exhort their contemporaries to a total observance of nonviolence as essential to Christian living, often suffering greatly. Christian understanding and practice of nonviolence gradually matured in confronting the different faces of violence in the world, most especially in response to the horrors of war and engagements in military activities.

---

1. For simplicity, this chapter uses the two terms *nonviolence* and *pacifism* as described. Both words are sometimes used interchangeably and share some common attributes, but they are different, with varied nuance and understanding.

Honoring these ideals waxed and waned at different points throughout Christian history but found a remarkable flourishing and broader scope for practicing nonviolence by the twentieth century.

Part One: Practicing Christian Nonviolence in History

In Scripture

Grasping the practice of early Christian respect for nonviolent behavior requires an understanding of peace in both scriptural Testaments. Both of these were influenced somewhat by the classical Greek understanding of peace that referred to the tranquility existing between the all-but-inevitable wars of the ancient world. Peace also can refer to an individual's peaceful attitude rather than a violent or belligerent one. As we shall find, the Hebrew and early Christian sense of peace offers something new, each in its own way.[2]

The Old Testament

Much of the foundation of Christian attitudes toward peace and nonviolence appears in the collection of Old Testament writings. The people of Israel understood the state of peace as associated with their salvation, a gift from God, which should be an enduring condition for God's people and possible through their faithfulness to the covenant. The first chapter of Genesis sets the stage for God as the creator of all life and the architect of humanity, and it reveals the manner of human life pleasing to God. Abraham accepts his role to be the father of all nations (Gen 15:5), and Israel is to live as a community gathered before God and in harmony with one another (Isa 2:2–4). The Hebrew word *shalom*, peace, evokes many nuances of meaning; its chief message calls the human family of many tribes to live as people of one faith, one unifying hope to live as one human family while also in harmony with all of creation. *Shalom* is an elusive vision, God's blessing and gift rather than something they could themselves produce, which the people strive to keep and which God offers them in the words of their prophets. Ezekiel, for instance, reminds them that God will ultimately fulfill that which they seek:

2. Carlson, "Peace," 1634–35.

> I will make with them a covenant of peace and banish wild animals from the land, so that they may live in the wild and sleep in the woods securely. I will make them and the region around my hill a blessing.... The trees of the field shall yield their fruit, and the earth shall yield its increase. They shall be secure on their soil. ... I will provide for them a splendid vegetation.[3]

God offers the peace and harmony of *shalom* to every believer, to live by this peace with one another and all of creation. The people perceive *shalom* as a reality that would finally be established through the promised messiah, the "prince of peace" (Isa 9:6–7).

Unfortunately, the challenge to live *shalom* occurs in ages of war between people and ruptures of harmony between persons and with the rest of creation, consequences of human propensities to self-assertion, avarice, and violence.[4] This frequent warring reality among the people helps to explain the paradox of the Old Testament in which God is frequently described with warrior qualities. Images abound in metaphors of God as savior and potent protector, calling and guiding leaders to enact the divine vision for the people.

The pilgrimage of God's people from the time of Abraham encountered many episodes where, in the eyes of faith, God called them to arms for reasons such as defending against enemy peoples (e.g., against Amalek in Exod 17:8–13) or for retribution (e.g., against the Midianites in Num 31:1–12). Certain moments called the Hebrew people to violence while trusting in their God who was leading them gradually into the fullness of *shalom* for which they longed, their God of mystery and paradox, possessor of unfathomable wisdom and justice. Though early Judaism was not generally a warlike religion, establishing and restoring *shalom* sometimes involved inflicting violence and death.

The New Testament Way to Peace

Jesus's proclamation that the reign of God had arrived fulfilled the prophetic announcements of the Hebrew Testament, with a twist. Whereas the Old Testament people looked forward to the final establishment of an earthly and just peace on earth, Jesus announced that the reign of God had already begun, in which his disciples could live by accepting their salvation

---

3. Ezek 34:25–29a.
4. Brueggemann, "Living Toward a Vision," 2–3.

through him and following his way of life. Life according to this reign would facilitate peace (in Greek, *eiréné*), a gift of the Spirit and the sign of the Spirit's presence within a community of believers. This life is difficult because cultivating the peace of Christ is not universally welcomed; it is a two-edged sword that cleaves Christian disciples of peace from others in society whom it challenges and who stand to lose status or some other advantage. Even within established Christian communities, peace is fragile and frequently lost due to human weakness and sin.

Understanding the early Christian sense of peace helps clarify how God challenged disciples to live in a way that honored and maintained the peace offered by Jesus and the reign of God. Jesus frequently insisted that one essential way to find the peace of his reign was by refusing to commit any acts of violence toward offenders, thereby not responding to evil with more evil. But Jesus's teaching does not call Christians to respond passively, as implied in some English translations. Scriptural professor Walter Wink interprets a creative "third way" for responding to adversaries, neither with violent response nor mere passive acceptance, but a creative and potentially life-giving way that can lead opponents to reflect on their actions.

Wink illustrates with examples of Jesus's teaching in Matthew's Gospel. Should someone strike a disciple on the left cheek (Matt 5:39), only possible with the superior's backhanded slap using the right hand, that disciple could best respond by offering the other. The socially inferior disciple's action would require the superior to use the left hand for another slap, a legally punishable affront since the left hand was used only for socially impure actions. Another example is when a Roman soldier would legally impress a disciple to walk one mile to help carry his field pack; Jesus instructs that the disciple should offer to transport it for a second (Matt 5:41), a move that would likely confound the soldier's expectations and, at the least, might cause him to consider the disciple's motive. In both cases, the disciple responds to injustice by exceeding mere compliance. Rather than prompting violence, escalating injustice may be overcome by a superior response that, surely, would at least stymie and disorient the offender and could break the cycle of violence. Resorting to the nonviolent love of God offered to all, friend or foe, could thereby prevail over evil (Matt 5:43–45).[5]

That disciple is blessed who follows in the way of poverty of spirit, meekness, earnestly seeking righteousness, mercy, purity in heart—the way of peacemakers who prefer suffering over rupturing the peace offered

---

5. Wink, *Jesus and Nonviolence*, 9–26.

by living in the reign of God (Matt 5:1–10). Jesus taught his disciples, "Love your enemies and pray for those who persecute you. . . . Be perfect, therefore, as your heavenly Father is perfect" (Matt 5:43–48). He exemplified this limitless divine response in moments of potentially violent confrontations with his opponents and, ultimately, in accepting his unjust condemnation, scourging, and crucifixion.

The only example of Jesus exhibiting any violence is the familiar episode of his cleansing the temple by overturning market tables and driving away the merchants and money exchangers from the courtyard where sacrificial animals and offerings were sold.[6] All four Gospels portray Jesus's outburst to restore the integrity of the temple as a house of prayer rather than a den of robbers, while John's Gospel includes the disciples' recalling the psalm phrase "Zeal for your house consumes me" (Ps 69:9). Critics of Christian nonviolence and pacifism point to this event and assert that even Jesus could sometimes justify violence. Jesus's anger in defense of temple sanctity offers an example of what we might call righteous anger in his bloodless response that is not always alien to the effort of establishing peace.

The earliest Christian disciples' overall sense of peace is evident in the opening greetings of several Pauline letters, such as in 1 Cor 1:3, Eph 1:2, and Gal 1:3. Peace, for Paul, is not merely wishing for some distant reality, following the Jewish custom. Paul's signature greeting of "Grace to you and peace to you from God our Father and the Lord Jesus Christ" attests to his belief in a present reality, offered as a divine gift to those who choose to acknowledge Jesus as Messiah and live in the reign of God.[7]

Christian Nonviolence in the Patristic Era

Early Christians sought to live according to Jesus's teaching in their daily social lives. Evidence from some of the early Christian church writings offer insight into how Christians practiced Jesus's way of love through living the Beatitudes and ways of nonviolence in at least three areas: in disciples' overall attitude of peacefulness that the churches professed, during the periods of persecution by the empire, and in the ambiguous attitude of early Christians toward participating in the Roman military.

---

6. This episode occurs, slightly rewritten, in Matt 21:12–13; Mark 11:15–17; Luke 19:45–46; and John 2:13–17.

7. Carlson, "Peace," 1634–35.

The Peaceful Nature of Christianity

The first followers of Jesus held a deep respect for the sanctity of human life, evident in many writings of the period. The second-century Christian apologist Athenagoras of Athens noted Christian sensitivity and aversion to bloodshed, contrary to the surrounding culture:

> Who does not reckon among the things of greatest interest the contests of gladiators and wild beasts, especially those which are given by you? But we, deeming that to see a man put to death is much the same as killing him, have abjured such spectacles.[8]

Other authors emphasized Christian respect for human life in religious proscriptions against murder, infanticide, abortion,[9] and suicide.[10]

Early Christianity sought to live according to Jesus's life example that embodied his attitude of peaceful coexistence and refusal to respond to evil with evil. Justin Martyr wrote to Emperor Antoninus Pius, expressing Christians' fundamental desire to live peaceably with all other people. Justin noted that Christians did not challenge the empire's rule by choosing to live in an otherworldly reign of God; on the contrary, they ranked first among Roman subjects most desirous of peace within the empire. Disciples had never sought violence against their adversaries, following the words of Isa 2:4 to beat their swords into plowshares and their spears into pruning hooks in anticipation of the peace of Christ that had already begun.[11] A document of Tertullian's, written about the year 197, also describes the innate peacefulness of Carthaginian Christians with a strong expectation among them of absolute peacefulness. Tertullian noted that Christians could only treat the emperor with respect and homage and wish him well, "for we are equally forbidden to wish ill, to do ill, to speak ill, to think ill of all men. The thing we must not do to an emperor, we must not do to any one else."[12]

---

8. Athenagoras, *Plea for the Christians* 35.
9. *Did.* 2.
10. Lactantius, *Inst.* 3.18.
11. Justin, *1 Apol.* 11–12; 39.
12. Tertullian, *Apol.* 36.1.

THE CHALLENGING PRACTICE OF CHRISTIAN NONVIOLENCE

Living Peaceably in Times of Persecution

Christians believed that the eternal reign of God did not stand at odds with the Roman Empire but served to guide Caesar's empire in its earthly mission of ruling and maintaining order. Disciples should observe the authority and commandments of their heavenly ruler of everlasting life while seeking to comply with the empire's governance. Their principle of nonviolence meant that Christians submitted to Roman law even to the point of sacrificing their earthly life to serve the incorruptible and eternal one.

This attitude helps to shed light on why early Christian nonviolence extended to how disciples reacted to Roman authority in times of persecution. The early writings contain no mention of encouraging Christian violence toward their unjust persecutors during the first centuries, instead promoting nonviolent behavior. Justin Martyr wrote that following divine teaching, Christians sought to live peaceably with all, even their persecutors.[13] Tertullian wrote that each disciple's life rested in the hands of the all-knowing God who could use every event to bring about good from evil, not least of which was the witness value of martyrs' perseverance and suffering.[14]

Early Christians and Military Service

Christian attitudes toward service in the Roman military have been much discussed among academics and vary in intensity among the few early Christian writings that address the issue. Asserting the assistance of an early church pacifist tradition based primarily on wanting to avoid violence and bloodshed is difficult to support and has been hampered by theological biases of Christian denominational conclusions.[15] Nowhere in the Gospels does Jesus specifically challenge his listeners to avoid military service; in fact, the Gospels do not record Jesus saying a word about military service or abstaining from it. An underlying desire to follow Jesus's directive to love others by avoiding violence toward all, including enemy warriors, surely must have guided at least some disciples. Literary evidence, though slim, suggests other pressing reasons for avoiding Roman military service, including Roman soldiers' worship of idols and pagan Roman deities such as Mithras. Another concern was that the periodic episodes of Christian

---

13. Justin, *1 Apol.* 12.
14. Tertullian, *Fuga* 4.
15. Helgeland, "Christians and the Roman Army," 149.

persecution could place Christian soldiers in a position of having to seek and prosecute their fellow disciples.[16]

Christian exhortations supporting or opposing disciples' military participation varied in intensity from region to region. The Alexandrian ascetic Origen (d. 253) also wrote that "we no longer take up 'sword against nation,'" nor do we "learn war any more."[17] Christians supported the emperor by offering instead their prayers and spiritual sacrifices for the emperor's success.[18] In North African Carthage, Tertullian acknowledged that Christian soldiers were present in Roman garrisons ("camps").[19] References to Christian soldiers in later works of Tertullian are more contentious, likely influenced by his growing anti-military sentiment in the wake of severe persecution and his more demanding asceticism. Besides having to contend with idolatrous practices of the Roman military, Tertullian noted that such Christian disciples would ultimately have to choose between two military banners vying for their loyalty—those of God and Rome, representing the two realms of good and idolatrous evil—which was impossible for disciples living simultaneously as Christians and Roman soldiers.[20] Tertullian also wrote that no Christian could accept positions that might require making decisions of bloodshed, particularly as soldiers or as legal authorities with the power to impose imprisonment, torture, or execution.[21] The early third-century Roman *Apostolic Tradition* instructed that Christians in military authority must agree never to execute another person or take idolatrous military oaths.[22]

Despite these limitations, at least some Christians served in the Roman military before the early fourth century. However, it is impossible to determine what percentage of those serving were soldiers before baptism and how many were Christian disciples who enlisted. Clement of Alexandria noted military service as one of several occupations in which disciples were engaged.[23] The first documented evidence of disciples' military service is in a report that a large contingent of Christians had

---

16. Fahey, *War and the Christian Conscience*, 42.
17. Origen, *Cels.* 5.33.
18. Origen, *Cels.* 8.73.
19. Tertullian, *Apol.* 37.
20. Tertullian, *Idol.* 19.
21. Tertullian, *Idol.* 17.
22. Hippolytus, *Trad. Ap.* 16.
23. Clement, *Protr.* 10.

enlisted in defense of the region, serving in the Legion of Thunder at Caesarea around the year 180.[24] The great persecution of Christian disciples by the Emperor Diocletian between 303 and 313 reportedly extended to the many disciples in military service, compelled to worship the emperor and observe other idolatries.[25]

Serving as a Roman soldier for a designated period had enticing rewards of Roman citizenship, a monetary pension, and a plot of land. It is reasonable that these advantages would attract at least some Christian disciples to enter the military, especially as the need grew for personnel on both foreign and domestic fronts. Demand for soldiers increased with the increasing menace of barbarian attacks and other activities, likely forcing the need for increased Roman military strength into the third century.[26] Not every Roman soldier served in the legions defending the frontier but also in local contingents charged with military or law enforcement service.[27]

Disciples could certainly act on a change of heart. Early Christian literature contains several accounts of disciples who either refused to serve in the army or eventually left for reasons of their faith. Maximilian, around the year 295, refused a position in the Roman army on the grounds that his faith prohibited him; it is unclear whether his refusal was to avoid bloodshed or the menace of idolatrous practices.[28] Traditionally considered among pacifists as the first conscientious objector on religious grounds, Maximilian was beheaded.[29] Other disciples who shared his faith stance included Nicander and Marcianus (both d. 297), and Ischius (d. 303).[30]

Changing Attitudes to Military Service Following Legalization of Christianity

The normalization of Christianity in 313 dramatically changed Christians' status within the empire and eventually challenged some of their reasons for avoiding military service. The 314 Council of Arles decreed

24. Helgeland, "Christians in the Roman Army," 157.
25. Helgeland, "Christians in the Roman Army," 159.
26. Ryan, "Rejection of Military Service," 13–14.
27. Helgeland, "Christians in the Roman Army," 162–63.
28. Hornus, *It Is Not Lawful*, 133–35.
29. Maximilian is traditionally counted among Christian martyrs; however, historians including Helgeland assert that the soldier did not die specifically for his faith but for insolence. Helgeland, "Christians in the Roman Army," 158.
30. Hornus, *It Is Not Lawful*, 139.

that eligible Christians could no longer lay down their arms as they would earlier have done before when called to fight or enforce anti-Christian edicts.[31] The Emperor Theodosius decreed in 380 that Christianity would henceforth be the only permissible religion in the empire; by 470, only Christians could serve in the military, removing the excuse for avoiding military service due to idolatrous practices.

Christians considered their newfound religious legitimacy as a divine blessing through the hands of the General-made-Emperor Constantine. The emperor's victory and legalization of their religion enabled the prospect of a peaceful existence that had eluded them for almost three centuries. Eusebius of Caesarea (d. 339), who served as Constantine's bishop and spiritual advisor, loftily praised the emperor as a divinely guided agent of God's word to the nations and keeper of the empire's stability. Consequently, Eusebius justified the emperor's use of military power to remove causes of imperial division, whether from the threat of barbarians or spiritual division caused by religious heresy.[32] Eusebius also justified Christian participation in the military in service to God's instrument on earth to defend the empire and sustain Christian flourishing and growth, serving the temporal reign in service to the eternal one.[33] Christians who enjoyed the freedoms and other benefits of the emperor's rule should have been willing to serve in military service for such a just and reasonable cause.

"Justified" Warfare

A gradual Christian ethical guideline regarding warfare emerged that strengthened the justification of morally acceptable Christian military participation. Bishop Ambrose of Milan conceived a related and broadened view of Christian military service, asserting that war could be considered justifiable and perhaps even praiseworthy when the action (1) was to defend the weak and oppressed, (2) avoided the death of innocents, (3) was legally declared (by recognized rulers), and (4) did not involve priests and monks

---

31. Canon 3, the meaning of which has been debated, is generally accepted as upholding Christian soldiers' responsibility to participate in justified military service. See Canon 3 with footnote 1 in "The Canons from the Council of Arles..." in bibliography.

32. Eusebius, *Laud. Const.* 7.12–13; 8.7.

33. In so doing, the bishop also helped set the foundation for considering future Christian monarchs as extensions of divine rule on earth with additional responsibility to further the spread of the Christian church.

in bloodshed.³⁴ He also reasoned that the emperor's role included defending and eliminating spiritual threats to imperial unity, thus condoning Valerius's military attempts to destroy the divisive Arian heresy.³⁵

Augustine of Hippo further shaped the principles for just wars, offering five conditions that would justify warfare: (1) The war has a just cause such as defense of sovereign territory or restoring what has been stolen. (2) The war was declared by a legitimate ruling authority. (3) The ruler had a right intention. (4) The war was conducted only as a last resort. (5) The war was conducted lawfully concerning the treatment of non-combatants and disposition of their property. Augustine's thought carried the day in subsequent Christian military activity through the next several centuries.

Military Pacifism

A few appeals to Christian military pacifism persisted into the early medieval period. One, coming from the pseudonymous *Canons of Hippolytus*, likely a fourth- or fifth-century Egyptian Christian document, proscribed disciples from assuming livelihoods as magistrates or soldiers since they both involved the likelihood of bloodshed, although a Christian might be legally compelled to enter military service. The document also acknowledged the reality of Christian soldiers; those who did engage in military violence must observe a period of penance in atonement for the evil of shedding another's blood.³⁶

Martin of Tours (315/316–397) remains another favorite saintly example among Christian pacifists. According to tradition, Martin adopted a Christian life while a teenager, though he chose to defer baptism until later in life (a common fourth-century practice). Since his father was a veteran military soldier, Martin was required by law to enlist for a time and serve in the cavalry. One day at the city gate, Martin encountered a poor beggar with little clothing, at which point the soldier took his sword and divided his tunic in two to share with the needy one. After that, Martin dreamed that he had served Christ in clothing the beggar, leading the eighteen-year-old soldier to seek baptism. Recall that Christians could serve in the military but not to the point of shedding blood, which Martin observed for another two years until shortly before a major battle, when he resigned due to his religious

---

34. Fahey, *War and the Christian Conscience*, 87.
35. Ambrose, *Fid.* 2.16.
36. *Canons of Hippolytus* 13 and 14.

conviction. Accused of cowardice and desertion that merited death, Martin agreed to stand at the front line without bearing arms; however, the battle was canceled, and he was allowed to leave his service. Recognizing this as a miraculous event, Martin subsequently adopted the life of an ascetic and gathered other monks around him; before long, however, he was appointed bishop of Tours in Gaul. His popularity resulted in his being named a patron saint of Europe and later adopted by many Christian pacifists as an exemplary nonviolent disciple of Jesus.

To summarize this section, the later patristic centuries witnessed a dramatic shift in the widespread though irregular Christian observance of pacifism and abstention from interpersonal violence. Jesus's teachings provide a foundation for authentically Christian nonviolent discipleship; however, a firmly established, early universal church tradition of pacifism toward military service is more tenuous. While it is true that civilian disciples were barred from entering military warfare and other engagements because they involved violence and bloodshed, earliest church writings had greater concern for disciples contending with faith challenges of Roman idolatrous practices and temptations to apostasy in times of persecution. Christians from the fourth century gradually adopted justifiable conditions for warfare. Clerics and members of consecrated religious monks concerned themselves with establishing the reign of God on earth, leaving the burden of military service and warfare to the vast number of unconsecrated laity.

Christians and Nonviolence in the Medieval Centuries

Both Eastern and Western Christian traditions have long recognized that disciples live in an imperfect world and that people, sadly, incite both interpersonal and large-scale armed conflict. Western Christianity sought to limit military violence by establishing means for minimizing the inevitable occasions of war and the scope of its destructiveness. The notably violent character of feudal Europe compelled countless Christian disciples to take up arms in warfare, eventually spawning a number of popular movements advocating a return to Jesus's way of nonviolence.

Christians and Warfare in the Feudal Period

The collapse of the Roman Empire by the sixth century carried with it the loss of centralized imperial means to provide for basic needs and security for its people, leading to the rise of feudalism. This hierarchical structure relied on the loyalty of common people (serfs and vassals) defending and serving under their immediate lords, to whom they owed their ability to exist, and ultimately to their monarch at the head of the structure. Christians of all classes were integral components of this military system, guided at least in principle by the just war strictures of Augustine and later shaped by Thomas Aquinas and other theologians. European feudalism all but obliterated ideas of individual pacifism toward war, lasting until its gradual demise in the bloody fourteenth century that witnessed the devastating Black Death, the prolonged Hundred Years' War, and popular uprisings such as the Peasants' Revolt.

The church and the monarchy observed a co-beneficial division of authority. The church attended to the spiritual needs of the reign of God, while royalty concerned itself with earthly political ruling and power that bore the responsibility of securing and protecting church assets and other worldly concerns. During this period, bishops began to have greater political influence in their need to safeguard church land and other material assets, further aggravating the violence-ridden period.

Efforts to Cultivate Peace in Violent Lands

Several peace initiatives arose between the tenth and fourteenth centuries that attempted to limit the ravages of feudal wars. The southern regions of tenth-century France experienced a weakening of control among its royal family members and their respective concerns, aiding the Western Christian church to grow in political power and influence. One initiative, the tenth-century Peace of God decree, sought to limit combatant damage or violation of church property and possessions of the poor, and prohibited the assault of clergy; this had some effect into the thirteenth century.[37] The eleventh-century Truce of God decree sought to limit military warfare by banning violence on certain days of the week and during festive periods. Although these rulings were somewhat effective over the next few centuries, ensuing

---

37. The Council of Charroux especially showed these effects. Jedin and Dolan, *Age of Feudalism*, 345.

violations led to the justification for creating armed church military units, ironically known as "peace armies," to enforce the decrees.[38]

The establishment of military structures by the pope and many bishops supported the growing acceptance of the Christian church's ability to declare wars for material and spiritual reasons. It opened the way for the papacy's accepted right to stage military engagements to retrieve and protect Christian land, populations, and other interests. This authority was most visibly evident in the eight "Holy Wars" or Crusades to the Holy Land between 1096 and 1291, excursions leading to all-out warfare to free the Holy Land from Saracen (Islamic) control.[39] Church use of military power in worldly realms to protect spiritual and material interests also justified the several periods of the Inquisition between the thirteenth and sixteenth centuries in Europe, extending into the colonized regions of the Americas. Tragically, the Inquisition sought to preserve Christian peace and stability in confronting and sometimes supporting the violent suppression of heretical individuals and movements.[40]

As the Christian church evolved during this time as a formidable political and earthly force, there grew considerable Christian sympathy among the faithful for bringing an end to church-sanctioned military war and violence. The Bianchi movement and pilgrimage peace marches of 1399 captured the zeal of countless ordinary Christians. The third-order branch of the Franciscans (lay individuals who followed their spiritual program without the permanent commitment of vows) prohibited its members from taking up arms in acts of war and between individuals, while following the nonviolent principles of Francis of Assisi and his first followers.[41]

In addition to large-scale peaceful reactions to violence, many persons initiated local peace between individuals, notably in fourteenth- and fifteenth-century Italy. The third-order Dominican Catherine of Siena served several times as a mediator between rival city-states of her day. She also made the arduous journey to Avignon and, in her characteristically forceful manner, exhorted Pope Gregory VI to return to Rome in 1376 and resolve local and larger conflicts aggravated by the long papal absence. Popular

---

38. Jedin and Dolan, *Age of Feudalism*, 345–46.

39. Jedin and Dolan, *Age of Feudalism*, 347–48.

40. Fahey, "War and the Christian Conscience," 129–36. Church involvement in the Inquisition did not involve itself directly in torture or bloodshed, leaving those activities to the local governments.

41. Fahey, *War and the Christian Conscience*, 48–49.

preachers, such as the Franciscan Friar Bernardino of Siena (1380–1444), strongly proclaimed the need for penance and reconciliation with God as a foundation for any lasting peace between aggrieved parties.[42] Some disputing families, particularly among the fourteenth- and fifteenth-century nobility, also resorted to arranging marriages to preserve peace between them. Other Italian individuals, often women, interceded between families or individuals to settle local causes of violence, such as interpersonal feuds between families or long-standing desire for vengeance.[43]

In summary, medieval-era Christianity retained the desire for political and personal peace despite having deviated from its initial nonviolent beginning. As we shall find, appeals to recovering nonviolent Christian society would begin to accelerate over the next centuries.

Christian Nonviolence Developments in the Modern Era

Humanism and Protestant Reformation Developments

Notable authors in the fifteenth-century tradition of Christian humanism appealed to avoiding the violence of war at all costs.[44] The English Sir Thomas More (1478–1535), in his novel *Utopia*, envisioning an ideal society and government, wrote that virtuous rulers should abhor the violence of war as brutality more worthy of the lower animal kingdom but was sometimes necessary for defense against aggressors or tyranny. Even so, governments should avoid the brutality of war by any available means.[45] Another humanist-inspired Christian, Desiderius Erasmus (1469–1536), noted,

> War always brings about the wreck of everything that is good, and the tide of war overflows with everything that is worst. . . . War breeds war; from a small war a greater is born, from one, two; a war that begins as a game becomes bloody and serious . . . infects neighbors too and, indeed, even those far from the scene.[46]

42. Jansen, *Peace and Penance*, 22–24.
43. Kumhera, *Benefits of Peace*, 205–12.
44. Christian humanism focuses on the innate goodness of the human person, created by God as good and, as other created animals, meant to live at peace with one another and the rest of creation.
45. *Utopia*, book 2, section addressing military practices. More, *Essential Works*, 199–203.
46. Erasmus, *Education of a Christian Prince*, quoted in Hauerwas, *Christian Peace*

One should note, however, that both philosophical and religious perspectives shaped Erasmus's views; he, also, was willing to accept justified and defensive wars at times.[47]

Martin Luther, significantly influenced by works of Erasmus, held pacifist views and espoused nonviolent behavior toward any evil. Luther held a "two kingdoms doctrine": God ultimately reigned in both the spiritual one through the church and the earthly reign through the actions of the state, contrary to what church and state had become. He also supported just wars, underscoring that such action must be defensive. Luther wrote:

> Christ says that we should not resist evil or injustice but always yield, suffer, and let things be taken from us. If you will not bear this law, then lay aside the name of Christian and claim another name that accords with your actions, or else Christ himself will tear his name away from you, and that will be too hard for you.[48]

This principle was binding on all Christians, not only monks or clergy, to live as Christ in their particular time and place.

Luther's attitude toward the Peasants' War in Saxony (1524–25) was two-edged. On the one hand, he believed that the peasants' revolt was just since their overlords were unjust toward them; on the other, he also judged that the peasants had not acted as true Christians called to refrain from violent activity toward others. However, Luther ultimately sided with the aristocracy in endorsing their violent suppression of the bloody German peasantry revolt, believing that the ruling class had the duty to preserve social peace.

John Calvin's thoughts concerning a just war generally followed those of early and medieval Christian thinkers, with a few exceptions. Unlike Luther's view that would suppress the possibility of popular revolt, Calvin held that there could be times when revolutionary action against governing authority was justifiable. He reiterated that Christians must always remember that their allegiance to God as their spiritual king took precedence over any earthly rulers, even while recognized as instruments of divine authority on earth. Thus, Calvin also allowed for disobedience against royal commands when they were deemed immoral and unjust, including unjust military conflicts.[49]

---

and Nonviolence, 71.

47. Bender, "Pacifism," 130.
48. Luther, "Admonition to Peace," 28–29.
49. Pellerin, "Calvin," 35–59; Bax, "From Constantine to Calvin," 168–69.

The "Historic Peace Churches"

A group of church communities arose between the sixteenth and nineteenth centuries desiring a return to original Christian nonviolence observances that, to them, had included military pacifism. These more radical Protestant expressions also sought a fuller embrace of the early Christian religious tradition, from which sprang the worship communities of the Anabaptists in the sixteenth century, the Society of Friends in the seventeenth, and the Churches of the Brethren in the eighteenth, each movement holding the observance of nonviolence and pacifism as core values.

Other individuals and quasi-religious organizations during the nineteenth and early twentieth centuries also embraced the ideals of nonviolence. The Russian author Leo Tolstoy (1828–1910) adopted pacifism and a nonviolent response to evil against him, shaped by a personalized interpretation of Christianity and philosophical principles. Tolstoy's thought would later influence the nonviolent stance of Mahatma Gandhi and other nonviolent movements.

Summary Observations of Traditional Christian Nonviolence

Our survey of Christian nonviolence tradition has uncovered several key observations:

Nonviolence as part of Christian discipleship. The early Christian tradition taught the importance of nonviolent discipleship. Historically, the particular case of military pacifism evidently received the lion's share of attention. Military pacifism developed much more gradually in the shadow of the ever-present and evolving construct of what constituted a "just" war that compromises absolute pacifism for disciples who are also royal and political subjects. Perhaps a better identifier for just war would be "justifiable war."[50]

Questions about the applicability of nonviolence. Christian history records many voices who spoke against the violence of warfare in terms of its ultimate folly and the ensuing terrible destruction of lands and people. Some called for a complete renunciation of personal and military violence, while others have recognized that exceptions do arise that call for some forceful response.

---

50. Bax, "From Constantine to Calvin," 169.

A gradual and tentative development of Christian military pacifism. A tradition of military abstention on pacifist grounds rooted in Jesus's call to nonviolent discipleship probably had some limited presence in the early Christian centuries and all but disappeared during the feudal centuries. A stronger position began to take firmer hold in the later medieval period and gained more recognition during the Reformation decades into the early twentieth century.

Part Two: Practicing Christian Nonviolence Today

Called to Proclaim the "Gospel of Peace" in a Violent World

The period from the early twentieth century to the present has proved, at times, to be especially catastrophic and destructive. Two world wars claimed untold millions of lives among military and civilians caught between warring parties. Millions have died in concentration camps, prisons, and as forced factory laborers. Other regional wars have added to the toll of people killed, maimed, and emotionally scarred, along with their homes and property being destroyed. Wars of any type, offensive or defensive, have wreaked untold carnage and loss in terms of persons, wellbeing, and damage to the rest of nature.

The Questionable Place of Just War Principles in the Contemporary World

Appeals to Christian just war guidelines can ring hollow in a world where the gospel message is increasingly muted. The topic is too complex to be represented here, but suffice to note that many voices have sought in recent decades to articulate a contemporary just war theory. For instance, the Roman Catholic *Catechism of the Catholic Church* (1992) lists four traditional conditions to exist if a military conflict to be considered as morally just: (1) the damage inflicted by the aggressor on the nation or community of nations must be lasting, grave and certain; (2) all other means of putting an end to it must have been shown to be impractical or ineffective; (3) there must be serious prospects of success; and (4) the use of arms must not produce evils and disorders graver than the evil to be eliminated.[51] However,

---

51. *Catechism of the Catholic Church*, para. 2309.

twentieth-century technology and weapons research have produced armaments that, if unleashed, would have disastrous consequences for the world. For many people, any thought of rationalizing a war as "justifiable" that carries even the threat of massive nuclear carnage to nations and the environment is utterly reckless and morally obscene.

Political and Domestic Violence

The violence of national political and social revolutions purportedly for the betterment of people has too often induced enormous suffering due to violent behavior in the name of a greater good. The 1914 Russian Revolution, with its many assassinations of political foes and ordinary people perceived as threats to the new order, still reverberates today. African overthrows of colonial powers have often produced mixed results for the betterment of their ethnic and tribal populations. Popular liberation uprisings in parts of South and Central America beginning in the 1950s can appear to exchange one political structure of suffering for another, a questionable result at the cost of considerable bloodshed and social upheaval. Violence in our world extends also into local and even domestic realms. In the United States alone, one source reports that "an average of 24 people per minute are victims of rape, physical violence or stalking by an intimate partner in the United States—more than 12 million women and men over the course of a single year."[52] Many believe that shifting religious and social values exacerbate violence of spousal abuse, sexual crimes, urban street violence, and abuse of children. As the culture heaves politically left and right toward an uncertain future, growing segments of politically and religiously minded people believe that the instability could conceivably lead to increasingly destructive civil conflict.

The Christian Challenge to Live as Nonviolent Disciples

What *is* contemporary Christian nonviolence, in the face of all this?

Over the past several decades, Christian and other moral thinkers have grown to appreciate that nonviolence has a broader application of personal harm than simple bloodshed. The twentieth century has witnessed a broadened understanding of violent behavior in its many forms beyond physical

---

52. National Domestic Violence Hotline, "Domestic Violence Statistics."

expressions, as well as how the Christian call to nonviolence can work to confront the many forms of contemporary personal and social violence.

People claim to be nonviolent for different reasons. Many individuals have claimed to follow Christian nonviolence and sought to better their world and society. But what makes their way particularly Christian? Some popular movements rooted in other religious movements or recent political philosophies may contain only a trace of Christian underpinning in service to deeper political beliefs that ultimately prove self-serving to a particular social group. Authentic Christian social engagement seeks to image the love of God for all of God's creation, beginning with upholding the dignity of each person.

Given the above admittedly bleak view of the twentieth- and early-twenty-first-century world, how might the Christian disciple adopt a personal mode of nonviolence in the face of such suffering and evil? The remainder of this chapter explores the varied understandings, approaches, and challenges to living by the gospel counsel to cultivate lives of nonviolence in the face of the many contemporary expressions of violence.

Suggested Forms or Categories of Violence Today

A quick online search uncovers many classifications of violence within particular contexts, sometimes present in one another. For our purposes, here is a collection of principal ways to inflict violence on others, consciously or unknowingly, each containing a very brief description.[53] While these forms primarily describe interpersonal violence between persons, they also can appear embedded in institutional or governmental systems as expressions of structural violence.

Physical violence toward another person can range from murder and physical torture to striking them directly, pushing or shoving, to other intimidating actions such as slamming one's fist on a table. Physical violence may be directed to strangers, associates at work, friends, from one spouse to another, or toward one's children.

Psychological violence can seek to gain control over other persons by belittling, insulting, or otherwise to instill feelings of inferiority.

---

53. There are many other online resources that consider this topic. Most of these violence forms listed in the text are addressed at the English-language website of the Government of Quebec. Gouvernement du Québec, "Forms of Violence."

Verbal violence aims to demean other people. They may be insults, hurtful sarcastic statements, sexist or racist remarks, and shouting.

Economic violence is a broad category, but its aim is generally to inhibit another person's financial independence, including the control of another's access to credit cards, not allowing a person to have full access to their resources, or hiding a victim's passport and visa to keep the person financially dependent on the perpetrator. Some government policies and structures can also inhibit citizens' prosperity and normal development, resulting in forms of *ideological* violence.

Sexual violence can injure a victim in what is the most intimate dimension of human life, whether physically (rape, forms of sexual assault, sexual trafficking), psychologically (sending unwanted emails or photos of a sexual nature), or even physiologically (refusing to inform a sexual partner beforehand about the presence of HIV, AIDS, or other sexually transmitted disease).

Some Representative Families of Christian Nonviolence Movements

Christian attitudes and expressions of nonviolence form a spectrum of possible responses. As authors Cramer and Werntz note, "Christian nonviolence has never been monolithic but has always included merging and diverging streams; it is therefore best understood as a dynamic and contested tradition rather than a unified and settled position."[54] The authors present a very helpful way to consider the myriad expressions of nonviolence.

Generally speaking, the first four approaches to nonviolence embrace a foundational belief that Jesus's earthly mission calls disciples to employ his teaching of gospel nonviolence while struggling to bring forth the reign of God on earth. Critics of this first set contend that, since proponents have their primary objective of promoting this reign centered on Jesus's teachings, they fail to adequately engage and seek to transform the structures supporting social evil. Cramer and Werntz isolate four principal strands of thought and response.

Nonviolence of Christian discipleship. These community-based, well-known actions are mostly the path of church communities or

---

54. Cramer and Werntz, *Field Guide*, 2. Their book is very useful for beginning to understand the multifaceted efforts of contemporary Christian nonviolence efforts and was invaluable for writing this chapter section.

denominations who regard nonviolence as a fundamental teaching of Jesus for disciples to cultivate as they encounter personal and communal threats and actual violence. Influential figures include André Trocmé, Dietrich Bonhoeffer, and John Howard Yoder.[55] Adherents to these religious-based associations can demand an absolute practice of personal nonviolence and military pacifism.

Nonviolence as Christian virtue. Proponents of this class regard nonviolent living as a particular quality of Jesus that, when cultivated by disciples, renders them more authentically Christlike in their quest to establish a foundational and abiding peace. The desire for peace should be paramount, guiding disciples' lives and choices to further its presence in the world at all times, especially when personally confronting moments of violence. Its adherents include twentieth-century prophetic figures Dorothy Day, Leonardo Boff, and Stanley Hauerwas.[56]

Nonviolence of Christian mysticism. Many practicing proponents of nonviolence find that their convictions arise from their ever-deepening lives rooted in divine love. They recognize that social strife proceeds from individual imperfections, the inner wounds and scars of sin and alienation. Only when God's love overcomes this disorder may the world find an end to what drives them to violence. Their struggle through prayer and contemplation fosters the ongoing transformation of their inner hearts to dwell more harmoniously with the love of God, described in the experiences of nonviolence mystic writers including Howard Thurman, Dorothee Sölle, and Thomas Merton.

Apocalyptic nonviolence. Members ascribing to this field seek to address the underlying powers of human organizations, also within political and administrative structures. To the degree that these structures are not animated by the reign of God, they are unwitting channels of contrary values such as human self-promotion, secular striving, and control, all the qualities represented in the collective word *Death*. While Death cannot be confronted directly, apocalyptic nonviolence followers work to transform the instruments and implements serving Death, following the words of Joel 3:10, as swords into plowshares. While most apocalyptic nonviolence disciples oppose violent actions against individuals, some proponents justify the bloodless

---

55. Although indisputably influential, Yoder's standing in the nonviolence field was greatly damaged following the revelation of personal difficulties. Cramer and Werntz, *Field Guide*, 25–26.

56. Cramer and Werntz, *Field Guide*, 27–42.

destruction of military-associated property, including draft records, missiles, and other weaponry. Perspectives range from influential figures such as Daniel and Philip Berrigan to William Stringfellow.

The second set of four movement families contain elements of Jesus and the Gospels but are more oriented to promote social change for alleviating different causes of human suffering. The following categories also share the characteristic of arising from social inequalities of limited regional geographic areas:

Realist nonviolence. These movements maintain that Jesus's teachings for living in the reign of God, as beautiful as they may be, offer only an ideal to which disciples can hope to gradually realize them over time. Examples include the highly optimistic though not highly successful nineteenth-century "social gospel" movements to bring Christian ethics to bear on social ills and the advances in late nineteenth-century military pacifism that lost considerable popular ground during the First World War. Since then, realist nonviolence proponents have learned to include sophisticated study in topics including a sociological understanding of various social ills and trends, along with international and ethnic studies that help to shape realistic goals and offer better hope for gradual success. A related focus area of realist nonviolence is *peacemaking*, which seeks to promote programs and changes at different social levels to minimize the ever-present specter of military aggression and conflict. Contributors to realist nonviolence include Baptist theologian Glen Stassen and Roman Catholic ethicist and professor Lisa Sowle Cahill.

Political nonviolence. Political nonviolence movements embrace aspects of Jesus's life and the gospel message with two objectives of raising awareness of social bias and fostering the transformation of prejudicial and other unjust laws or social structures. The anti-racism efforts of Martin Luther King Jr., one of the best-known proponents of political nonviolence, brought the issue of racial discrimination in the United States into the public eye through nonviolent marching demonstrations and massive public prayer events, often in the face of racial antagonism and violence toward them. King abhorred any reciprocating acts of violence or vengeance, overall maintaining a stance of peaceful nonresistance despite considerable pain, suffering, and even death, to bring the plight of Black Americans into wider social awareness. Other figures who followed this approach include Desmond Tutu in South Africa and Mahatma Gandhi of India. Gandhi's efforts exemplified an underlying truth of the political nonviolence movements:

human dignity and freedom were universal human rights shared by the human family beyond any Christian denomination. As a result, political nonviolence efforts can attract countless disciples from a wide range of Christian creeds and other non-Christian participants.

Liberationist nonviolence. This collection has roots in Latin American liberation theology developments beginning in the 1950s, seeking to free untold millions of its lower-class populations from relentless grinding poverty supported by prevailing societal structure. Initially the work of Anabaptists and Roman Catholics, this Christian "new way of being church" uses nonviolent means to educate its populations in the ways that poverty has systemic roots in government, laws, and social attitudes that perpetuate their bondage while favoring the more affluent upper classes. Influential writers include Adolfo Pérez Esquivel, Dom Hélder Câmara, and Leonardo Boff. The transformation has not come easily, notably in the accounts in El Salvador, evident in the life and death of Archbishop Oscar Romero (1917–1980).

Romero has received notable recognition for his preaching and living the gospel on behalf of the Salvadoran poor (largely people who were land-less due to the large-scale coffee production industry, where 0.5 percent of the population controlled 90 percent of national wealth). Romero initially sided with the more traditional, conservative side of the church that was mostly unsympathetic to their plight while more concerned with rising Communist agitation. From 1975, the new Bishop Romero began speaking out more in defense of basic human rights and dignity of the poor. He denied that he was simply politicizing the gospel message. In fact, he was critical of other liberation figures who tended to lose the gospel message through political involvement and even condoning retaliatory violence for government atrocities.

Romero was appointed archbishop of San Salvador in 1977, at the time when military repression and murder of both radical church figures and innocent victims was raging. He was particularly vocal about the growing violence of Marxist extremists on one side and government violence on the other and labored to head off a looming civil war. Addressing soldiers and government forces in his weekly broadcast homily, Romero said that "no soldier is obliged to obey an order against God's law . . . in the name of God, then, and in the name of this suffering nation, whose increasingly tumultuous cries rise to heaven, I beg you, I plead with you,

I command you in the name of God: Stop the repression!"[57] The next day, March 24, 1980, he was assassinated at the altar while celebrating a funeral mass for a friend's mother. Romero's martyrdom for the gospel words of nonviolence offers one shining example of courage and faith among many others who were killed.[58]

Returning to our nonviolence categories, the collection of Christian *"anti-violence"* efforts address the victimization and marginalization of women and other vulnerable gender groups who suffer the brunt of sexual violence. Their focus is not only on that which occurs due to military violence but also addresses the many underlying social biases and stigmas that reinforce attitudes toward them as victims or pariahs. Influential voices include Elizabeth Soto Albrecht, Carolyn Marie Fortune, and Traci West. Disciples practicing anti-violence also address how seemingly innocent religious expectations and dogmas can place conflicting expectations on victims as they journey their often long and painful paths toward recovery and integration.

One additional category concerns movements of *environmental nonviolence*, particularly Christian actions in this area. Individuals from a wide range of natural and other disciplines have devoted themselves to addressing the many human ways and attitudes that tend to inflict unnecessary damage to elements of nature. For many Christians, concern for environmental protection seems out of place when compared to traditional Christian concerns of salvation, redemption, the reign of God, etc. Indeed, concern for environmental nonviolence finds echoes in the Hindu observances of ahimsa (whose proponents endeavor to cause no harm to any creature) and in other indigenous religions and philosophies, causing some Christian disciples to keep the issue at arm's length. But one can easily perceive a Judeo-Christian and Scripture-rooted opening to care for creation. This attitude requires disciples to recognize that the naturally created world, and the human family as part of it, comprise a source of freely given gifts and blessings from God.

The interdependent and life-sustaining biosphere of the created world and its resources are meant to be graciously received rather than commercially exploited by dominant nations or international corporations. Jesus was a Jew whose people lived close to the land and seasons for survival; it is reasonable to believe that he held at least some attitude of respect for the surrounding nature, whose images and elements

---

57. Morozzo della Rocca, *Oscar Romero*, 213.
58. Morozzo della Rocca, *Oscar Romero*, 213–16.

he would use in his preaching, teaching, and healing. Disciples who can embody Jesus's various personal strengths and virtues, especially humility and gratitude, gradually can recognize that human life with the rest of creation flow from the bounteous love of God, calling us to accept the created world with attitudes of reverence and thanksgiving rather than simply as consumable natural resources.

Just two notable individuals from among the growing number of people who have contributed to the field of Christian care for creation and natural resources are Anne M. Clifford and Denis Edwards.

Conclusion

Christian history reveals a nonviolence tradition that has slowly developed as different periods observed nonviolence through the centuries. The admittedly few earliest written artifacts exhorted disciples to avoid occupations or other situations that involved the potential of shedding another person's blood. How far this teaching was applied to Christian military service is debatable for the first few centuries before adopting a "just war" understanding that recognized the inevitability of occasional military conflict. Observing the just war theory, with a few exceptions, contained the issue of military violence before the arrival of Anabaptist and other peace churches beginning in the sixteenth century. The nineteenth and twentieth centuries have witnessed a broadened awareness of how violence can manifest itself and a range of nonviolent ways to confront it, offering additional pathways for Christian disciples to extend the love of Christ and uncover the reign of God.

A final word of caution: Studying the history of Christian nonviolence reveals that acting to change the flow of personal and communal violence has been costly, even deadly, for many individuals. Assuming a public mantle of nonviolence is to accept a form of prophetic calling. This special call of the Holy Spirit summons from disciples particular inner resources, including regular prayer, personal discipline, humility, prudence, discernment, and a good deal of self-honesty regarding one's motives and motivations. This latter quality would seem especially important, for the arena of nonviolent social witness can contain a confusing mixture of personal ideals, not all of which align well with the Christian disciple's fundamental call to help establish the reign of God on earth. History from the past several centuries reveals more than one noble effort for social change and revolution that became compromised by individuals espousing social change for secular or even sinister aims. Evil can thrive in a milieu of confusion and division. In short, Christian disciples pursuing nonviolence should be attentive while going about as people of faith and hope.

Questions for Reflection

1. What do you think of the concept of a "just" war? Does this have relevance today? What would be some difficulties in observing this today?

2. Can you imagine some scenario of injustice toward you or another person in which you could formulate a "third way" of active yet nonviolent response?

3. Military pacifism: What do you think about this absolute stance of nonviolence? Is it feasible in today's world?

Suggested Further Reading

Cramer, David, and Myles Werntz. *A Field Guide to Christian Nonviolence: Key Thinkers, Activists, and Movements for the Gospel of Peace.* Grand Rapids: Baker Academic, 2022.

Wink, Walter. *Jesus and Nonviolence: A Third Way.* Minneapolis: Fortress, 2003.

Bibliography

à Kempis, Thomas. *The Imitation of Christ*. Translated by Ronald Knox. New York: Sheed and Ward, 1960.
Ambrose of Milan. *De virg.* In *NPNF*^{2} 10:363–87.
Athanasius. "Life of Anthony" [*Vit. Ant.*]. In *NPNF*^{2} 4:195–221.
Athenagoras of Athens. "A Plea for the Christians." In *ANF* 2:129–48.
Augustine of Hippo. *City of God* [*Civ.*]. In *NPNF*^{1} 2:1–511.
———. *Confessions* [*Conf.*]. In *WSA* 1.1.
———. "Exposition on Psalm 120 [*Enarrat. Ps.* 120]." In *WSA* 3.19:510–26.
———. "Exposition on Psalm 147 [*Enarrat. Ps.* 147]." In *WSA* 3.20:441–75.
———. "Faith, Hope and Love" [*Enchir.*]. In *ACW* 3:95–96.
———. "Sermon 207." In *FC* 38:89–92.
Austin, Nicholas. "The Virtue of Asceticism." *Thinking Faith*, Mar. 8, 2011. https://www.thinkingfaith.org/articles/20110308_1.htm.
Baqutayan, Shadiya Mohamed S., et al. "The Psychology of Giving Behavior in Islam." *Sociology International Journal* 2.2 (2018) 88–92. http://dx.doi.org/10.15406/sij.2018.02.00037.
Bax, Douglas S. "From Constantine to Calvin: The Doctrine of the Just War." In *Theology and Violence: The South African Debate*, edited by Charles Villa-Vicencio, 147–71. Grand Rapids: Eerdmans, 1988.
Bender, Harold S. "The Pacifism of the Sixteenth Century Anabaptists." *Church History* 24.2 (1955) 119–31.
Benedict of Nursia. *St. Benedict's Rule for Monasteries*. Translated by Leonard J. Doyle. Collegeville, MN: Liturgical, 1948. https://www.gutenberg.org/files/50040/50040-h/50040-h.htm.
Bonhoeffer, Dietrich. *Discipleship*. Dietrich Bonhoeffer Works 4. Minneapolis: Augsburg Fortress, 2001.
Bounds, Edward M., and Homer W. Hodge. *The Necessity of Prayer*. New York: Fleming H. Revell, 1929. https://archive.org/details/x-necessity-prayer/page/9/mode/2up.
Bouyer, Louis, et al. *The Spirituality of the New Testament and the Fathers*. History of Christian Spirituality 1. Kent, UK: Burns & Oates, 1986.
Brooke, Christopher. *The Age of the Cloister: The Story of Monastic Life in the Middle Ages*. Mahwah, NJ: Paulist, 2003.

BIBLIOGRAPHY

Brooks, David. "America Is Having a Moral Convulsion." *The Atlantic*, Oct. 5, 2020. https://www.theatlantic.com/ideas/archive/2020/10/collapsing-levels-trust-are-devastating-america/616581/.

Brown, Peter. *The Body and Society: Men, Women, and Sexual Renunciation in Early Christianity*. New York: Columbia University Press, 1988.

Brueggemann, Walter. "Living Toward a Vision." In *Christian Peace and Nonviolence: A Documentary History*, edited by Michael G. Long, 2–7. Maryknoll, NY: Orbis, 2011.

Buckley, Michael J. "Discernment of Spirits." In *The New Dictionary of Catholic Spirituality*, edited by Michael Downey, 274–81. Collegeville, MN: Liturgical, 1993.

Cabié, Robert. *The Eucharist*. The Church at Prayer 2. Collegeville, MN: Liturgical, 1986.

Cadoux, Cecil John. *The Early Christian Attitude to War: A Contribution to the History of Christian Ethics*. New York: Seabury, 1919.

Caesarius of Arles. "Sermon 196." In *FC* 66:41–44.

Callahan, Annice. *Spiritual Guides for Today: Evelyn Underhill, Dorothy Day, Karl Rahner, Simone Weil, Thomas Merton, Henri Nouwen*. New York: Crossroad, 1992.

"The Canons from the Council of Arles (A.D. 314)." https://www.fourthcentury.com/arles-314-canons/.

Carlson, David. "Peace." In *Baker* 4:1634–35.

Carroll, Patricia. "Moving Mysticism to the Center: Karl Rahner (1904–1984)." *The Way* 43.4 (October 2004) 41–52.

Cassian, John. *Conf*. In *ACW* 57.

Catechism of the Catholic Church. https://usccb.cld.bz/Catechism-of-the-Catholic-Church.

Caussade, Jean Pierre de, and John Joyce. *Self-Abandonment to Divine Providence: Also Known as Abandonment to Divine Providence*. Rockford, IL: TAN, 1987.

Chrysostom, John. "Homily 2." In *NPNF*[1] 9:186–90.

Clement of Rome. "Epistle to the Corinthians" [1 Clem.]. In *ACW* 1:9–49.

———. "On the Vanity of Idols" (*Idol.*). In *FC* 36:349–60.

Cotter, Francis. "Franciscan Spirituality." In *The Search for Spirituality: Seven Paths within the Catholic Tradition*, edited by Stephen J. Costello, 159–90. Dublin: Liffey, 2002.

Council of Trent. In *Canons and Decrees of the Council of Trent*. Translated by Henry Joseph Schroeder. Rockford, IL: TAN, 1978.

Cramer, David, and Myles Werntz. *A Field Guide to Christian Nonviolence: Key Thinkers, Activists, and Movements for the Gospel of Peace*. Grand Rapids: Baker Academic, 2022.

Cross, Frank Leslie, and Elizabeth A. Livingstone, eds. "Asceticism." In *Oxford Dictionary of the Christian Church*, 114–15. 3rd rev. ed. New York: Oxford University Press, 1997.

Cyprian of Carthage. "On the Lapsed" [*Laps.*]. In *FC* 36:55–88.

Davis, Adam J. "The Charitable Revolution." *Christian History* 101 (2011). https://christianhistoryinstitute.org/magazine/article/charitable-revolution.

Day, Dorothy, and Daniel Berrigan. *The Long Loneliness: The Autobiography of Dorothy Day*. San Francisco: Harper & Row, 1981.

de Sales, Francis, and John K. Ryan. *Introduction to the Devout Life*. New York: Image, 1966.

"The Despised Class." *Christian History* 101 (2011). https://christianhistoryinstitute.org/magazine/article/what-was-leprosy.

Dey, Hendrik W. "*Diaconiae, Xenodochia, Hospitalia* and Monasteries: 'Social Security' and the Meaning of Monasticism in Early Medieval Rome." *Early Medieval Europe* 16.4 (2008) 398–422.

Dickens, Charles. *A Christmas Carol*. New York: Hodder and Stoughton, 1911. https://www.read.gov/books/pageturner/2003bit37729/#page/38/mode/2up.

"Didache" (Did.). In *ACW* 6:15–25.

Duhr, Joseph. "Confrèries." In *DS* 3.2:1469–79.

Eusebius. *Hist. eccl.* In *NPNF*² 1:81–387.

———. "In Praise of Constantine" [*Laud. Const.*]. In *NPNF*² 1:581–610.

Evagrius. *Talking Back: A Monastic Handbook for Combating Demons*. Translated by David Brakke. Collegeville, MN: Liturgical, 2009.

Fagerberg, David W. "C. S. Lewis on Asceticism and Holiness." CERC. https://www.catholiceducation.org/en/religion-and-philosophy/apologetics/c-s-lewis-on-asceticism-amp-holiness.html.

Fahey, Joseph J. *War and the Christian Conscience: Where Do You Stand?* Maryknoll, NY: Orbis, 2005.

Fanning, Steven. *Mystics of the Christian Tradition*. New York: Routledge, 2002.

Farrow, Jo. "Discernment in the Quaker Tradition." *Way Supplement* 64 (Spring 1989) 51–62.

Francis of Assisi. *Francis and Claire: The Complete Works*. Translated by Regis Armstrong and Ignatius C. Brady. Classics of Western Spirituality. New York: Paulist, 1982.

Gouvernement du Québec. "Forms of Violence." https://www.quebec.ca/en/family-and-support-for-individuals/violence/forms-violence.

Gramlich, John. "Young Americans Are Less Trusting of Other People—and Key Institutions—Than Their Elders." Https://www.pewresearch.org/fact-tank/2019/08/06/young-americans-are-less-trusting-of-other-people-and-key-institutions-than-their-elders/.

Guillet, Jacques. "Discernement spirituelle: dans l'Écriture." In *DS* 3:1222–47.

Hagan, Harry. "Prayer in the Old Testament." In *The Tradition of Catholic Prayer*, edited by Christian Raab et al., 3–20. Collegeville, MN: Liturgical, 2007.

Hall, Brian P., and Benjamin Tonna. *God's Plans for Us: A Practical Strategy for Communal Discernment of Spirits*. New York: Paulist, 1980.

Hauerwas, Stanley. *Christian Peace and Nonviolence: A Documentary History*. Edited by Michael G. Long. Maryknoll, NY: Orbis, 2011.

Helewa, Giovanni. "Ascesi paulino." Lecture publication for graduate-level course. Rome: Teresianum, ca. 1996.

Helgeland, John. "Christians and the Roman Army AD 173–337." *Church History* 43.2 (June 1974) 149–63 and 200.

Helm, Paul. "Prayer." In *Baker* 4:1745–50.

Hermas. *The Pastor*. In *ANF* 2:9–55.

Hippolytus. *Trad. Ap.* In *The Apostolic Tradition of Hippolytus*. Translated by Burton Scott Easton. Cambridge: Cambridge University Press, 1934.

Hornus, Jean Michel. *It Is Not Lawful for Me to Fight: Early Christian Attitudes Toward War, Violence, and the State*. Revised ed. Scottdale, PA: Herald, 1980.

Ignatius. *Letters of St. Ignatius of Loyola*. Edited and translated by William J. Young. Chicago: Loyola University Press, 1959.

Jamart, François. *Complete Spiritual Doctrine of St. Therese of Lisieux*. Translated by Walter Van de Putte. New York: Alba House, 1963.

Jansen, Katherine Ludwig. *Peace and Penance in Late Medieval Italy*. Princeton, NJ: Princeton University Press, 2018.

Jedin, Hubert, and John Dolan, eds. *The Church in the Age of Feudalism*. History of the Church 3. New York: Seabury, 1980.

Jerome. "Commentary on Isaiah." In *ACW* 68:67–880.

———. "Letter 22." In *NPNF²* 6:22–41.

John of Damascus. *The Orthodox Faith [De fide orth.]*. In *FC* 37:165–406.

John Paul II. "Canonization of Six New Saints." Funeral homily for Gianna Beretta Molla (1922–1962). https://www.vatican.va/content/john-paul-ii/en/homilies/2004/documents/hf_jp-ii_hom_20040516_canonizations.html.

Joseph, Peter. "Traditions of Giving in Buddhism." *Alliance*, Dec. 1, 2000. https://www.alliancemagazine.org/analysis/traditions-of-giving-in-buddhism/.

Jungmann, Joseph. *Christian Prayer through the Centuries*. New York: Paulist, 2007.

Justin Martyr. "First Apology" [*1 Apol.*]. In *ANF* 1:163–87.

Keirsey, David W. and Marilyn Bates. *Please Understand Me: Character and Temperament Types*. Del Mar, CA: Promythius Nemesis, 1984.

Kolb, Robert, and Timothy J. Wengert, eds. *The Book of Concord: The Confessions of the Evangelical Lutheran Church*. Translated by Timothy J. Wengert et al. Minneapolis: Fortress, 2000.

Kumhera, Glenn. *The Benefits of Peace: Private Peacemaking in Late Medieval Italy*. Leiden: Brill, 2017.

LaBelle, Joseph T. *From Strength to Strength: Seven Timeless Virtues for Christian Discipleship*. Eugene, OR: Wipf & Stock, 2020.

Leaney, A. R. C. *The Rule of Qumran and Its Meaning: Introduction, Translation, and Commentary*. London: SCM, 1966.

Leonard, Richard. *Why Bother Praying?* New York: Paulist, 2013.

Liebert, Elizabeth. *The Way of Discernment: Spiritual Practices for Decision Making*. Louisville: Westminster John Knox, 2008.

Lienhard, Joseph T. "On 'Discernment of Spirits' in the Early Church." *Theological Studies* 41.3 (1980) 505–29.

Liguori, Alphonsus de. *Uniformity with God's Will*. Translated by Thomas W. Tobin. Charlotte, NC: TAN, 2013. https://archive.org/details/uniformitywithgo0000ligu/page/14/mode/2up.

Lindberg, Carter. "'There Will Be No Poor among You': The Reformation of Charity and Social Welfare." In *The Protestant Reformation of the Church and the World*, edited by John Witte Jr. et al., 139–58. Louisville: Westminster John Knox, 2018.

Luther, Martin. "Admonition to Peace: A Reply to the Twelve Articles of the Peasants in Swabia." In *LW* 46:17–43.

———. "Large Catechism." In *The Book of Concord: The Confessions of the Evangelical Lutheran Church*, edited by Robert Kolb et al., translated by Charles Arand et al., 377–480. Minneapolis: Fortress, 2000.

———. *A Simple Way to Pray*. In *LW* 43:193–211.

Markschies, Christoph. *Between Two Worlds: Structures of Earliest Christianity*. London, UK: SCM, 1999.

McNamara, Martin. "Discernment Criteria in Israel: True and False Prophets." In *Discernment of the Spirit and of Spirits*, edited by Floristán Samanes Casiano et al., 3–13. Concilium 119. New York: Seabury, 1979.

BIBLIOGRAPHY

Mercer, Calvin, Jr. "Faith." In *Mercer Dictionary of the Bible*, edited by Watson E. Mills et al., 289–92. Macon, GA: Mercer University Press, 1990.

Merton, Thomas. *Contemplative Prayer*. Garden City, NY: Doubleday, 1971.

Merton, Thomas, and Sue Monk Kidd. *New Seeds of Contemplation*. New York: New Directions, 2007.

Michael, Chester P., and Marie C. Norrisey. *Prayer and Temperament: Different Prayer Forms for Different Personality Types*. Charlottesville, VA: Open Door, 1991.

Moberly, R. W. L. "'Test the Spirits': God, Love, and Critical Discernment in 1 John 4." In *Holy Spirit and Christian Origins: Essays in Honor of James G. D. Dunn*, edited by Graham N. Stanton et al., 296–307. Grand Rapids: Eerdmans, 2004.

More, Thomas. *The Essential Works of Thomas More*. Edited by Gerard Wegemer and Stephen W. Smith. New Haven: Yale University Press, 2020.

Morozzo della Rocca, Roberto. *Oscar Romero: Prophet of Hope*. Boston: Pauline, 2015.

National Domestic Violence Hotline. "Domestic Violence Statistics." https://www.thehotline.org/stakeholders/domestic-violence-statistics/.

Noffke, Suzanne. *Catherine of Siena: The Dialogue*. NY: Paulist, 1980.

Origen of Alexandria. "Against Celsus" [*Cels.*]. In *ANF* 4:395–669.

Orsy, Ladislas M. *Discernment: Theology and Practice, Communal and Personal*. Collegeville, MN: Liturgical, 2020.

Pellerin, Daniel. "Calvin: Militant or Man of Peace?" *The Review of Politics* 65.1 (winter 2003) 35–59.

Perdue, Leo G. "Assurance." In *Mercer Dictionary of the Bible*, edited by Watson E. Mills et al., 71. Macon, GA: Mercer University Press, 1990.

Perkins, Pheme. "The Gospel According to John." In *New Jerome Biblical Commentary*, edited by Raymond E. Brown et al., 942–85. Englewood Cliffs, NJ: Prentice Hall, 1990.

Perrin, Norman, and Dennis C. Duling. *The New Testament: An Introduction*. 2nd ed. New York: Harcourt Brace Jovanovich, 1982.

Ponio, Judy. "How Mother Teresa Changed the World Through Charity." *Our Father's House Soup Kitchen*, Sept. 21, 2023. https://ofhsoupkitchen.org/mother-teresa-charity.

Racokzy, Susan. "Transforming the Tradition of Discernment." *Journal of Theology for Southern Africa* 40.139 (March 2011) 91–109.

Riquet, Michel. *Christian Charity in Action*. New York: Hawthorn, 1961.

Risner, Vaneetha Rendall. "When Praying Hurts: How to Go to God in Suffering." *Desiring God*, Dec. 23, 2022. https://www.desiringgod.org/articles/when-praying-hurts .

Root, Andrew. *Faith Formation in a Secular Age: Responding to the Church's Obsession with Youthfulness*. Grand Rapids: Baker Academic, 2017.

Ryan, Edward A. "The Rejection of Military Service by the Early Christians." *Theological Studies* 13.1 (March 1952) 1–32.

Ryan, J. A. "Charity and Charities." In *The Catholic Encyclopedia*, edited by Charles George Herbermann et al,. 592–604. 15 vols. New York: Robert Appleton, 1908. https://archive.org/details/catholicencyclop0003unse_x6i4/page/592/mode/2up.

Salenson, Christian. *Christian de Chergé: A Theology of Hope*. Translated by Nada Conic. Cistercian Studies 247. Collegeville, MN: Liturgical, 2012.

The Sayings of the Desert Fathers: The Alphabetical Collection. Translated by Benedicta Ward. Rev. ed. London: Cistercian, 1975.

Smith, Scott. "Top 45 Best Quotes from Blessed Pier Giorgio Frassati on Faith, Joy, Nature, the Eucharist, Charity, Holiness, and Life." *The Scott Smith Blog*, Aug. 10, 2021. https://www.thescottsmithblog.com/2021/08/top-45-best-quotes-from-blessed-pier.html.

"St. Patrick's Breastplate Prayer." *IrishCentral*, Mar. 9, 2023. https://www.irishcentral.com/roots/st-patricks-breastplate-prayer-irelands-patron-saint.

Staatz, Reinhart. "Asceticism." In *Encyclopedia of Christianity* 1. Edited by Erwin Fahlbusch, et al. Grand Rapids: Eerdmans, 1997.

Stanley, David. *Boasting in the Lord: The Phenomenon of Prayer in Saint Paul*. New York: Paulist, 1973.

Steele, Joshua, and Jacob Davis. "The Book of Common Prayer." https://anglicancompass.com/the-book-of-common-prayer-bcp-a-rookie-anglican-guide/.

Stendl-Rast, David. *A Listening Heart: The Spirituality of Sacred Sensuousness*. 2nd ed. New York: Crossroad, 1999.

Studzinski, Raymond. "*Lectio Divina*: Reading and Praying." In *The Tradition of Catholic Prayer: The Monks of Saint Meinrad*, edited by Christian Raab, et al., 201–21. Collegeville, MN: Liturgical, 2007.

Sugirtharajah, Sharada. "Traditions of Giving in Hinduism." *Alliance*, Sept. 1, 2001. https://www.alliancemagazine.org/feature/traditions-of-giving-in-hinduism/ .

Teresa of Avila. "The Book of Her Life." In *The Collected Works of St. Teresa of Avila*. Translated by Kieran Kavanaugh, et al., 53–365. Washington: Institute of Carmelite Studies, 1976.

Tertullian of Carthage. "Apology" [*Apol.*]. In *ANF* 3:17–55.

———. "On Flight from Persecution" [*Fug.*]. In *ANF* 4:116–25.

———. "On Idolatry [*Idol.*]. In *ANF* 3:61–76.

———. "To the Martyrs" [*Mart.*]. In *FC* 40:17–29.

Theodoret of Cyrrhus. *A History of the Monks of Syria*. Translated by R. M. Price. Kalamazoo, MI: Cistercian, 1985.

Thérèse of Lisieux. *Story of a Soul: The Autobiography of St. Thérèse of Lisieux*. Translated by John Clarke. Washington: ICS Publications, 1996.

Thomson, J. G. G. S. "Presence of God." In *Baker* 4:1750–52.

Ukpong, Justin S. "Pluralism and the Problem of the Discernment of Spirits." *Ecumenical Review* 41.3 (July 1989) 416–25.

Vatican News Service. "Gianna Beretta Molla (1922–1962)." https://www.vatican.va/news_services/liturgy/saints/ns_lit_doc_20040516_beretta-molla_en.html.

Vauchez, André. *The Laity in the Middle Ages: Religious Beliefs and Devotional Practices*. Edited by Daniel Ethan Bornstein. Translated by Margery J. Schneider. Notre Dame: University of Notre Dame Press, 1993.

Vischer, Lukas. *Tithing in the Early Church*. Philadelphia: Fortress, 1966.

Waal, Esther de. *The Celtic Way of Prayer*. New York: Doubleday, 1997.

Wakefield, Gordon S. "Anglican Spirituality." In *Christian Spirituality: Post-Reformation and Modern*, 259–63. World Spirituality 18. New York: Crossroad, 1989.

Wansink, Craig S. *Chained in Christ: The Experience and Rhetoric of Paul's Imprisonments*. Sheffield, UK: Sheffield Academic, 1996.

Webb, Kirk. "What Is Celtic Spirituality?" http://www.thecelticcenter.org/what-is-celtic-spirituality.
Wesley, John. "Sermon 29." http://www.godrules.net/library/wsermons/wsermons29.htm.
White, R. E. O. "Love." In *Baker* 3:1357–60.
Wink, Walter. *Jesus and Nonviolence: A Third Way.* Minneapolis: Fortress, 2003.
Wright, Timothy Cotton. "Hidden Lives: Asceticism and Interiority in the Late Reformation, 1650–1745." PhD diss., UC Berkeley, 2018. UC Berkeley. ProQuest ID: Wright_berkeley_0028E_18119. Merritt ID: ark:/13030/m5034gpp. Retrieved from https://escholarship.org/uc/item/3vh3r3x2 .

Name Index

à Kempis, Thomas (*Imitation of Christ*), 41, 64–65, 87n26, 116–17
Ambrose of Milan, 108–9, 162–63
Anthony of Egypt, 62–63, 85–86
Athanasius of Alexandria, 33–34, 110
Athenagoras of Athens, 158
Augustine of Hippo, 20, 34, 63–64, 84–85, 111–12, 136–37, 163
Augustus (emperor), 106
Austin, Nicholas, 122

Bates, Marilyn, 23n32, 25n34
Benedict of Nursia, 9, 86, 110–11
Beretta Molla, Gianna, 94–95
Bernardino of Siena, 167
Bonhoeffer, Dietrich, 124–25

Caesarius of Arles, 112
Calvin, John, 142, 168
Cassian, John, 9, 35, 63
Catherine of Siena, 14, 40–41, 71, 116, 166
Caussade, Jean-Pierre de, 91
Chergé, Christian de (and brother monks), 95
Christ (see Jesus)
Chrysostom, John, 34
Clement of Rome, 33
Constantine (emperor), 138, 162
Cramer, David, 173, 174n55
Cyprian of Carthage, 83, 105–106
Cranmer, Thomas, 18

Day, Dorothy, 71, 147–48
de Sales, Francis, 42, 90–91
Dixon, A. C., 20–21
Dominic of Guzman, 38, 115

Eckhart, Meister, 38–39
Elizabeth of Hungary, 140–41
Erasmus, Desideratus, 167–68
Evagrius of Pontus, 35
Eusebius of Caesarea, 162
Ezekiel (prophet), 154–55

Francis of Assisi, 37–38, 87, 115
Frassati, Pier Giorgio, 20

Gandhi, Mahatma, 169, 175–76
Gregory the Great (pope), 86

Helena, 138
Hermas, 60–61
Hilton, Walter, 39–40

Ignatius, of Loyola, 18, 65–66, 72, 89–90, 143
Isaiah, 78

James (scriptural author), 80–81, 103–4, 107
Jeremiah, 78
Jerome, 109–10, 140
Jesus (Christ), 4, 13–14, 20, 22, 30–34, 46–48, 79–82, 98, 103, 129, 131, 155–57, 159, 177–78

NAME INDEX

Job, 79
John (evangelist), 58–59
John of the Cross, 14, 16
John of Damascus, 1
John Paul II (pope), 95
Justin Martyr, 81–82, 135, 158–59

Keirsey, David W., 23n32, 25n34
King, Martin Luther, 175

Lawrence of the Resurrection, 43
Liebert, Elizabeth, 72n30, 73n31
Liguori, Alphonsus, 19, 91–92
Luther, Martin, 17–18, 88, 142, 168

Magdalene of St. Joseph, 16
Martin of Tours, 163–64
Maximilian, 161
Mary (mother of Jesus), 12, 13n19–20, 79
Mechtilde of Magdeburg, 71
Melania the Younger, 138
Merton, Thomas, 1, 148
Michael, Chester P., 25, 25n34
Molinos, Miguel de, 42n18
Montanus (and disciples), 106
More, Thomas, 167

Norrisey, Marie P., 25, 25n34

Olier, Jean-Jacques, 19
Origen of Alexandria, 9, 61, 160

Paul (of Tarsus, apostle), 4–5, 31–32, 56–58, 103, 107, 132, 157
Peter (Simon), 31

Risner, Vaneetha Rendall, 126n25
Romero, Oscar, 176–77

Simeon the Elder ("Stylites"), 112–13

Tertullian of Carthage, 7, 82–83, 105–6, 135–36, 158–60
Teresa of Avila, 14, 16–17, 42, 90
Teresa of Calcutta, Mother, 147–48
Thérèse of Lisieux, 1, 43–44, 92
Theodosius, 162
Tolstoy, Leo, 169

Underhill, Evelyn, 44–45

Werntz, Myles, 173, 174n55
Wesley, John, 88–89
Wink, Walter, 156

"The Bible can be difficult to understand unless one sees it as presenting the story of God centered on Jesus Christ. In this book Jim Hopwood's careful arrangement of passages enables the reader to follow that story in all its richness and drama. But be ready: he also gets you to think about what you read, often in new and surprising ways. If you want a very understandable, at times challenging, and always fruitful engagement with Scripture and the God of which it speaks, this is the book for you."

—**Henry H. Knight III**, Professor Emeritus of Wesleyan Studies and Evangelism, Saint Paul School of Theology, Leawood, Kansas

"*Day by Day* offers an accessible and compelling approach to the Bible's blueprint of divine love. Written with humor, humility, and first-class hermeneutics, Jim has captured the essence of the meta-narrative of Scripture, focusing not on the details, but on the storyline that consistently points toward God's inclusive and radical love for humanity. The format of daily readings is adaptable to an individual's desires or a small group's time frame. If you're looking for an overview of the Bible, you won't find better than *Day by Day*."

—**Angie McCarty**, Location Pastor, Church of the Resurrection, Leawood, Kansas

"With the investigative powers of a newspaper man and the spiritual sensitivity of a pastor, this wonderful text for biblical study provides exactly what people need. The introduction alone is worth the price of the book. From there we receive an outline of each book of the Bible, with brief, illuminating comments and just enough questions to take one deeper into the text. I recommend it with enthusiasm."

—**Tex Sample**, Robert B. And Kathleen Rogers Professor Emeritus of Church and Society, Saint Paul School of Theology, Leawood, Kansas

"I love Jim Hopwood! His approach to scripture study combines the curiosity, research and storytelling of a great journalist with the devotion, passion and theological acumen of thoughtful pastor. *Day by Day* is a great resource for individuals and groups hoping to hear the word of the Lord in the words of scripture."

—**Adam Hamilton**, author of *Making Sense of the Bible*